PILLOWS

PILLOWS

DESIGNS · PATTERNS · PROJECTS

MARY ELIZABETH JOHNSON

Oxmoor House, Inc.

Birmingham

Copyright © 1978 by Oxmoor House, Inc.
Book Division of the Progressive Farmer Company
Publisher of *Southern Living*, *Progressive Farmer*,
  and *Decorating & Craft Ideas*™ magazines.
P.O. Box 2463, Birmingham, Alabama 35202

Eugene Butler *Chairman of the Board*
Emory Cunningham *President and Publisher*
Vernon Owens, Jr. *Senior Executive Vice President*
Roger McGuire *Executive Vice President*

Pillows: Designs, Patterns, Projects

Designers: Viola Andrycich, Steve Logan
Photographers: David Matthews, Steve Logan, Glea Adams,
  Armen Kachaturian, Bob Lancaster
Illustrators: John Anderson, Carol Tipton
Copy Editor: Candace Conard Franklin
Consultants: Tappy Folts, Janet Roda
Interiors designed by: Elaine Kartus, William H. Whisnant &
  Richard Tubb, Alan Picard & Teeny Brannon, Sandra Hood,
  Ann Whitson Baker, Alexandra Eames, William Walter
Project designers: Dolly Fehd, Mary Grunbaum, Margaret Richmond,
  Linda Blackburn, Sandy Hunter, Melva Miller, Mary Sherrill,
  Bette Prigoff, Adalee Winter, Patricia Mabry, Lonnie Stern,
  Lynda Sangster, Betty Moon, Lynda Bagwell, Kathleen Moore,
  Anne Marie Dallis, Mary Connell, Dottie Binnion, Mary V. Moore,
  Wally Colia, Karen Hope

Photographic credits:
Pages 13, 16-17, 22—Martex, West Point Pepperell
Page 29—The Metropolitan Museum of Art
Pages 137, 154—Transworld

Special thanks to Mrs. Jacqueline Rea of the Cooper-Hewitt
  Museum; The staff of *Decorating & Craft Ideas;* Andrea
  Carmicheal for providing locations; and to Jane Hayes for helping
  with the initial concept of this book.

Library of Congress Catalog Number: 77-75687
ISBN: 0-8487-0477-0

Manufactured in the United States of America
Second Printing 1978

CONTENTS

LIVING WITH PILLOWS

Pillows are so much a part of our daily comfort as to be taken for granted, yet their importance in household furnishings has made them practically indispensable. We sit on them, sleep on them, scent our drawers and closets with them, use them as a catchall for pins and jewelry, play with them, use them to keep moths out of the closet, and give them as greetings and gifts. In addition, we use them for Christmas decorations; we hang them on the wall as objets d'art; and most frequently, we display our most cherished needlework on them. In fact, we often count on them to carry the decor of a room, and sometimes use them as a complete substitute for furniture.

Besides being so versatile and useful, this quite beautiful article is easy to make. For many of us a pillow was the very first sewing or craft project we undertook, because we found it so simple to stitch together two pieces of fabric of the same size and stuff something inside for the desired plumpness. To this basic pillow, we can add embellishments to our heart's content. Of course, the most natural place to add these is on the pillow top itself, which can be ornamented by almost any kind of needlework imaginable. In the project section of this book, you will find pillow tops of needlepoint, crewel embroidery, whitework, blackwork, ribbonpoint, cutwork, smocking, quilting, and many other techniques.

But corners and edgings also offer a great place for a little creative self-expression. A pillow can be the perfect showplace for some intricate hand-tied fringe or for some delicate crocheted edging you found in granny's trunk or for tassels you make yourself. See the Portfolio of Pillow Techniques for more ideas.

You also have a wonderful array of choices when it comes to stuffing your pillow. While you just can't beat feathers and polyester fiber fill for stuffing most of your pillow projects, you can also use other interesting things such as rose petals, potpourri, balsam, and even hair, depending on the function you want your pillow to perform. So you have another creative decision to make here — again, see the Portfolio of Pillow Techniques.

We invite you to come with us now to learn how to make the most out of the pillows you live with — learn how to make the best use of them in decorating your home, how to use them to get more from your furniture, how to enjoy making your own, how to finish your own needlework into pillows. At last, your imagination is your only limit — you can make any pillow you want, any size and shape you want. And if you run out of ideas of your own, try some of ours. Pillow-making is a most satisfying pastime!

An otherwise colorless corner is brightened cheerfully by a trio of appliquéd pillows which are tied in theme, color, and fabric selection to an appliquéd wall hanging. The pillows show some of the buildings and trees that might be hiding in the scenic landscape. Note that all of the pillows have the same eyelet ruffle, which adds to the unity of the grouping.

Room interiors today are becoming more and more reflective of the kind of relaxed, less formal life-style many of us take for granted. Gone are the stiffly-arranged period rooms where all the furniture had to be of the same style and everything seemed to have been designed around a basic crate shape. Plushness, lushness, softness, and comfort are integral to an appealing, attractive environment. Chairs and sofas invite you to snuggle into them and relax, or alternatively, to recline and stretch out. We live more on the floor than ever before. As our furniture gets lower, closer to the floor, we find ourselves sitting, sleeping, and eating directly on the floor.

If you study room settings in magazines, in department store displays, and in advertisements, not only will you spot the trend just described, but also you will become aware of the tremendous part pillows play in making this look work — or, in making it possible at all. Pillows add the richness, the softness, the air of luxury and comfort, whether they are on a banquette, a bed, a sofa, or the floor. In fact, much of modern furniture is nothing more than upholstered platforms with plush pillows added for comfort.

And one of the best things pillows can do for any of us is to provide an inexpensive means of having this look for our own, using the furniture

we already possess. Even in the very formal, very refined, Empire period of France (1800-1830), bolsters and pillows of all sizes and shapes were added to the very clean, perfectly proportioned straight and formal lines of the couches. So, even if your taste runs to the more classic look, you can soften and subtly update it without sacrificing design integrity.

Let's see how pillows work in different rooms to add beauty and to make the rooms and furniture in them more versatile.

THE LIVING ROOM

One of the most taken-for-granted additions pillows make to a living room is to add spots of color to complete a color scheme. We will examine color schemes more closely later on, but suffice it to say now that pillows are probably one of the most effective accessories for completing or enhancing a particular scheme. In addition to adding color, pillows provide a means of adding texture and surface interest to a space that may be filled with a number of smooth, uninteresting surfaces. The roughness of Haitian cotton or the luxury of fur may be just what is needed to provide a special spark of interest to a room. Along with this, pillows are the best way to provide a room with a seasonal change. You don't have to change a slipcover; just change your pillows. You can have a selection of different pillow covers to carry out the color scheme of the seasons.

Still another valuable thing pillows can do in a living room is to alter the personality of a rather uninviting piece of furniture by making it appear more comfortable. A row of softly invit-ing pillows across the back can change even the most unfriendly sofa into a tempting place to sit and relax. The secret is to allow for plenty of pillows and make them luxurious in size — don't skimp. Sometimes the throw pillows can even be larger than the back of the sofa, thus changing the line of the sofa even more dramatically. A natural progression of this idea is to slipcover your sofa, then make plenty of matching pillows to stuff into corners and plump up across the back. Your sofa will look like a brand-new piece of furniture, will be more comfortable, and you will have spent very little in comparison with what you would have had to invest in a new piece of furniture. Look at your present sofa and see if you can't benefit from this idea. Even a style of sofa as classic as the Chippendale (or camelback, as it is also called) can be improved and updated with the addition of new upholstery and pillows.

A rather obvious use for pillows in a living room is to provide additional seating. Used singly or in a stack, floor pillows can be covered in a fabric to coordinate with any type of room decorating scheme, whether formal or casual. Floor pillows add a lot to the general "softening up" of a room, and they serve the very practical purpose of providing the most inexpensive extra seating available. Children like nothing better than a big pillow, perhaps in a wonderful animal shape, to lie on while they watch television. A stack of floor pillows can serve as an ottoman or a footrest, also.

Pillows in a living area can be the only furniture, a very inexpensive way to outfit a first home or a second, vacation-type home. All that is required are simple platforms of plywood which are covered in a fabric or otherwise finished to your personal design, and a quantity of cushions, upholstered pads, and accent pillows. The platforms can be planned to be movable and accessible from all sides or they can

A profusion of patchwork pillows with a French flavor makes an unabashedly sumptuous display. Sometimes you can't get too much of a good thing — and if you're one of those people who is addicted to a certain needlework technique, this should make you feel less inhibited about stitching away to your heart's content. Notice that there is a certain discipline, however. Patchwork is the medium, the colors are mostly red and blue, and every pillow has a ruffle of chintz or gingham. These common themes keep the assortment from seeming uncoordinated.

be built out from a wall, as you desire. You can add backs or not, as you wish. The pillows and cushions will soften everything and make the furniture inviting. (This idea is applicable to other rooms — it is perfect for a bedroom.)

THE BEDROOM

Concurrent with the new decorating concept of the unmade bed, pillows have become more important in the bedroom. No longer just to lay our heads on when we go to sleep, pillows in the bedroom serve as a substitute for a headboard on the bed. This use complements another theme of interior decorating going on today — that of using each room for more than one purpose. The concept of the "live-in" bed is becoming more and more acceptable, as many people have found that their bed serves not only as a place to sleep, but also as a center of operations or an office. The telephone is usually close at hand and it's very easy to prop yourself up in bed with a profusion of pillows and then write letters, pay bills, and make phone calls. There's that little extra fillip of luxury to think that you're doing it all while still in bed!

The type of bed just described usually has up to a dozen pillows on it. If you count the pillows on a modern bed, you will find at least two "business pillows," that is, the ones you actually sleep on; two or four larger pillows, which are usually covered with pillow shams; at least two "European square" pillows, those which measure about 22" (55.9cm) square; two or more neckroll or boudoir pillows; and, perhaps, a couple or four "elbow" pillows. Sometimes some of the pillows are replaced by wedge-shaped bolster-type pillows, or by backrest pillows with arms. All of the pillows are usually covered in sheeting fabric to match those sheets used on the bed. When the bed is "made," the pillows are all massed at one end, and a matching comforter or "duvet" is spread across the top — thus the term "unmade" bed. The traditional bedspread which tucks around

two pillows at the head of the bed has been replaced. The posh effect of the unmade bed comes from the sheer number of pillows used in the grouping. The sheeting fabric is a utilitarian covering, so you have luxury combined with practicality.

Even if you don't go the whole route as described above, you must admit that there is nothing more luxurious about a bed than plenty of plump, inviting pillows. And if you are the type who reads in bed at night before going to sleep, you will find that a little pillow tucked into the small of your back and a neckroll pillow placed behind your head will greatly increase your comfort and enjoyment at this quiet time of your day.

Pillows in the bedroom provide the perfect place to use eyelet, lace, ruffles, and other feminine indulgences that may be out of place in other rooms in the house. Also, pillow shams are a wonderful showplace for needlework skills such as crochet, knitting, cutwork, and embroidery. So if you've been looking for a new application for a favorite needlework skill, consider the pillow sham.

Melville, *Moby Dick, Chap. 14, "With the landless gull, that at sunset folds her wings and is rocked to sleep between billows; so at nightfall, the Nantucketer, out of sight of land, furls his sails, and lays him to his rest, while under his very pillow rush herds of walruses and whales."*

Who needs a headboard when you can pile up four pillows and be just as comfortable? Placing the head of the bed against built-in bookshelves solves the problem of how to have all your favorite things near when you go to bed; four plump pillows provide softness and support while you read in bed. The two back pillows are covered with tailored pillow shams and the two front pillows have pillow cases on them.

As the temperature outside changes from hot to cold, the inner climate of your room adapts easily with a change of pillows and accessories. The smooth, cool textures of summertime, found in the crisp cotton/polyester sheeting on the cushions and in the natural straw matting, give way to the velvety, snuggly textures of winter, as seen in the velour toweling cushion covers and wooly sheepskin rug.

The cushions make a quick changeover whenever you wish because the covers are zippered across one entire end for quick and easy removal. Notice that even the accent pillows change their covers.

Welcome each new season with a fresh look. It's not necessary to have several sets of pillows — just several sets of pillow covers! Color alone will achieve the desired effect of speaking of the season, but don't ignore the persuasiveness of a change of texture, also.

Tucker, *Lt. Nat., 1768-74. "It will be very difficult to get a man up from his pillow . . . if he has nothing to do when he is up."*

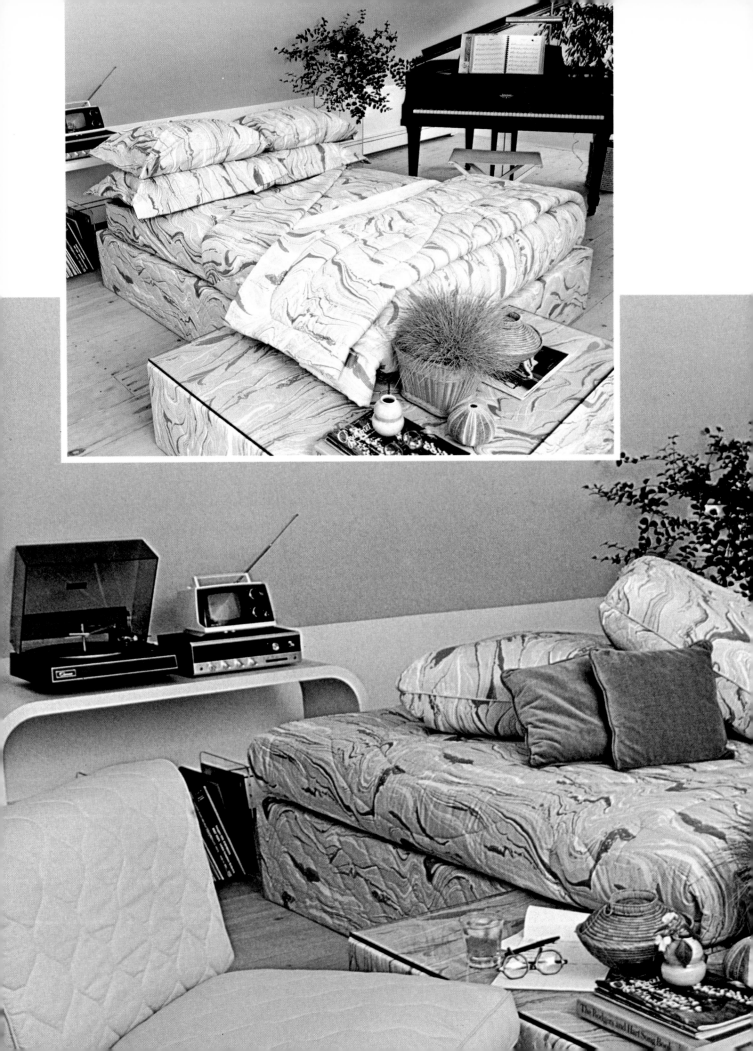

Shakespeare, *Cymbeline III, vi, 33. "Weariness / Can snore upon the flint when resty sloth / Finds the down pillow hard."*

Here is a glamorous, modern, and thoroughly workable approach to the timeless combination bed and sofa. Instead of buying a sofa which folds out into a bed, buy a bed and use it for seating during the day. Pile it high with accent pillows of the right size for lounging. At night, fold down the bed covering and add big comfortable sleeping pillows.

THE STUDIO GUEST BEDROOM OR ONE-ROOM APARTMENT

There is a whole new concept at work today in decorating an all-purpose room. The question used to be how to hide the bed — you hoped it folded up into the wall. If it didn't, you bought a sofa with a pull-out bed, or you built a loft and put the bed up there out of sight. Fortunately, the idea now is not so much to hide the bed as to make it a center of interest in the room. Sometimes it even takes the physical center of the room so that it can be approached from all four sides. The lavish use of pillows makes this concept work. During the times when the bed is used for seating, piles of pillows are used in the center of the bed to provide each person with as many pillows as he/she needs to be comfortable. These pillows are squishy so they can be punched into the desired shape around the body.

Floor pillows are also important in decorating a one-room apartment. If there is not room for a dining table, you can sit on the floor on a pillow with a footed tray in your lap and dine quite comfortably, Japanese-style.

One more idea for how to use pillows to make the most of a small living area — use them for storage! Make sure your pillows have zippers, and you can stuff all kinds of things, such as towels, sheets, and even out-of-season clothes in them!

Pillows efficiently transform this double bed into a splendid sofa for comfortable seating during the day. The big, sleeping-sized pillows are covered with a polished cotton fabric, and the mattress is covered with the same fabric, quilted to make a sturdy covering.

Useful as well as beautiful, the pillows on this sofa fill in across the back so that it is comfortable to sit and dine at the sofa. This is an easy way to have the newest look in dining room seating — the banquette. Because they are so luxuriously comfortable, banquettes are making a reappearance after many years of oblivion, and they work best with lots of pillows. Adapt this idea for your kitchen as well as your dining room. The bright crayon colors are a perfect accent for the lively floral print of the sofa.

THE BATHROOM

Aha! you say. There's no place a pillow comes into use in the bathroom. Well, have you ever treated yourself to one of those plastic inflatable pillows that fit behind your head and allow you to completely relax and enjoy yourself while you soak in the tub? If not, you are missing a true sybaritic experience. It's even nicer if you cover the pillow with a soft velour cover made from a towel or bath cloth. Also, you can make wonderful little pillows filled with bath salts to drop into your tub for marvelous fragrance and the very last word in luxury.

HOW TO PLAN PILLOW GROUPINGS FOR MAXIMUM EFFECT

It is not hard to understand how pillows add to our comfort and how they help certain pieces of furniture turn double duty. It is more difficult to fully recognize what makes one grouping of pillows look absolutely smashing and another grouping look lifeless and uninteresting. The major fault with most groupings of pillows, particularly those which march across the backs of many sofas, is that the only thing common to the grouping is that they are all pillows. Not one other thing works to provide any kind of unity — no similarity of shape, size, color, or technique. Additionally, the pillows quite often are not tied to the color of the furniture or floor or walls of the room. The result is a hodge-podge of styles and colors effectively preventing the eye from focusing on any aspect of the grouping.

You must be as critical of the pillows you choose to put in a grouping as you are of the art pieces you choose to hang together on a wall. It is vital that there be something that is common to each pillow — a unifying element. This unifying element can be color, size, shape, type or treatment of the pillow top, texture of the fabric, the way the edges are finished, or a combination of any of these factors.

Color, Pattern, and Texture

Color is probably the single most vitalizing element of a pillow. Even the absence of it, as in neutral or white pillows, can be exciting. Pillows are a natural to bring in accent color to a room and have been traditionally used as room brighteners. One important thing to remember is that while pillows are invaluable as accents for a color scheme, they cannot carry the color scheme for the whole room. They are too small to do the entire job by themselves. You must count the floor and wall colors, as well as the color of the furniture on which the pillows will sit, and any other major contributors of color, in the total room scheme.

When you are aware of the color scheme of your room, you can use pillows to pack a little extra punch into the overall look of things. Because of the accent pillow's relatively small size, you can make it a much brighter and more vivid color than you could use in a large area of a room. The same theory holds true when it comes to choosing patterns and textures for the accent pillows. Because the general area you are working with is small, you can indulge your yen for fantasy fabrics and textures such as fur,

A quaint collection of early twentieth-century filet lace doilies make an amusing addition to a sofa when these striking bits of nostalgia are put on the front of solid-color pillows. Notice that only two colors — red and yellow — are used for the backgrounds on the pillows, allowing the delicate tracery of the needlework to be the center of interest. In this case, the pillows were made, then the doilies were sewed in place on the pillow tops.

damask, or brocade, if they fit into the overall scheme of your room.

Always it is important to have a color plan in mind for your grouping of pillows. Make a rule for yourself and stick to it: don't cheat to allow just one little thing in, or you will spoil your carefully planned effect. Your rules don't mean that your color plan has to be dreary. You can say to yourself that you will use only primary colors, for example. That is in no way limiting, because you can use yellow, red, orange, blue, green, and purple — all at the same time, as long as they are all crayon-bright and of the same intensity. You might say to yourself that you want to work only with pastels — think of the lovely pinks, baby blues, peaches, violets, and pale aquas that you have to plan around. The important thing is that you stick to a plan that will produce harmony and will give a thread of consistency to your grouping of pillows. The pillow tops can be different — of any kind of needlework you want, and of different designs, as long as there is something that holds the pillows together as a group. One of the simplest ways to achieve this unity is to back and finish all the pillows with the same color and trimming.

Having determined an effective color scheme, however, does not mean you cannot vary it. Changing the color of your pillows is the easiest way in the world to give your room a seasonal boost. And the easiest way to change the color of the pillows is to change their covers — make several sets of covers in the desired colors and use zippers for the closures. Nothing could be simpler, and the covers will last for many years since you will rotate them so often. And best of all, the luxury of a different look for each season is much cheaper and easier to attain this way than with a complete change of slipcovers!

Texture should also be a consideration if you plan a seasonal change of pillows. Crisp, polished textures seem right for warm seasons, while soft, fluffy textures are better for cool months. You may even find that texture by itself can make the difference — your pillows in primary colors could be made in polished cotton for the summer and in corduroy or velveteen for the winter.

If you work with a completely neutral color scheme, texture becomes even more important than usual. Varying the texture from one pillow to the next keeps the interest up and adds excitement to the grouping.

Size and Shape

Size and shape go hand in hand in determining the amount of visual weight a pillow takes up. Also, size and shape are very important in determining the function of the pillow or in assuring that the intended function of the pillow will be served. With today's pillow furniture, you should make sure that you have pillows in several different sizes and shapes so that they can be arranged to feel good when you sit on them.

Keeping all the pillows in a grouping to the same size and same basic shape will provide unity. If you know that you are going to use your pillows as accents in a certain place, it can be very dramatic to make the pillows all of one size, especially if they are very large, or if there are a great many of them.

When you plan the size of a pillow, it is a good idea to plan it for a specific piece of furniture, if possible. That way you can make sure that the proportions are right. For example, today's big overstuffed furniture requires fairly large accent pillows; small ones get dwarfed.

Don't forget your pillows when you live outside! This deck is made more comfortable and inviting with a bevy of beautiful pillows. Placed in the small of a back or behind a tired head, they add that little touch of comfort so often missing from outdoor furniture. These pillows are covered with very practical sheet fabric, so they can be quickly washed and returned to use.

One more point about size and shape of pillows: it is a fact that squares, rectangles and circles are rather static shapes. More exotic shapes, even triangles, and especially irregular shapes, provide enough visual excitement by their shape alone; thus, as a rule, pillows of these shapes should be of solid fabric. If there is too much more going on, the pillow loses a design center of interest.

Design of the Pillow Top and Type of Edge Finish

Another element that can unify a grouping of pillows is the design of the pillow tops. If, for example, the pillow tops are all smocked, or all woven, or all needlepointed, this common thread will serve to unite the pillows, as long as there is some sort of harmony from one design to the next. A famous television actress indulges in a passion for needlepoint by stitching flowered designs for pillow tops. She has masses and masses of pillows, and they are of all different colors, but the effect is charming because the designs are all flowers and they are all executed in needlepoint.

You can also stitch needlework into pillows with a variety of sizes and with a number of different design themes as long as the colors are the same throughout. Many of us are addicted to crewel, or quilting, or blackwork, or knitting, or crochet, and pillows provide a perfect place to display our finished pieces. But remember that in order for them to look their best and garner the compliments they deserve, they must be finished and displayed to best advantage — and that means there must be some kind of harmony if they are displayed as a grouping.

Intensely personal, this collection of lacy and doll-like portrait pillows
underlines the pillow's potential as a collectible. Some very fine artists are
using fabric and thread as their medium, and often their original work can be
found on pillow tops such as the ones shown here. These pillows point out how
close is the bond between soft sculpture, doll-making, appliqué, and pillowmaking.

Sometimes pillows provide the perfect finishing touch to a beautiful quilt. The
pillows were made especially to complement, not overwhelm, the delicate
beauty of this unusual quilt. This is achieved partly by the fact that the pillows
are white, trimmed with blue ribbon, which accents the white pattern of the
quilt. It would have been a mistake to try to make the pillows match the color of
background of quilt — the contrast of reverse coloring is much more effective.

An entrance hall and a lovely old bentwood deacon's bench become a gallery-like setting for a stunning collection of bargello pillows. Because of the intricacy of the bargello patterns, the finishing of the pillows has been kept to a minimum — all are made with a simple knife-edged seam which has no additional trimming. A bevy of solid blue pillows, matched exactly to the carpeting of the stairs, helps to soften and unify the overall effect.

Pillows provide a place to indulge a desire for colors and patterns which are too vivid and too intense to use in big areas. In this artist's studio the backgrounds are neutral colors so that the myriad pillows can be wild with exotic colorings and textures — there is even one of white rabbit. The skillful combining of stripes and paisley-type fabrics is possible because the print is more subtle in coloring than the stripe; therefore, it does not compete, but blends with the bolder pattern.

The type of edge finish you choose for a group of pillows can help to make the pillows work together as a whole. Along with this, the fabric used for the backing of the pillow may be the same on each pillow, and that makes for a nice pre-planned effect. The sameness of edge finish and back fabric leaves the eye free to appreciate the needlework on the pillow top.

ARRANGING PILLOWS IN A GROUPING

The standard positioning of two pillows on a sofa is one for each corner. If there are four pillows, two go in each corner. There is nothing really wrong with this arrangement — it applies the principle of formal balance — but it can become repetitious. And when you think that you can get more impact from your pillows simply by the way you place them in an area, it is a shame not to try different combinations.

To begin with, it is much easier to make a pleasing arrangement with an odd, rather than an even, number of pillows. Even if you know you want to line a bunch of pillows up straight across your sofa back, it is easier to make it work out if you start with five, or seven, or nine, rather than four, six, or eight. (And while you're at it, try standing your square pillows on one corner when you line them up on the sofa.)

The most important factor at work in coming up with a pleasing arrangement is assigning a visual weight to each pillow. While this sounds at first like an abstract idea, it won't take you long to see that it works very well to place two small pillows at one end of the sofa and one larger one at the other end. You might also find that a cluster of small pillows of varying sizes works well at either end. The important thing is that the grouping is balanced visually because there is an equal distribution of visual weight.

Pleasing arrangements can be made that work with uneven visual weights. Pretend that you have two pillows of equal size and a third smaller pillow. If you put the equal pillows in either corner of the sofa, you will soon see that it won't work to put the smaller pillow in the center because it will look lost. A much better idea is to place the smaller pillow to one side or the other of the center line of the sofa, close to the other pillow. The arrangement will look balanced because the empty space on the other side of the center line will serve as a visual counterbalance to the small pillow. You need to remember that empty spaces are very important in planning a pleasing arrangement, especially when you are working with an informally balanced grouping, as just described.

Work with your pillows until you have a pleasing arrangement, keeping in mind all the time that very often the arrangement that offers the most comfort to the body when it is actually using the pillows is also the most pleasing aesthetically. Above all, don't let your arrangements look too uptight and forced — that goes against the very nature of the pillow!

Confucius, *551-479 B.C. "With coarse rice to eat, with water to drink, and my bended arm for a pillow — I still have joy in the midst of these things."*

PILLOWS, CUSHIONS, CURIOSITIES

The pillow, or cushion, has been a common article of the household for time immemorial, although some of the forms and materials our familiar pillow has taken seem strange and unusual to us today. Genesis 28:11 and 18 refer to Jacob sleeping on pillows of stone. We could assume that Jacob made do with a stone pillow because he was traveling, but wouldn't most of us rather just do without altogether? The difference in our attitude and Jacob's has to do with the purpose that pillows were meant to serve at that time. The headrest found in the tomb of King Tutankhamun of Egypt was meant to elevate the head, thus allowing a plentiful supply of air around the head, which was considered the seat of life. The Chinese regularly slept on porcelain pillows, such as the one illustrated, in the belief that the use of these pillows for sleeping kept the eyes clear and preserved the sight, ''So that even in old age fine writing can be read.'' Porcelain pillows, as well as those of porcelain combined with other materials, were often found in ancient Chinese tombs. Japanese women would place their heads on porcelain or rattan blocks with a concave upper surface when they retired for the purpose of preserving elaborate hairstyles. Since earliest times, natives of other countries, specifically Africa, have used pillows of wood and bamboo and other hard materials as neck and head supports.

A form of the pillow has traditionally been the only furniture available to nomadic tribes, such as those of North Africa. As these people traveled with all their possessions loaded onto their donkeys and camels, the saddlebags were actually giant pillows, stuffed with clothing, tents, and so on. The saddlebags were taken inside the tents at night to serve for seating and sleeping.

Not only have pillows been made of unusual materials, but intriguing beliefs have been associated with pillows. The *Dictionary of Mythology, Folklore, and Symbols*, Volume 2, defines

Stoneware pillow from the Sung Dynasty, 960-1280.
The Metropolitan Museum of Art, Gift of Mrs. Samuel T. Peters, 1926.

Ivory headrest from the tomb of King Tutankhamun, Egyptian, XVIII Dynasty.
The Metropolitan Museum of Art, Photograph by Harry Burton.

Pillow painted with iron brushwork on white slip depicting boy riding on toy bamboo horse, from the Sung Dynasty, 960-1280.
The Metropolitan Museum of Art, Harris Brisbane Dick Fund, 1960.

Pillow as a "Talisman for prevention against pain, sickness, suffering. It is placed with the dead as a protection against violation of the tomb. Symbolic of comfort, luxury." The *Encyclopaedia Brittannica* tells us that at one time in the Spanish court a cushion or pillow was regarded as a peculiarly honorable substitute for a chair, and that in France, to kneel upon a cushion in church behind the king was a right jealously guarded and strictly regulated; this type of cushion was known as a *carreau* or square. The position of keeper of the house and its attendant prestige was clearly denoted in medieval times by a large pincushion, or pin pillow, worn about the waist.

Without a doubt, the most popular reason for pillows of the soft, inviting kind we are familiar with was that they added comfort and provided extra seating. It is certain that crude pillows were in use in Neolithic times, and they were accounted among household inventories in ancient Egypt. It is interesting to note that in many Egyptian chairs, as an economy measure, stones were often dressed with plaster and painted to represent fabric cushions. The very wealthy had soft cushions, and a small rest was frequently found at the head of the couch to fit under the neck. In the Greek and Roman civilizations, circa 750 B.C., cushions and pillows were the only upholstery, and the wealthy used an abundance of them, as familiarly portrayed in banquet scenes where the participants are illustrated lounging on soft cushions and bolsters while they eat. In the third century B.C. pillows of various shapes were in use, and they were covered with linen, wool, leather, or silk and filled with refuse wool, vegetable fiber, or feathers. Throughout medieval times cushions and pillows were valued items in a somewhat limited domestic inventory. Often pillows and cushions were carried about in chests and laid on top of the chest at night to make a bed. Inventories of household goods from the early 1500s show intricately embroidered pillow covers, known as "pillow beres." (Needlework continued as the most popular type of pillow cover until the eighteenth century. In Victorian times, beadwork became popular, and damask

and similar fabrics which matched the room decor came into favor.)

One of history's most enchanting pillows, and it is still in use today, is the windowsill pillow. Its purpose is to cushion the elbows during that time honored pastime of people-watching, carried on in the grandest old European manner from your own front window.

There were more than twenty spellings of the word "pillow" in Old English, among them "plye," "pele," "pilewe," "pylow," "pelloe." The word, in one or the other of its various forms, gradually worked its way into the slang or common usage in several periods of history. At one time the phrase, "To take counsel of, or consult with, one's pillow," meant to take a night to consider a matter of importance — in other words, to sleep on it. Similarly, "To sew pillows under people's elbows" meant to give a sense of false security. And, of course, we still hope to "cushion a blow" or somehow make bad news easier to take.

"Pillow lace" is a type of lace that is worked upon a cushion that serves as the easel upon which the lace takes form. A "pillow sword" was a European sword so named because it hung at the bedside of the master of the house.

Chaucer, *Troylus III, 1374.* *"He tornede on his pylwes ofte." Later on in the same work, "Save a pilwe, I fynde naught tenbrace."*

Chronicles of England, 1480. "They put on his mouth a pilowe and stopped his breth."

Caxton, *Chesse 21, 1474. "She put in a pelowe of fethers a serteyn somme of money."*

Sir H. Johnson, *River Congo, 1884. "Many pretty little things are carved in wood: — pillows or headrests are made, much like those used by the ancient Egyptians."*

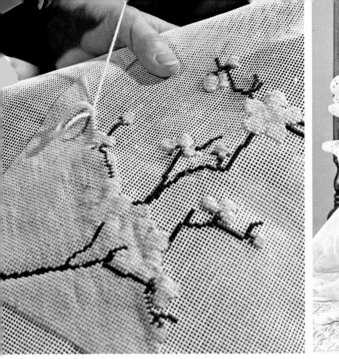

PORTFOLIO OF
PILLOW TECHNIQUES

The exciting thing about pillow-making is that, no matter what shape or size you make a pillow or how you fill it, all you need to know to make one is a few basic sewing skills. Many of these skills are probably already well known to you if you've done any sewing at all. If you can make a plain seam, you can make a pillow. Of course, the challenge of pillow-making comes with the many variations on the plain seam! This chapter reviews some of the basic techniques for you and also lets you in on some of the tricks that professional pillow-makers, or "finishers," use.

One of the objectives of this chapter is to reveal the secrets of blocking and finishing needlework, which will enable you to make your needlework into pillows yourself, rather than paying someone else to do the job for you. It is not difficult at all to finish your own needlework, and the money you save means you have more to spend on another project. It's good for you to realize that the fancy needlework you do for the pillow top takes a lot more skill than the finishing!

Perhaps the primary purpose of this chapter is to let you know how easy pillow-making is and how many different ways there are to make a perfectly lovely pillow. If, for example, you are not skilled in needlework, you can make absolutely stunning pillows with purchased fabric and trimmings. As with any other craft, you can begin with simple projects and work up to the more difficult ones.

Pillows are intriguing in that by changing just one element, such as the size or shape or stuffing, you can change the whole purpose of the pillow and give it a completely different end use. Knowledge of pillow-making means knowing how to make toys, soft sculpture, pincushions, sachets, simple furniture, doorstops and draft-stoppers, just as a beginning.

Look at the difference the stuffing makes: Fill a rectangle with feathers and you have an inviting place to lay your head; fill a smaller rectangle with dried aromatic flowers and you have a sachet; use sand and you have a doorstop or draft-stopper; choose vermiculite to make a pincushion. Each article is sewed up in exactly the same way, using the same techniques. The only difference is what you put inside!

Consider how simply varying the shape makes pillows with different end uses. While most of us think of pillows in terms of regular shapes such as circles, squares, and rectangles, there's no rule saying you can't cut any shape you want. If you cut a giraffe shape with a long neck, then stitch it and stuff it, you have a perfectly wonderful stuffed toy. And, you're also on your way to learning soft sculpture! Almost all soft sculpture has its beginning in a shaped pillow. The details are added as desired with yarn, paint, or scraps of fabric.

The variety of sizes in which you can make a pillow also contributes to the versatility of the art of pillow-making. Mammoth pillows can be used on the floor for seating; tiny pillows can be hung on padded hangers in the closet to perfume clothing and keep away moths.

Now that you are turned on to the difference pillows make in your environment and to their versatility, let this Portfolio of Pillow Techniques turn you on to how easy it is to make them!

PLANNING A PILLOW

Remember that the success of any project is dependent on clear and detailed advance planning. You will want to plan your entire project before you start the first step. Consider the finished purpose of the pillow, and from that, make the decisions regarding the type of edge finish, corners, trimmings, stuffing and closure. This way, you will be able to see in advance that all the elements work together to produce a unified effect.

One of the first things you must ask yourself is: How do you plan to use the finished pillow? Will it serve a functional purpose such as cushioning a chair seat, or will it simply sit prettily in the corner of a sofa? Think about the wear the pillow will take. For example, if your cushion is to be a pad for a chair seat, you would not want to use a pillow top with long or raised embroidery stitches that could be snagged or flattened with use. On the other hand, if you are looking mainly to add a spark of interest to a chair or sofa, that finely-stitched, brightly-embroidered pillow is exactly what you need. Think also what the end use of the pillow will mean in terms of washing or cleaning. If you plan to make a pile of pillows for poolside or patio, you will want a fabric such as terrycloth, which washes beautifully, or a vinyl or leather-like fabric that is easily wiped clean. What kind of support do you require from the pillow? If you need a small pillow to tuck behind your back to make a certain chair more comfortable, that little pillow should be stuffed rather firmly so that it supports your back correctly. If pillows are to substitute for furniture, they need to be both comfortable and able to hold their shape.

TECHNICAL CONSIDERATIONS

All pillows consist of a top and a back that are held together with a seam involving some sort of edge finish, and a stuffing. The edge finish may be a simple seam, or it may incorporate cording, ruffles, flanges, fringes, tassels, or other decorative trimmings. Additionally, an extra piece of fabric called boxing may be inserted between the pillow top and the pillow bottom, adding height. The inclusion or exclusion of this extra strip of fabric determines which of the two basic types of pillow, either boxed or knife-edged, you will make. When the top and the bottom of the pillow are sewed directly to one another, the pillow is knife-edged. When boxing is sewed between the top and bottom, as just described, the pillow is boxed. Either pillow type may be embellished with any sort of edge finish desired; the difference is that the boxed pillow requires twice the cording or whatever, since both the seam at the top and the one at the bottom of the boxing must be decorated. A boxed pillow generally gives a tailored appearance and is particularly appropriate for simple upholstery projects. Also, you will find that circular pillows must almost always be boxed; knife-edged circular pillows have a habit of puckering. (The exception is when a ruffle or other rather weighty edge finish is added to a circular knife-edged pillow.)

The decision must be made at the beginning of your project about how you will fill your pillow, whether it be with a rigid pillow form, loose stuffing, or an inner pillow you make yourself. If, for example, you plan to make a boxed windowseat cushion, you must know in advance that you can find a piece of solid-core foam that you can cut to that desired size, as a solid form is the only really appropriate filler for that particular type of pillow.

Additionally, the type of filler you select for your pillow will help determine what kind of closure must be used. The easiest, and perhaps the most appropriate for a pillow that will not require frequent cleaning, is the hand-sewn closure. A loose filler would be fine for this kind of pillow. However, if the cushion or pillow will need to be laundered often, it would be wise to sew in a zipper or other type of closure. You would not want to put a loose filler in this type of pillow—a much better choice is a separate inner pillow.

Unless you are making a round pillow, you will have to make a decision about what type of corners you want; there are several choices, as you will learn in the section on corners. Corners may also be left plain, or they may be trimmed with tassels.

AESTHETIC CONSIDERATIONS

A pillow top is in many ways like a soft painting, and the methods you choose to sew the pillow together act much as a mat or frame does for a painting. Consider the feeling you want the finished pillow to have. Do you want it to be feminine, masculine, tailored, frilly, casual, formal? All the fabrics and trimmings used in your pillow will contribute their measure to the final appearance and feeling of the pillow. A piece of dainty embroidery is surely more beautiful when set off by a delicate lace edging than with a wide ruffle in a bright plaid. On the other hand, a needlepointed mallard duck intended for a man's den might be further enhanced by a bold plaid ruffle.

Each element of your pillow must work to complement the others for an effective finished creation. Almost always, the pillow top is the center of interest, even if it is a solid color fabric. Therefore, all the

when a beautiful hand-tied fringe or wide lace is used with a plain or very small pillow. In these cases, the trimming is visually more important than the pillow top, and it is the purpose of the pillow to show it off. It is, however, the exception, rather than the rule, for the trimming to become more important than any other part of the pillow.

Remember also that each element within the pillow has a personality. Turkish corners give a certain type of feeling, as does ruffled eyelet trim, and the two feelings are so distinct and different that it is hard to imagine using the two together. Be aware of what each element is going to add to the pillow.

One more word: oddly-shaped pillows, even fairly simple ones such as triangles, usually make such a strong statement with their shape that they are best left untrimmed and covered in a subtly patterned fabric.

decorative trimmings should be planned to enhance the pillow top. The fabric chosen for the back, and the boxing, if any, should be of a texture and color to accent, not overwhelm, the pillow top. Additionally, any cording, ruffles, or fringes should be of a color and a size to bring out the best in the pillow top. Notable exceptions to this general rule are when cording in a contrasting color is used on a solid color boxed pillow, or

THE PILLOW BACK

The type of fabric you choose for a pillow back depends on the look you want to achieve, on the weight of the pillow top, and on the purpose of the pillow. The more formal types of fabric are velvet, velveteen, upholstery velvet, suede cloth (which gives the effect of velvet but is easier to work with and available in more colors), satin, antique satin, or a piece of the upholstery fabric from the sofa or chair on which the pillow will rest. Other suitable fabrics for pillow backs include linen, linen-look synthetics, corduroy, monk's cloth, and, especially with counted cross stitch and work of that nature, Aida or hardanger cloth. Gingham and calico are popular and very effective, but make certain they are of a heavy enough weight to match the pillow top.

Again, the choice of fabric for the pillow back, and in many cases, the matching cording or ruffle, should be made to fit the intended use of the pillow, the decor of the room in which it will be used, and the pillow top itself. You might find it advantageous to pick out the backing fabric when you select the threads or yarn to make a needlework piece. It is usually safe to choose the backing fabric to blend with the background of the needlework. If an exact match is not available, go for a darker tone of the same color. A more dramatic approach is to select backing fabric to pick up an accent color in the pillow top.

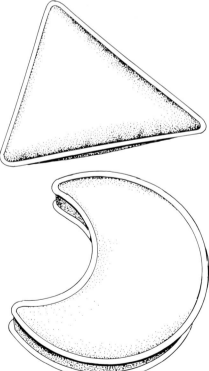

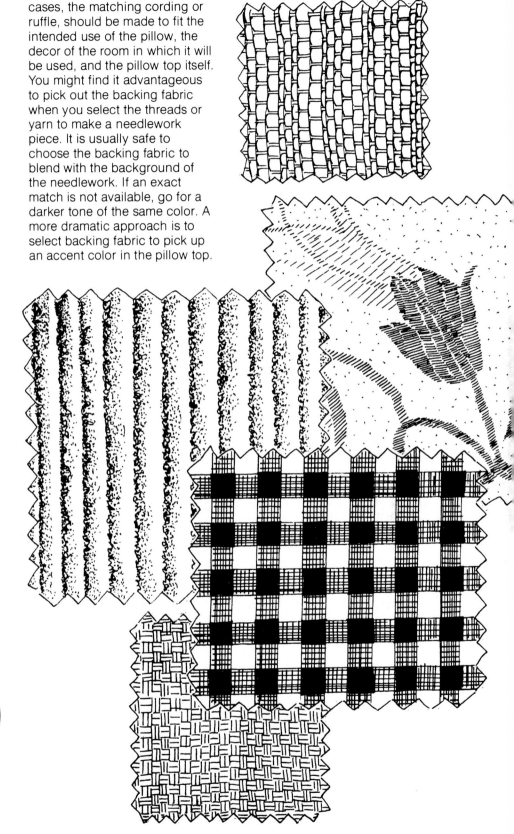

THE PILLOW TOP

Proper preparation of the pillow top is perhaps the most important step in the construction of a good pillow. No matter whether your pillow top is needlepoint, crewel, crochet, knit, quilted, handwoven, or whatever, you will want to make sure it is as perfectly constructed as possible. A pillow is a showplace! If, however, your pillow top is made of fabric, your main concern will be that the fabric is "on grain"; that is, that the lengthwise and crosswise threads are straight and cross one another at right angles. Additionally, if the fabric is a print, the major motif of the print should be centered on the pillow, and if a set of pillows is made from a fabric, the location of the major motif should be the same on each pillow. This is particularly true in chair seats when you want all the chairs to look the same.

BLOCKING NEEDLEWORK

The first step for a pillow top of needlework is blocking it into shape. The purpose of blocking is to pull the threads of the canvas or fabric on which the needlework was done back to their original "on grain" position. Keep in mind that while blocking can make up for a multitude of mistakes made while working the piece, it cannot correct entirely a piece that has been worked so tightly that the canvas is stretched permanently out of shape. The moral is to work with an even, slightly loose tension. (This applies to *all* needlework, not just needlepoint.)

If a needlepoint piece is badly out of shape, it must be soaked in *cold* water. This step is to be avoided if possible, especially if a painted canvas was used. The colors of the painted canvas may bleed, not because of the paint or ink, most of which is guaranteed not to run, but because of the very necessary sizing which comes loose from the canvas and floats the colors through the piece. If a piece *must* be soaked, be sure to dry it flat, rather than upright, to give less chance of the colors bleeding onto one another.

Alternative methods for dampening a piece preliminary to pinning it to the blocking board are: rolling it in a wet towel until the piece is damp; or, spraying it with water. Steam pressing your work with a wet cloth, after the piece is pinned down, is usually enough for pieces which are not much out of shape, as is often the case with bargello and pieces worked on a frame or hoop.

The steps to be followed in pinning down a needlework piece are always the same except that wet pieces should be blocked right side up and pieces

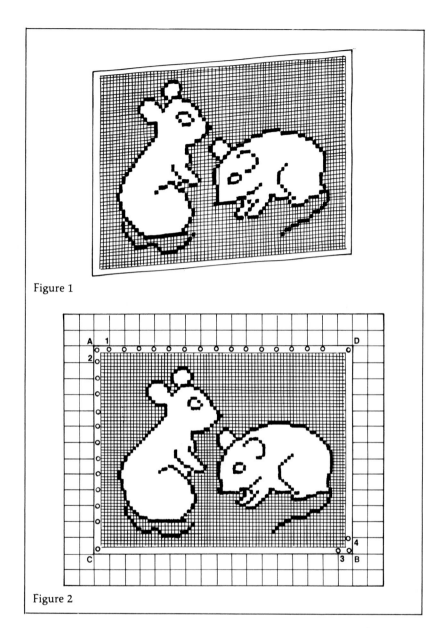

Figure 1

Figure 2

to be steamed should be blocked upside down. (The reason for this is to retain stitch texture and prevent flattening the face of the work.) Pinning down may be done on a plywood board, a drawing board, or a cutting board. If the piece is small, the ironing board may be used.

First, mark a square or rectangle the size of the canvas on the board or on paper attached to the board. (If you do a lot of blocking, it will be useful

to mark a board in 1″ [2.5cm] squares across the whole surface so that pieces of many different sizes can be blocked on the board.) Aluminum push pins are the best to use for blocking, because they are sharp and do not rust. Two precautions: make certain your pins are rustproof; and never, never pin into the worked part of the canvas.

Most needlepoint requiring blocking has become a little bit diamond-shaped. (See fig. 1.) To correct this, pin the needlepoint to the marked board as follows: Starting at A, pin the corner to the board at the upper left corner. Now place a pin at 1 and 2 in the same corner. At opposite corner B, repeat the procedure through 3 and 4. Now pin from 2 toward C, spacing pins about 1″ (2.5cm) apart. Stop the pins about 2″ (5.1cm) from corner C. Repeat from 1 to D, then from D to 4 and C to 3. (See fig. 2.) If the piece is soaking wet, allow to dry thoroughly—at least 24 hours. If the piece is face down, use a wet cloth and steam iron until it is damp through and allow to dry thoroughly. Drying is important because the needlepoint will revert to its original warped shape if removed from the blocking board while still wet.

Crewel and other embroidery work should be blocked on a heavily padded surface, such as can be formed with several layers of toweling. Work with the embroidery face down. Using a steam iron and a light spray starch, press and pull the embroidery to the correct shape with the backs of your hands. Let it dry in the correct shape before moving it.

Knitted, crocheted, and handwoven pieces should be blocked much the same as other needlework, that is, dampened and pulled or pressed into shape. There is very seldom a need to pin pieces of this type onto a board. If washing is necessary, cold water and cold water soap is a must. Drying completely is the most important step here, as with needlepoint and embroidery.

MAKING A PATTERN

The shape of your pillow may be determined by any one of a number of factors. The shape of a particular piece of needlework, a chairseat, a particular space you wish to fill with a pillow, or a distinctive fabric design can determine the shape and size of your pillow. Other things that determine shape and size are existing pillow forms, pillows that must be re-covered, or the specific function of the pillow, i.e., floor seating. Regularly shaped pillows, such as squares and rectangles, do not really require a pattern as the fabric can easily be measured and marked. But if the shape is unusual—round, octagonal, or that of an odd-shaped chair or stool, a paper pattern must be prepared.

A round pattern can be easily marked on paper by using a compass. A string compass can be used for large circles. Fold a square of paper slightly larger than the diameter of the desired circle into quarters. Take a length of string that is equal to a bit more than the radius of the desired circle and tie a pencil onto one end of the string. Push a pin through the other end of the string so that the distance

between the pin and the pencil is exactly equal to the radius of the circle. Place the pin at the folded corner of the paper and, holding the string taut, draw the outer edge of the circle. (See fig. 3.) Add a seam allowance of ½″ (1.3cm) and cut pattern out. Use the pattern to center the design of the pillow top, to cut the pillow back, and to cut out sheet foam rubber if used.

To cut a perfect octagonal pattern, fold a square of paper in half, in half again, then in half on the diagonal and in half a fourth time. Cut a straight line from one side to the other. (See fig. 4.) When this is opened, a perfect octagonal will have been formed. (See fig. 5.)

To make an oddly-shaped seat or back cushion fit exactly into a chair, use aluminum foil and make careful measurements. Aluminum foil fits easily into the curves and indentures that are so typical of many types of antique chairs. Mold the foil carefully into the shape of the chair seat, creasing the outer edge with your fingernail or a pencil. Lift foil from chair and trim away excess foil on the crease line. Trace the aluminum foil pattern carefully onto paper. Check the measurements of the

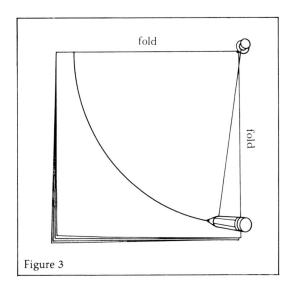

Figure 3

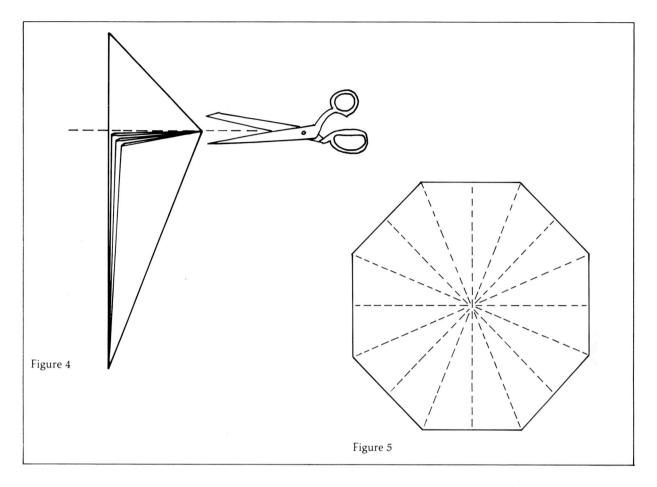

Figure 4

Figure 5

paper pattern against the chair, especially the back-to-front measure and then the widest and the narrowest side-to-side measures. Add ½" (1.3cm) seam allowances all around.

When measuring a pillow form or existing pillow for a cover, measure from seam to seam, front to back and side to side, then add ½" (1.3cm) all around for seams. Plan for the cover to be 1" (2.54cm) *smaller* all around than the pillow form or existing pillow. This will ensure a smooth, well-fitting cover. For example, if the pillow form measures 16" (40.6cm) square, the pillow top should be 14" (35.6cm) square when finished. However, you must allow ½" (1.3cm) seams all around, so you would cut out a 15" (38.1cm) square.

LINING THE TOP

If the pillow top is knitted, crocheted, or of a sheer fabric, a lining is necessary both to add body and depth to the pillow top and to hide construction details such as seam allowances. The color of the lining may be chosen to match the color of the pillow top, or it may contrast with the pillow top for a different effect. Machine-stitch the lining to the pillow top along the outer seamlines, then treat the lining and top as one piece during the construction of the pillow.

ENLARGING A PILLOW TOP

If your pillow is to be made of fabric, the chances are that you can cut the pillow top to the desired size without adding a border. However, sometimes a piece of needlework is not the size you want the pillow to be, and there are ways to make it bigger and have it look like that was what was intended all along. If you want to enlarge a piece of needlepoint, you can add a canvas strip to the worked canvas as follows: Overlap the original piece of canvas and the strip to be added by four stitches, matching the threads of the canvas exactly. Needlepoint your border design through both thicknesses. A contrasting color or a patterned stitch will make the piecing less obvious. (See fig. 6.)

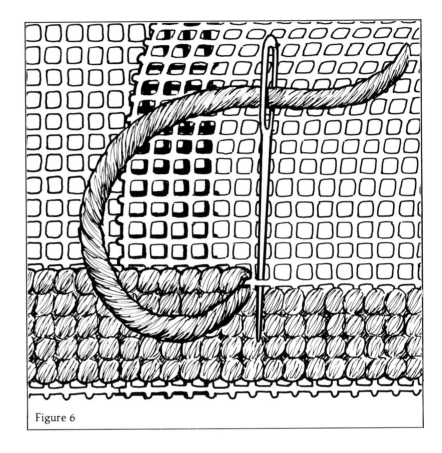

Figure 6

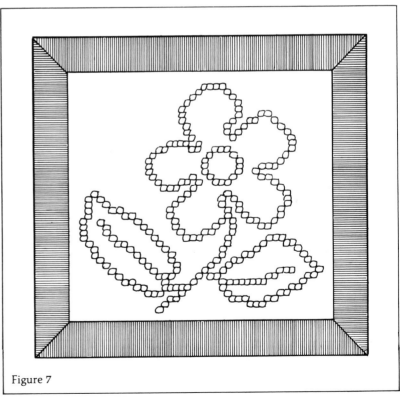

Figure 7

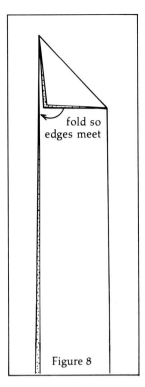

fold so
edges meet

Figure 8

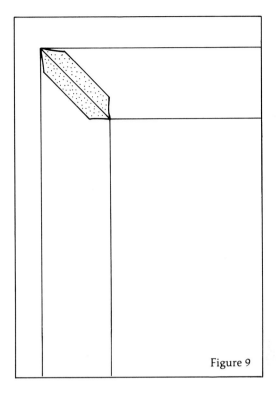

Figure 9

You may also frame the piece of needlework with the same fabric as the pillow back or with braid or ribbon. (See fig. 7.) To make a frame, first measure on the seamline around the outside edges of the piece to be enlarged and add to length and width measurements the width of the frame at both ends. For example, if you want to add a 3″ (7.6cm) wide frame to a piece of needlework that measures 5″ by 7″ (12.7cm by 17.8cm) on the stitching lines, two strips of the frame would need to be 11″ (27.9cm) long and two strips would have to be 13″ (33cm) long. Make the frame, and miter the corners at the same time like this: place the ends of the strips right sides together, then fold a true diagonal from the corner to one side and press. (See fig. 8.) Stitch exactly on pressed line; trim away excess fabric; press seam open, and open out the strip for a perfect miter. (See fig. 9.) Repeat on all four corners to

make a frame, then set the needlework piece into the frame. A fabric frame requires seam allowances in addition to the fabric needed for the width of the frame. The seam allowance should be left out of the mitering so the frame will fit onto the needlework. A braid or ribbon frame may be topstitched in place on the needlework.

EDGE FINISHES

PLAIN SEAM

The simplest and fastest way to join the pillow top and bottom together is with a plain seam. Place the top and bottom of the pillow together, right sides facing, outer edges matched all around the pillow. Begin stitching in the center of one side, preferably the lower edge, if the pillow top has a one-way design. Stitch around the outer edge of the pillow along the seamline, which is usually ½'' (1.3cm) in from the cut edge. Stitch slowly up to the corner; at the last stitch, leave the needle lowered into the fabric, then lift the presser foot and pivot the fabric on the needle until the second side is in line for stitching. (See fig. 10.) Lower the presser foot and stitch to the next corner. Continue until the entire perimeter of the pillow has been stitched except for an ample opening (at least as wide as your hand) through which you will turn the pillow right side out and insert the pillow form or stuffing. Backstitch or double stitch on either side of the opening for strength. (Note: If a pillow form is to be inserted, leave most of one whole side of the pillow open. Stitch the corners, but leave the rest of the side open. This will give plenty of room for inserting the form but will ensure that all the corners look the same.) You may cut off the seam allowances or not, as you desire, but professional finishers often do not trim away any seam allowance no matter how many thicknesses because this extra fabric adds body to the outer edge of the pillow. This is a particularly useful hint if loose stuffing is used, because it is difficult to stuff for a crisp edge. You should, however, trim away

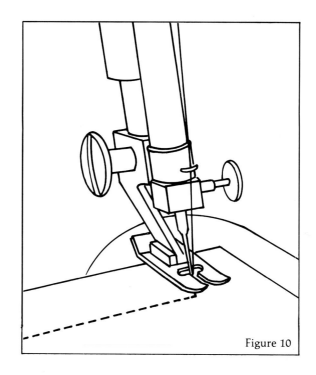

Figure 10

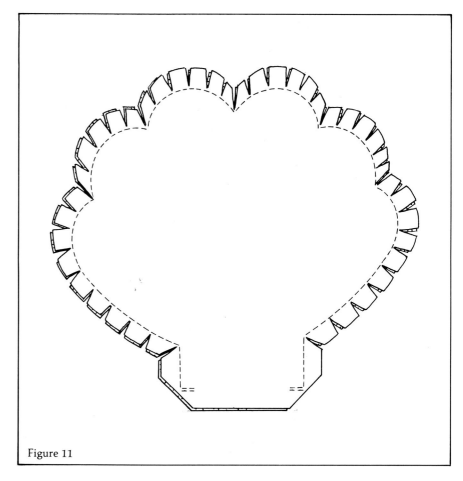

Figure 11

excess fabric across the corners, and if there are any curved portions to the seam, clip the seam allowance in these areas to the stitching line so the seam allowance will lie flat when the pillow is turned right side out. (See fig. 11.) A plain seam on a knife-edged circular pillow will not give good results; the outer edge of the pillow will be rippled.

Before turning the pillow right side out, press all the seams flat (as stitched), to embed the stitching. Turn pillow right side out. Roll the seam between your fingers to position the seam exactly on the edge of the pillow. If the fabric is difficult to work with, baste around the entire outer edge of the pillow through both thicknesses of fabric to hold the seam exactly on the edge for the final pressing. Pull the corners square with a pin or blunt needle, taking care not to snag threads of the fabric. Metal rulers or a right angle placed inside the pillow at the seam edge act as guide to pressing a good corner. Press the pillow carefully, keeping the seam exactly on the edge. Remove any basting before stuffing the pillow.

CORDING

Cording is the most popular decorative edge finish for a pillow. Used alone, it adds a tailored, professional look to a hand-made pillow. Used in combination with other edge finishes such as ruffles or flanges, cording adds a note of luxury. When it is sewed into a pillow seat that receives a lot of wear, cording strengthens the edges of the pillows where friction is the worst, thus adding to the life of the pillow.

Cording is made by covering an inner core cord, known as cable cord, with fabric. (Cording is distinguished from piping in that piping has no inner cord.) Cording may be purchased ready-made by the yard in a variety of colors and sizes, but it is not difficult to make yourself. Cable cord is available almost everywhere fabrics or notions are sold. Cable cord can be made of cotton or polyester; it can also be made of several plys of yarn twisted into a rope, or of one single ply. The least expensive and most versatile is a cotton cord covered with a cheesecloth type netting. This type cord turns corners most easily and does not show ridges when covered with a lightweight fabric. All of the different types of cords come in different diameters, from very tiny—almost like string—to large rope-like sizes.

When covering cord for your pillow, you might want to match a color in the pillow top, or you may choose to make the cording and the pillow back of the same fabric. Whatever the color or pattern or size of the cording, it should complement the overall plan of the pillow.

Fabric strips for covering the cable cord should be cut on the bias to wrap smoothly around the cord and to conform to the shape of the pillow. In some cases, however, the pattern of a particular fabric may be destroyed by cutting the strips on the bias. In those cases, use the crosswise grain of the fabric, but be prepared for more difficulty in stitching the cording around corners; the cording will have to be clipped frequently, close to the stitching, in order to make up for the flexibility lost by not using bias. With knit fabrics, the most flexible direction in the fabric construction is the crosswise, so the cording strips should be cut from the crosswise of a knit fabric.

To determine how wide the fabric strip should be to go around the cable cord, add 1¼″ (3.2cm) to the circumference of the cord. (Find the circumference of the cable cord by wrapping a tape measure loosely around it. The circumference is also printed on the dispenser from which the cord was purchased.) The length of the bias strips should be enough to go around the outer edge of the pillow top plus 4″ (10.2cm) for joining the ends. Ideally, you would be able to cut one long bias strip that would be the exact length needed but that is almost never the case. Here are two ways to cut and piece bias strips.

Individually pieced bias strips: This method should be used if just a small amount of bias is required.
1. To find the true bias of a rectangular piece of fabric, fold the crosswise edge of the fabric down, and align it perfectly with the lengthwise threads, or the selvage. Press the fold. (See fig. 12.)
2. Using tailor's chalk, draw lines parallel to the true bias fold line making the lines the same distance apart, that distance being equal to the width bias strip needed. Measure and mark

as many strips as are needed to cover the length of cord. (See fig. 13.) Cut along the fold; then cut along the chalk lines.

3. Bias strips should always be joined on the lengthwise grain, which creates a flat, less noticeable diagonal seam across the strip. If the ends of any strips have been cut on the crosswise grain, fold those ends on the lengthwise grain, and cut off the triangle that forms.

With right sides together, lap the ends so that the points extend ½" (1.3cm) and the strips are at right angles to each other. Using ½" (1.3cm) seams, stitch ends of strips together. (See fig. 14.) Press seams open and trim to ¼" (6mm).

Continuously pieced bias strips:

This method is a true time-saver, especially if a lot of bias must be cut. All the seaming is done in one step.

1. Find the true bias of a rectangular piece of fabric as outlined for individually pieced bias strips. Cut along the true bias fold line and discard the triangle.

2. Using tailor's chalk, draw lines parallel to the true bias fold line, marking off the width of bias strip needed. Measure and mark as many strips as are needed to cover the length of cord. Label opposite ends of each strip with corresponding letters. (See fig. 15.) Each line must begin and end on a side edge of the rectangle of fabric. Discard the excess corner triangle.

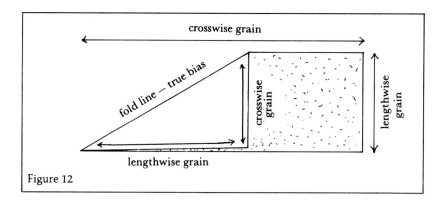

Figure 12

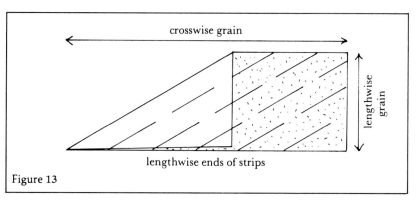

Figure 13

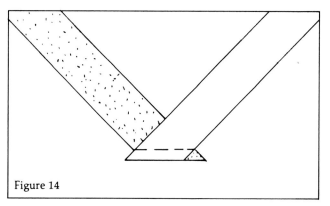

Figure 14

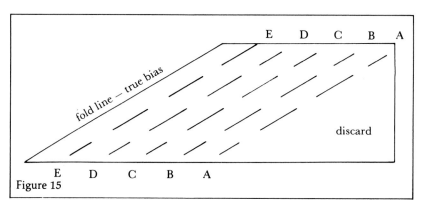

Figure 15

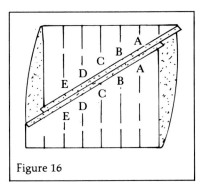

Figure 16

3. Form a tube by bringing right sides together so that A meets A, B meets B, etc. The marks should meet exactly so that one uninterrupted line spirals around the tube. Stitch edges together with a ¼" (6mm) seam and press open. (See fig. 16)

4. Begin cutting along line A and continue in a spiral fashion to the end.

Covering the cord: Wrap the bias strip around the cord, right side out. Make sure the raw edges are even. Using a zipper foot attachment, stitch the bias strip in place close to the cable cord, but be careful not to crowd the cord too tightly. (See fig. 17.) Gently pull the bias strip in front and in back of the needle as you stitch.

Sewing the cording to the pillow top: The seam allowances of the cording should be of the same width as the seam allowances of the pillow top. If they are not, trim them down to the same width—usually ½" (1.3cm). If the seam allowances on the cording are narrower than those of the pillow, you must take care to place the stitching line on the cording exactly on top of the seamline of the pillow. If you sew cording to needlepoint done in straight rows, the cording must follow one row of the needlepoint exactly. The same is true for any pillow top that has very definite straight lines; the cording must follow a straight line.

The ends of the cording will overlap 2" (5.1cm), so leave a 2" (5.1cm) "tail" on the cording when you start to stitch it on. Begin on any side of the pillow top and pin the cording in place so that the stitching line on the cording rests exactly on the seamline of the pillow top. Still using a zipper foot, sew the cording to the pillow top, using the stitching on the cording as a guide. (A zigzag presser foot on top of the cord can be used if necessary. One "toe" of the presser foot will rest on top of the cord.)

To go around a corner with cording, first stitch up to the corner and leave the needle in the fabric at the last stitch. Clip the seam allowance of the

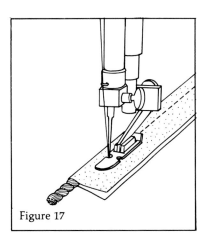

Figure 17

cording (four or five times, up to the stitching) so that the seam allowance can fan out around the corner allowing the cording to lie smoothly. With the needle still in the fabric, lift the presser foot and pivot the work on the needle so that the next side is ready for stitching. (Refer to fig. 66.)

To join the ends of the cording, open the stitching on one end and open up bias, exposing the cord. Cut away 2″ (5.1cm) of the cord so that the two ends of the cord meet exactly. Turn under ¼″ (6mm) on the raw end of the bias strip. Fold the bias strip around the 2″ (5.1cm) "tail" you left at the beginning and stitch in place through all thicknesses of fabric. (See fig. 18.)

An alternative method for taking care of the ends of cording goes as follows: On each of the 2″ (5.1cm) "tails", push the bias back so that the cord can be cut out. Overlap the flattened ends as shown and stitch through all layers. (See fig. 19.)

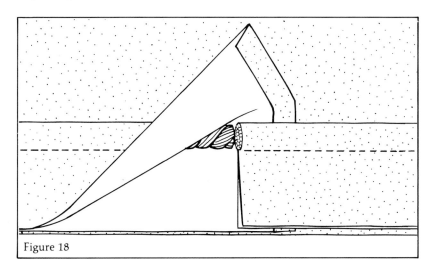

Figure 18

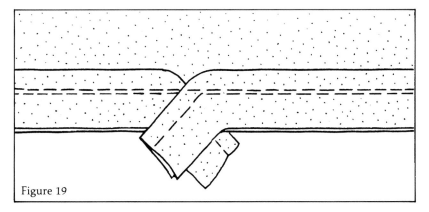

Figure 19

RUFFLES

Although we generally think of ruffles as feminine and frilly, they actually take on a number of different looks, depending on the fabric used and their width. An understated ruffle done in the right fabric, especially if combined with cording, can be just the right softening touch for a formal or masculine pillow style. Although the opulence of one big ruffle around the outer edge of a pillow makes quite a statement in itself, a wide ruffle can be used as a backdrop for an additional narrow, contrasting ruffle for a super-luxurious feeling. Or, instead of a ruffle, choose an eyelet or crocheted edging, or perhaps some bright ribbon or braid. The outer edge of the ruffle offers another place where trimming can be attached—a tiny rickrack on the edge of a calico ruffle may be just what the pillow needs to make it really distinctive.

Preparing the ruffle: A ruffle may be cut from one thickness of fabric and hemmed or otherwise finished along the outer edge, or it may be cut double width to become a self-faced ruffle. The length of fabric needed for a full, luxurious ruffle is 2½ times the distance around the outer edge of the pillow.

A self-faced ruffle may be cut from either the straight grain or the bias of the fabric. The bias is especially good for fabric that has a definite, regular geometric pattern, such as a check, stripe, or plaid. Cutting these fabrics on the bias sets the pattern on the diagonal and adds a note of interest. Cut the fabric twice the width of the desired finished ruffle plus two seam allowances. (See Cording for how to cut bias strips.) Fold the strips in half wrong sides together, and stitch the raw edges together—this makes gathering easier. (See fig. 20.)

A ruffle of a single thickness works best when the fabric does not have a distinct right and wrong side. The single thickness ruffle is also best when cut on the crosswise grain of the fabric; the free edge is much easier to hem. The single thickness ruffle must be cut in a width to equal the finished ruffle plus a seam allowance, usually ½'' (1.3cm), and a hem, which can be ¼'' to ½'' (6mm-1.3cm).

The hemmer attachment on your sewing machine is perfect for hemming the edge of a single ruffle. Or you may turn the hem allowance under twice to make a ¼'' (6mm) wide double hem, and top-stitch it. (See fig. 21.) A third alternative is to fold the hem allowance to the *right* side of the ruffle and topstitch a narrow trim in place over it. (See fig. 22.)

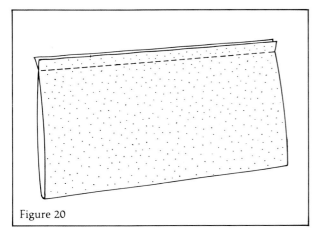

Figure 20

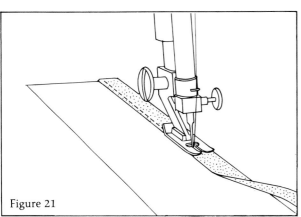

Figure 21

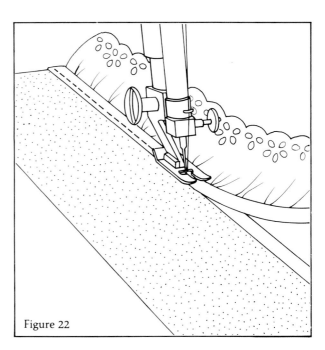

Figure 22

Of course, you can always handstitch the hem. A hand-rolled hem is particularly effective with sheer fabrics. Make a hand-rolled hem as follows:

1. Mark the fabric with tailor's chalk where the hemline is to be, and stitch ¼" (6mm) below the mark. Trim excess hem allowance ⅛" (3mm) below the stitching line. Press stitching. (See fig. 23.)

2. Fold stitched edge to wrong side of fabric, making sure the stitching line is just below the folded hem allowance. Working from right to left and using a fine needle with thread to match the fabric, take a small stitch through the fold. Then, diagonally ⅛" (3mm) below and beyond the stitch, pick up a few threads of the main fabric (See fig. 24.)

3. After several loose stitches have been made, carefully pull on the thread to roll the hem to the wrong side of fabric. (See fig. 25.)

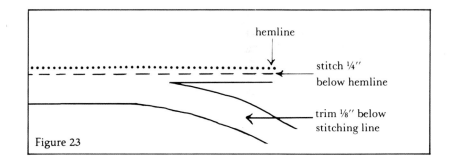

Figure 23

hemline

stitch ¼" below hemline

trim ⅛" below stitching line

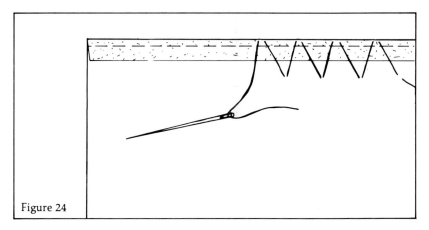

Figure 24

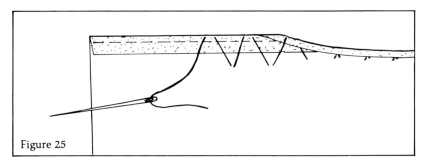

Figure 25

Gathering the ruffle: The ruffle strip may be gathered in one of several different ways. The easiest, but the hardest to gauge for fullness, is to use the ruffler attachment that is available for most makes of sewing machines. It automatically gathers and stitches the fabric, but it is difficult to be precise about how much fabric is gathered into the ruffle. Another method for gathering a ruffle is to run two rows of long machine stitching into the ruffle at the seamline and then ¼" (6mm) above it. Pull gently on the threads to gather the fullness. (See fig. 26.) The third method is to zigzag over a strong cord, then pull on the cord to gather the ruffle. The cord must be placed slightly above the seamline so the zigzag stitching does not go into the body of the ruffle. (See fig. 27.) The ruffle may also be gathered by hand, using a double thread and a short running stitch. Yet another method is to make a narrow casing (which can be done only with a double ruffle) and run a cable cord through the casing with a safety pin; then pull on the cord to gather. (See fig. 28.)

If you are going to put two ruffles or a ruffle and some other trimming on the pillow, gather each ruffle separately, then stitch one to the other along the seamline before sewing them to the pillow top. They may be treated as one piece after they are sewed together.

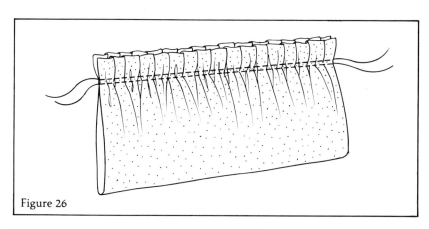

Figure 26

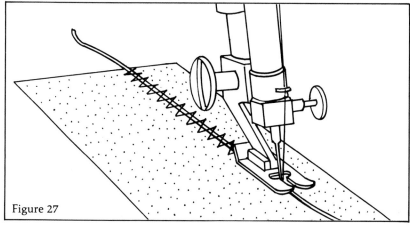

Figure 27

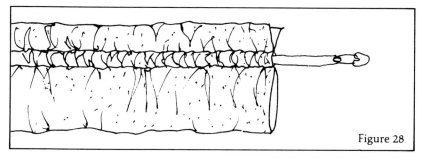

Figure 28

Sewing the ruffle to the pillow top:
Start in a corner, if there is one, and pin the ruffle to the top, raw edges of ruffle and top aligned, and with the finished edge of the ruffle toward the center of the pillow. Be sure to allow a little extra fullness at the corners. When the ruffle is almost completely pinned in place and the fullness distributed, sew the ends of the ruffle together with one of the following seams, both of which give a finished appearance; no raw edges remain.

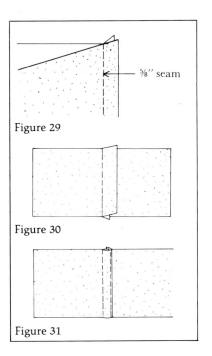

Figure 29

Figure 30

Figure 31

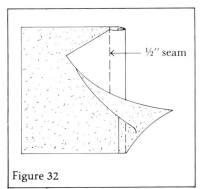

Figure 32

Flat-felled seam: This is a very sturdy seam, particularly good for use on heavy fabrics.
1. Using a ⅝″ (1.5cm) seam allowance, pin-baste wrong sides of fabric together, then stitch in place. (See fig. 29.)
2. Trim edge of one seam allowance to one-half its width. Press seam open, then press seam allowances to one side with the wider seam allowance on top. (See fig. 30.)
3. Turn the raw edge of the top seam allowance under ⅛″ (3mm) and stitch along the fold through all thicknesses. (See fig. 31.)
French seam: This seam becomes almost invisible, and it is a very good seam for sheer fabrics. The end result is much narrower than the flat-felled seam.
1. Pin-baste *wrong* sides of fabric together. Stitch, using a ¼″ (6mm) seam. Press seam to one side, then carefully press seam open with point of iron. Trim seam allowances to ⅛″

(3mm).
2. Fold right sides of fabric together so that the stitching line lies directly on the folded edge. Using ½″ (1.3cm) seams, stitch in place, enclosing the raw edges of the first seam. (See fig. 32.) Press the seam to one side.

When the ends of the ruffle are sewed together, the ruffle may be permanently stitched in place to the pillow top. Overlap stitching at beginning and ending of seam. Do not trim away seam allowances. (See fig. 33.) When stitching the pillow back in place, take care not to catch the ruffle in the seam. Leave the ruffle in position with the finished edge toward the center of the pillow, then pin the pillow back in place over it. Stitch the pillow back in place with the pillow top up, so that you can use the stitching which holds the ruffle in place as a guide. Sew on top of the ruffle stitching so that no extra lines of stitching show when the pillow is turned right side out.

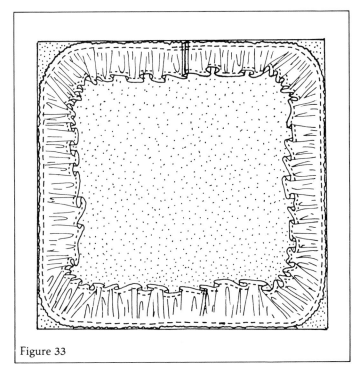

Figure 33

FLANGES

A flange is a straight, ungathered piece of fabric that is very much like a frame for the pillow. It provides a nice tailored edge to a pillow, and if you plan the flange when you are constructing the pillow, it is very easy to make. Following are instructions for a flange that is made all-in-one with the pillow.

1. Decide on the size you want the pillow to be and the width you want for the flanges. Cut out a piece of fabric with the following dimensions: Length—twice the width of the pillow plus four times the width of the flange plus 4″ (10.2cm). Width—twice the length of the pillow plus twice the width of the flange plus 1″ (2.5cm). (See fig. 34.)

2. Hem the short sides of the fabric rectangle by turning raw edges under ¼″ (6mm), then under 1″ (2.5cm); press, then stitch in place. (See fig. 35.)

3. Fold fabric wrong side out so that hemmed edges overlap each other by ¾″ (1.9cm) at center back of a tube that is formed. Stitch across each end of the tube with a ½″ (6mm) seam allowance. Clip corners, turn tube right side out, and press. (See fig. 36.)

4. Measure from the outer edges of the tube in toward the center of the pillow the width the flange is to be. Mark with chalk the flange width around the entire pillow, then stitch on marked line. Outer edge of flange may be topstitched if desired. Insert pillow from the back through hemmed opening. (See fig. 37.)

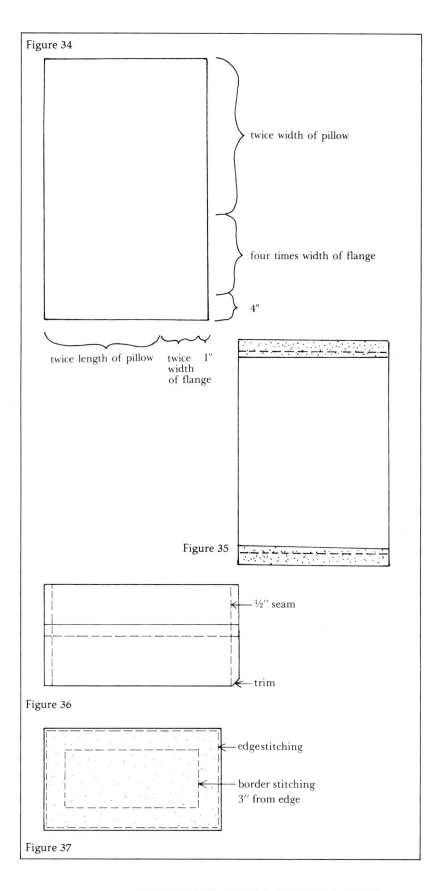

Figure 34

twice width of pillow

four times width of flange

4″

twice length of pillow   twice width of flange   1″

Figure 35

½″ seam

trim

Figure 36

edge stitching

border stitching 3″ from edge

Figure 37

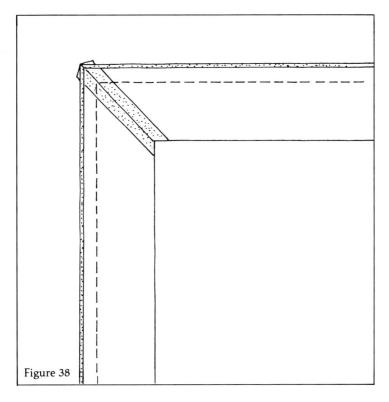

Figure 38

If you want to make a separate flange for your pillow, follow the instructions for framing a piece of needlework with braid or ribbon on page 41. You must make two separate frames, one for the front side and one for the back side of the pillow. Allow a seam allowance at both edges of the frames, then sew them together, right sides facing, around the outer edge. (See fig. 38.) Turn flange right side out, press, and sew to pillow top just as you would a ruffle, matching corners of flange to corners of pillow top. (See fig. 39.) Continue with construction of pillow.

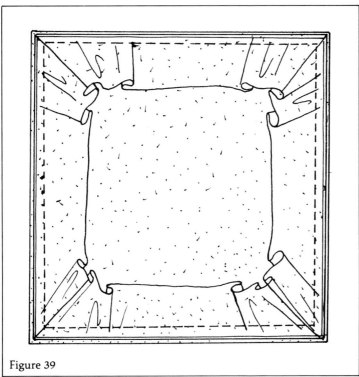

Figure 39

FRINGE

Handmade from fabric or yarn or bought ready-made by the yard, fringe comes in so many different styles that it's impossible to list them all. As with ruffles, a look of extra richness can be obtained by using a double row of fringe all around the pillow, perhaps with one row set into the seam and the other row hand-sewed on top. Of course, a more individual creation is achieved when you make the fringe yourself; several easy methods are described further on in this section.

Commercial fringe can roughly be categorized according to the type of heading it has. (See fig. 40.) Some types of heading are completely finished, much like a separate braid, and in this case the fringe may be sewed directly to the finished edge of the pillow, either by hand or machine. In other cases, the heading consists simply of several rows of stitching that hold the loops of the fringe in place. In that case, the fringe must be sewed into the seam at the edge of the pillow.

To determine how much fringe you need, measure around the outer edge of the pillow and add 1″ (2.5cm) for finishing the ends. Width, of course, is determined by what is available and the look you wish to achieve. With hand-made fringe you can have exactly the width you want.

To sew purchased fringe into a seam, follow the instructions for attaching ruffles, easing in some extra fullness at the corners. The way the ends of the fringe are sewed together depends on the type of fringe. The ends can be sewed together with a ½″ (1.3cm) seam, or the ends of a braid-type heading can be trimmed to meet one another exactly and securely hand-

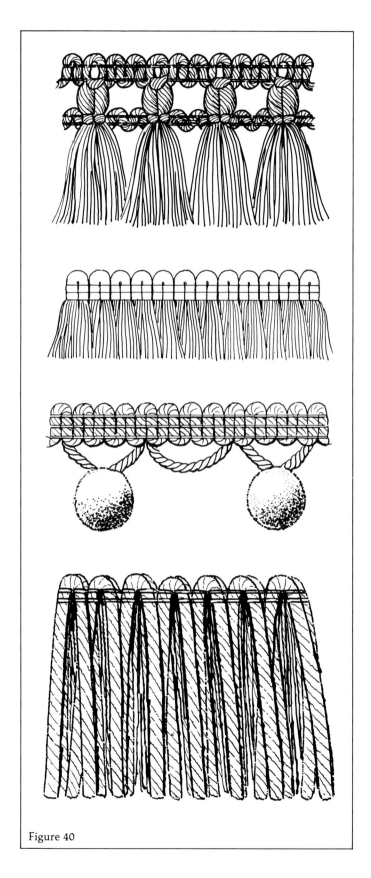

Figure 40

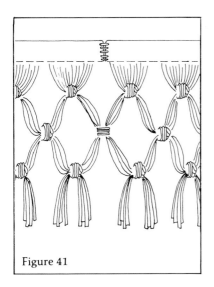

Figure 41

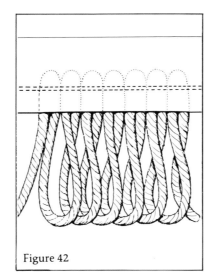

Figure 42

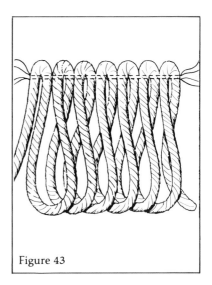

Figure 43

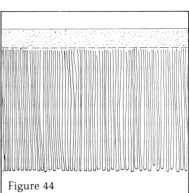

Figure 44

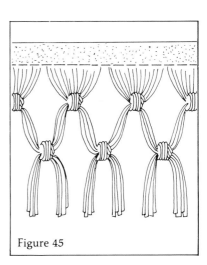

Figure 45

whipped together. If the fringe is very wide and knotted, it is a good idea to tack the knots to one another across the width of the fringe. (See fig. 41.)

To sew fringe in place on a finished pillow, first choose a fringe that has a braid-type heading. Using tiny hand whipstitches, sew the lower edge of the heading to the seam of the pillow. Tack ends of fringe to one another, then whip top edge of heading to pillow top, easing to fit where necessary.

Hand Made Fringes

Loop fringe: Choose yarn in a color to complement the pillow top. Measure around the outside of the pillow top to determine the length of fringe you will need. Cut a length of masking tape to this measurement. Loop the yarn so that one edge is on the sticky side of the masking tape, making the loops as large as you want, and placing them as close together as necessary for the desired thickness of fringe. Continue looping the yarn until the length of the masking tape is covered. Place another piece of masking tape on top and stitch through both layers of tape and the yarn. (See fig. 42). Stitch twice for extra security, then

gently remove the tape and you have a fringe made exactly to your specifications. (See fig. 43.) Leave it looped or cut it if you prefer straight fringe. Make two thicknesses of fringe by repeating the looping process a second time, placing the tops of the loops just slightly higher on the second row. Stitch through the tape and the yarn, being sure to catch in both layers in at least one row of stitching. Or, make several separate layers of fringe and sew all of them into the edge of your pillow.

Hand-tied fringe made from fabric: Cut a length of fabric slightly longer than the edge to which the fringe is to be applied and in the width desired for the finished fringe plus ½'' (1.3cm) for the heading. Cut the strip so the lengthwise threads of the fabric run the length of the strip. Do not sew strips together if you need a longer length of fringe than you have in one fabric piece; instead, make short lengths up through step 2, then join them at the heading, and continue from step 3.
1. Measure ½'' (1.3cm) in from

one long edge and run a row of short machine stitches (16-20 per inch) down entire length of fabric. This row of stitching will be at the top of the fringe.

2. Ravel all the lengthwise threads out of the fabric up to the line of stitching. (See fig. 44.)

3. Decide on the knotting pattern you want to use, then group the crosswise threads into equal bunches and tie them into the desired pattern. (See fig. 45.)

4. Sew finished fringe into pillow. Note: Lovely variations can be achieved by using two colors of fabric together. Simply sew the two lengths together in the first step and proceed from there.

Fringe in needlepoint canvas: This fringe should be worked next to the last row of needlepoint stitches. Be certain to keep the fringe out of the seam when you sew the backing to the needlepoint.

1. Choose a yarn color that complements your needlepoint design. Cut yarn into individual lengths slightly longer than you want finished fringe to be. An easy way to do this, since you will need so many individual lengths, is to cut a stiff piece of cardboard about ¼″ (6mm) wider than you want the finished fringe. Wrap the yarn several times around the cardboard, then cut along one edge. (See fig. 46.)

2. Fold each length of yarn in half. Using a tiny crochet hook, pull the loop of the yarn from front to back through one hole in the canvas, the same hole in which the last stitch of the needlepoint is placed. Then pull the loop to the front of the canvas, *two* holes underneath. Pass the two ends of the yarn through the loop and tighten up to make a knot on the front side of the canvas. (See fig. 47.) Continue around the perimeter of the needlepoint until all sides are finished with fringe. More than one thread may be used in each hole for a thicker fringe. Try mixing different colors of yarn for interesting effects.

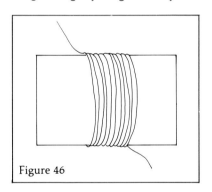

Figure 46

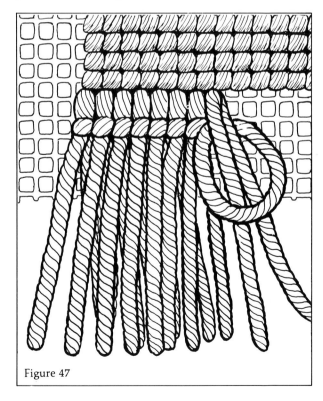

Figure 47

TWISTED CORD

One of the most elegant edge finishes for a pillow is twisted cord, especially if it is made of silk-like threads. However, one of the best examples of twisted cord, and one that can be used to great effect on pillows of a rather casual style, is plain old rope. Rope comes in all different sizes (diameters), and it gives a spritely nautical or rugged outdoor look when used as an edge finish. Twisted cord of other materials can be purchased, but it is easy and fun to make your own.

Although wool and acrylic yarns are the most easily available material for twisted cord, you can use macramé cord. Silk macramé cord twisted into a rope is lovely.

1. Cut yarn or thread three times the length needed. Cut as many strands in this length as desired; the more strands, the thicker the cord.

2. Secure all strands at one end to a doorknob or a chair back, or ask someone to hold them. (See fig. 48.)

3. Tie the other end of the strands around a pencil or ruler to help in turning. Holding strands fairly taut, twist pencil until strands begin to wrap together as one and when tension is released a bit, the cord wants to twist back upon itself.

4. When desired twist has been obtained, fold the cord in half, ends together, and allow the two lengths to wrap around each other. (See fig. 49.) Tie a knot in the end. The cord will stay twisted.

Note: A quick trick for twisting the cord is to use an electric hand mixer. Remove one beater and tie the strands of yarn to the remaining beater. Tie the other end of the strands to the door-knob. Turn the mixer on to a speed you can handle and

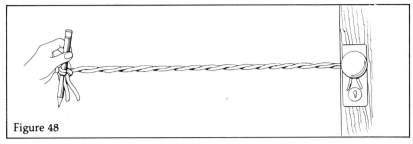

Figure 48

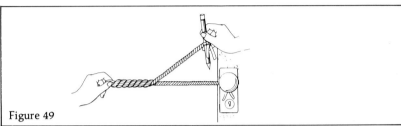

Figure 49

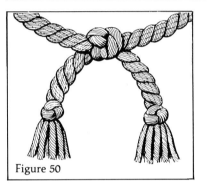

Figure 50

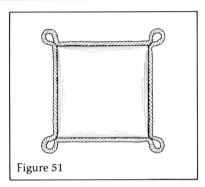

Figure 51

watch the yarn twist. This makes a very uniform cord with much less effort on your part.

To use twisted cord as an edge finish, simply whip it in place by hand over the seam that joins pillow back and front. Because it is very difficult to join the edges of the cord invisibly, the best way to handle the ends is to tie them together, then knot and loosen each end to form a little tassel. (See fig. 50.)

A special look can be obtained by making a loop of the cord at each corner of the pillow when you sew it in place. (See fig. 51.) The pillow can be hung on a hook by this loop if desired; this idea is particularly applicable to a daybed that must function as a sofa. The pillows will stay in place across the back of the daybed when they are hung from the wall.

TASSELS

Tassels can be made fat or thin, to match or contrast with the color of the pillow top, and of almost any material you choose—yarn, braid, embroidery floss, ribbon, or metallic cord. Put them at the corners of a pillow, or make several individual tassels and attach them all around the outside of the pillow as an interesting and different edge finish. No matter what size you choose for your tassels or how you sew them on to your pillow, they add a lively and sometimes exotic note wherever they are used. Although tassels can be purchased ready-made, they are simplicity itself to make.

1. Cut a rectangle of cardboard to the desired length of the tassel. Wind the yarn or ribbon (or whatever you are making your tassel with) around the cardboard twenty or more times, depending upon the thickness desired for the tassel. (See fig. 52.) It is better to lay the threads next to one another rather than stacking them on top of each other.

2. Thread a large-eyed needle with 8″ (20.3cm) of yarn or embroidery floss. Slide needle under top of tassel strands and tie strands together tightly. (See fig. 53.) Cut untied ends of yarn and remove from cardboard.

3. Tightly wrap a piece of yarn or floss several times around the tied strands, one-third of the way down from the top. Tie the ends securely. With a tapestry needle or crochet hook, pull the loose ends into the tassel. Trim the tassel evenly to the desired length. (See fig. 54.)

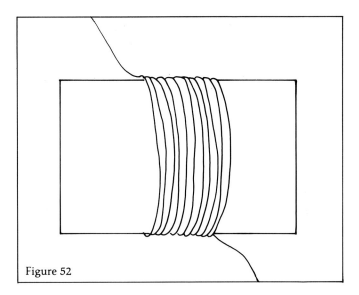

Figure 52

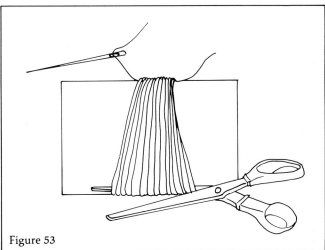

Figure 53

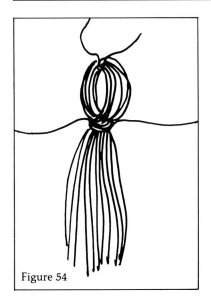

Figure 54

For a more elegant tassel, add a little crocheted cap as follows:
1. Using a crochet hook that is appropriate to the size yarn or floss you are using for the tassel, chain 3, work 6 single crochet in the second chain from hook, join with a slipstitch.
2. Work 2 single crochet in each stitch, join with a slip stitch (12 stitches).
3. Work 1 single crochet in first stitch, 2 single crochet in next stitch, repeat around (18 stitches).

Figure 55

4. From then on do one single crochet in each stitch until there are five rounds. Join and cut the yarn, leaving about 12" (30.5cm).
5. Pull the crocheted cap over the top of the tassel. Using the extra thread, whip the cap to the thread that is wrapped around the upper part of the tassel. (See fig. 55.)

To attach tassels to the pillow top, either sew them into the seam as you sew the pillow top and back together, or sew the tassels on after the pillow is completed. To sew them into the seam, position the tassels toward the inside of the pillow top with the double strand of yarn at the top of the tassel crossing the seamline. Sew twice across the double strands (see fig. 56), then pin pillow back in position and continue with pillow. To sew the tassel in place after the pillow is completed, thread a needle with the yarn at the top of the tassel and stitch the tassel securely in place.

BOXING

Boxing is a strip of fabric that is inserted between the pillow top and the pillow back, making the pillow thicker by the width of this additional strip. Boxing works best when a rigid form is used as stuffing; if loose stuffing is to be used, plan to stuff the pillow very firmly to achieve the desired shape. Boxed pillows are more tailored and formal-looking than knife-edged pillows. Boxing is good for bench pads, upholstered cushions, and circular pillows. Small square pillows or those with geometric patterns that give a squared look also benefit from boxing. Boxing is not good when a squishy, soft effect is desired.

To cut fabric strips for boxing, measure the circumference of the pillow form or the outer edges of the pillow top. (See fig. 57.) This gives you the length of the boxing strip; add 1" (2.5cm) for seam allowances. The width of the strip is determined by the height of the pillow form if one is being used; measure the form and add 1" (2.5cm) for seam allowances. If you are not using a form, plan to make the boxing at least 2" (5.1cm) wide; any narrower looks a little skimpy except in very rare cases.

If you must piece strips to get the length you need for the boxing, plan ahead for where the seams of the boxing will be. If the pillow is square or rectangular, place the seams in opposite corners. If the pillow is round or octagonal, place the seams halfway around the pillow.

Boxing is the perfect place to put the closure for your pillow. Plan to sew the closure, be it a zipper, or hook and eye tape, or whatever, into a flat piece of fabric that is 1" (2.5cm) longer than the closure and at least 2" (5.1cm) wider than the boxing

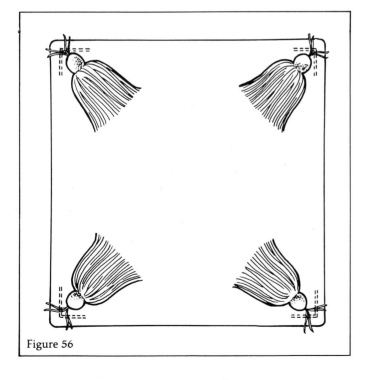

Figure 56

strip. Cut this piece of fabric in half the long way; then sew it back together with a 1'' (2.54cm) seam, and install closure according to package directions or the directions given in the Closures section of this chapter. Seam the remaining boxing strips to the ends of the closure. (See fig. 58.)

It is very important to follow the correct sequence of steps when sewing boxing into a pillow. One of the most frustrating occurrences with boxing is that sometimes the bottom and the top of the pillow don't seem to fit the boxing in the same way. You can avoid this problem by following these steps in order.

1. Apply your chosen edge finish, say cording, to the pillow top as usual.

2. Machine stitch on both long edges of the boxing strip, ½'' (1.3cm) from the edge. Pin-mark the boxing and the pillow top into four or eight equal sections, starting and ending at the seamline on the boxing.

3. Pin the boxing strip to the pillow top, clipping at corners or curved areas to stitching line. Match the pin-marks on the boxing to the pin-marks on the pillow top. Seam ends of boxing strip with a ½'' (1.3cm) seam. Stitch boxing to pillow top along seamline of pillow top.

4. Sew the cording for the bottom of the pillow to the *unstitched edge of the boxing.* (See fig. 59).

5. Pin the pillow back to the corded edge of the boxing strip, clip the corners, and stitch the back to the boxing. If a closure was not sewed into the boxing, leave an opening for turning the pillow cover right side out.

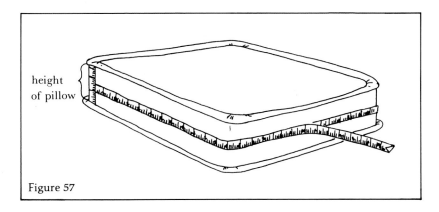

Figure 57

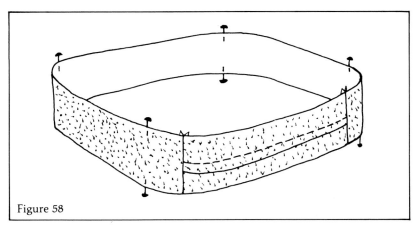

Figure 58

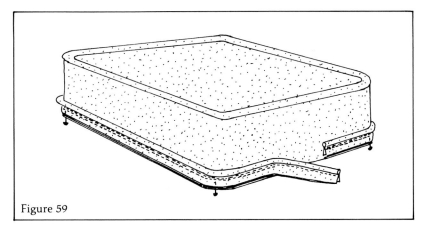

Figure 59

Boxing does not have to be just a straight strip of fabric. Interesting effects can be obtained by shirring the boxing before sewing it into the pillow. See page 89 in the Designer's Workbook for specific instructions on making shirred boxing. Following are instructions for a pillow with a shirred boxing that wraps around the edges of the pillow form to become a part of the pillow top and bottom. (See fig. 60.)

1. Decide on the size you want finished pillow to be, and plan for the pillow top to be at least 3″ (7.6cm) *smaller* all around than the finished pillow. Cut pillow top and pillow back to this size, allowing ½″ (1.3cm) seam allowances all around.

2. To cut boxing, plan for it to be three to four times longer than the distance around the outer edge of the pillow top. The width should equal the height of the pillow form plus 6″ (15.2cm) extra for wrapping over the top and bottom of the pillow, plus 1″ (2.5cm) for seam allowances. (See fig. 61.)

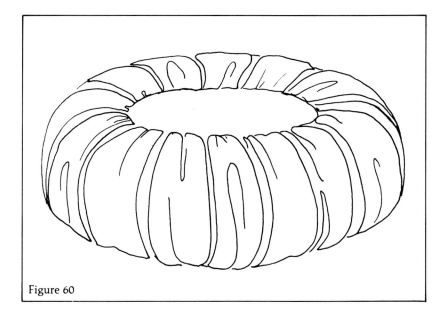

Figure 60

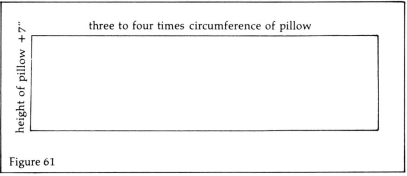

three to four times circumference of pillow

height of pillow +7″

Figure 61

Figure 62

3. Place a row of machine basting stitches (6-8 stitches per inch) at the ½" (1.3cm) seamline on both edges of the boxing strip. If fabric is heavy or thick, place another row of basting stitches ⅛" (3mm) away inside the seam allowance. Pull up on basting stitches on both edges until the boxing strip is equal in length to the outer edge of the pillow top.

4. Seam ends of boxing strip together with a ½" (1.3cm) seam allowance.

5. Pin-mark pillow top and shirred strip into fourths or eighths. With right sides together, pin boxing to pillow top, matching marks. If pillow is square or rectangular, adjust shirring so there is extra fullness at the corners. Stitch boxing to pillow top on seamline. (See fig. 62.)

6. Decide where the opening will be on the back of the pillow, and stitch seam tape on top of the shirring in this area to hold the gathers in position. (See fig. 63.)

7. Pin pillow back to the boxing, matching pin marks. Stitch, turn pillow right side out, and insert pillow form or stuffing.

BOLSTERS

Bolsters are essentially long, skinny boxed pillows with the bolster cover acting as the boxing. The ends of the bolster play the parts of the pillow top and pillow back. If you want a zipper in your bolster cover, place it in the seam. If the bolster is very narrow, you might not have enough room to put the zipper in the seam. In that case, plan to make the cover in two pieces so you can put the zipper in one of the seams while the piece is still flat.

The end pieces on a fitted bolster can either be flat, or they can be gathered or pleated. To make flat end pieces, simply measure the diameter and circumference of the end of the bolster and cut a piece to these measurements, allowing a ½" (1.3cm) seam allowance all around. Set end pieces into bolster after it has been sewed into a tube, following the directions for boxing.

To make a gathered end piece:

1. Cut a strip of fabric in a length to equal the circumference of the bolster plus 1" (2.5cm) for seam allowances. The width of the strip should be equal to *one-half* the diameter, or distance across, the end, plus 1" (2.54cm) for seam allowances.

2. Stitch the ends of the strip together with a ½" (1.3cm) seam allowance. Run two rows of machine basting (6-8 stitches per inch) into the strip at one edge, placing one row on the seamline and one row slightly into the seam allowance.

3. Set the edge of the strip without the machine basting into the bolster seam.

4. Pull up on the basting threads to gather the center of the end piece to fit. Tack the gathers securely in place by hand with needle and thread. (See fig. 64.)

5. Turn bolster right side out and sew a button or tassel in place at the center of the gathers.

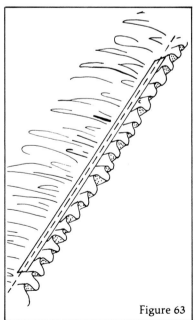

Figure 63

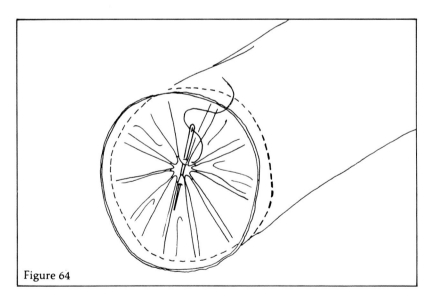

Figure 64

To make a pleated end piece:
1. Cut the strip the same as for a gathered end piece. Decide on the number of pleats that you want (usually five to seven) and divide this number into the length of the strip to determine how deep each pleat should be.
2. Mark one edge of the end piece strip into this number of sections of equal size.

3. Fold pleats, taking up the full depth at the center and tapering to nothing at outer edge so end piece will lie flat. (This will take some manipulation.) Baste pleats in place at center.
4. Sew end piece into bolster. Turn bolster right side out, and sew a button over center of pleats. (See fig. 65.)

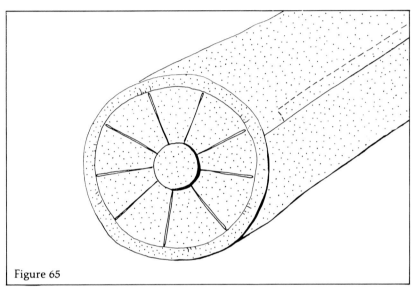

Figure 65

CORNERS

There are basically three kinds of corners common to pillow-making. The one used about ninety per cent of the time is the right-angle corner, in which you stitch up to the end of one side, lift the presser foot on the sewing machine, pivot the work 90 degrees on the needle to stitch the next side, and proceed until all corners are made. In some cases, it works better to make this corner slightly rounded, especially if thick cording is being used, as the cording simply cannot make a 90 degree turn without puckering. To round a corner with cording, clip the seam allowance of the cording every ½″ (1.3cm) or so and ease the cording around the corner. (See fig. 66.)

Corners that are gathered or pleated are very much the same in that they are used with a rigid pillow form when a softly boxed effect is desired. The pillow top and the pillow back are planned so that they will meet at the halfway point of the depth of the pillow, thus forming a sort of mock boxing.

GATHERED CORNERS

These corners are also called "kissing" corners and may be done one of two ways. The results are the same. (See fig. 67.)
1. Stitch pillow top and pillow back together, inserting desired edge finish in seam. Leave an opening for turning pillow right side out. At each corner, measure in 2″ (5.1cm) and make a mark. Pick up corner at mark and wrap securely with dental floss, fishing line, or string thread. (See fig. 68.) Tie off. Turn pillow right side out and stuff to desired firmness; sew up opening.
2. On all four corners of pillow top and pillow bottom, run a row

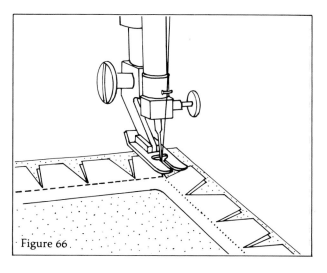

Figure 66

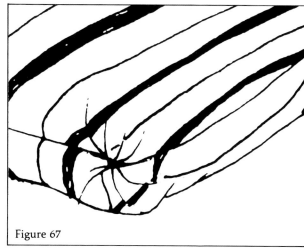

Figure 67

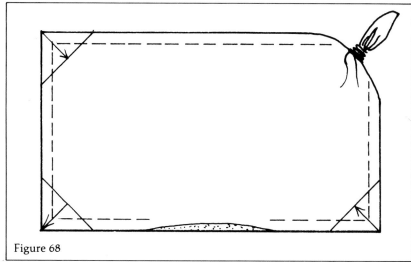

Figure 68

of machine basting (6-8 stitches per inch) around the corner on the seam line, rounding off the corner slightly. Pin pillow top and back together, right sides facing, and draw up the basting threads in each corner until desired fullness is obtained. Be sure to gather all corners the same amount. Pin in place and stitch on seamline all around pillow, leaving an opening for turning. (See fig. 69.) Turn, stuff, and sew up opening.

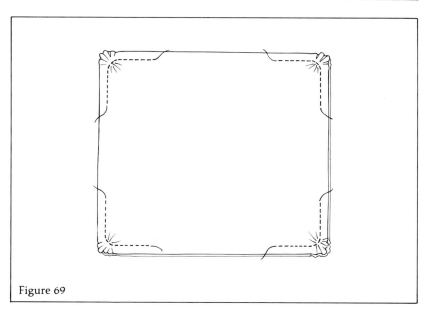

Figure 69

PLEATED CORNERS

The first set of instructions is for a stitched pleat, which doesn't show as a pleat from the right side, and the second instructions are for a loose, inverted box pleat, also known as a Turkish corner.

1. Sew pillow top and back together in the usual way, leaving an opening for turning. To form the corners and make mock boxing, fold the corners as shown (see fig. 70) so that the seamlines from one side to the next are perfectly matched. Decide on the depth you want for the mock boxing, and measure in from the point until a seam of that length can be stitched. Stitch seam two times for extra strength; trim off excess at corner. Turn pillow right side out, stuff, and sew opening closed. (See fig. 71.)

2. The loose pleats in this method are equal in depth to the desired mock boxing. At each corner of pillow top and back, fold in a pleat as shown (See fig. 72.), and stitch across it to hold it in place. When pleats have been formed at all corners of top and back, place the two pieces of fabric right sides together and match corner pleats exactly. Stitch around outside of pillow, leaving an opening for turning. Turn, stuff, and stitch opening closed. (See fig. 73.)

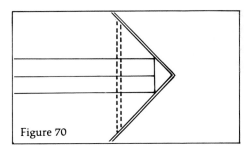

Figure 70

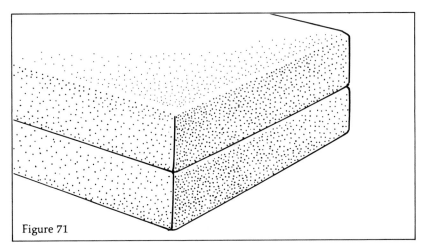

Figure 71

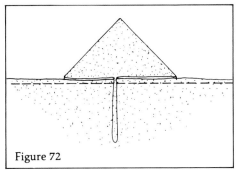

Figure 72

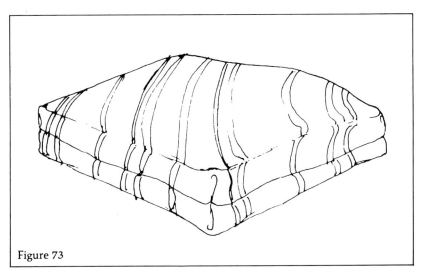

Figure 73

CLOSURES

Decisions regarding the type of closure you need for your pillow should be made after considering two things: the frequency that you expect to launder the pillow cover, and how big the opening in the pillow cover will be. Obviously, if you don't expect to be washing a pillow often, it saves you time simply to hand-sew the opening shut. But if you expect to take the cover on and off the pillow form regularly, you should take the time during construction to put in a zipper or tape closure or make a baby pillow closure.

The size of the required opening affects the type of closure in that the generally available zippers are limited to lengths not much greater than 22″ (55.9cm). If your project requires a larger opening, as might be the case with a large upholstered cushion, you will have to go to one of the tape fasteners: hook and eye tape, snap tape, or nylon loop and hook tape. At one time, before these fastener tapes were available, ties made of firmly constructed material such as twill tape were spaced evenly across the width of the opening and used to tie the pillow cover in place. (See fig. 74.) While this is certainly still an alternative, the tape fasteners hold the cover in place more securely.

The most important thing to keep in mind is that zippers and tape fasteners are infinitely easier to sew into a flat piece of fabric than into a pillow that has been sewed, even partially, together. Plan to sew fasteners into boxing before the boxing is constructed, or sew fasteners into the pillow back before the back is sewed to the front. You can put the fastener right down the center of the back, or you can locate it in the lower third of the back. (See fig. 75.) Cut the

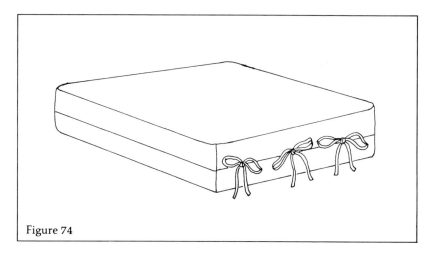

Figure 74

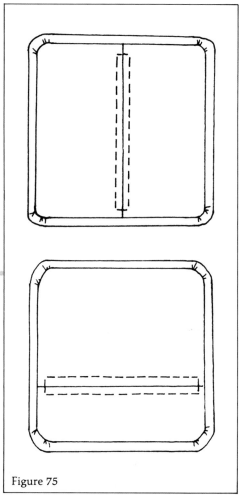

Figure 75

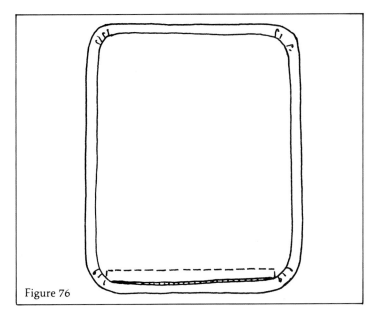

Figure 76

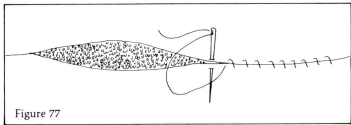

Figure 77

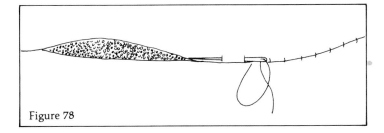

Figure 78

pillow back in two pieces, allowing seam allowances on all edges; when the fastener is sewed in place, the two pieces will equal the size required for the pillow back. It is much easier to put a zipper in the back of the pillow than on the edge of the pillow; however, instructions for sewing a zipper into a corded edge are included. (See fig. 76.)

HAND-SEWN CLOSURES

The quickest and easiest closure of any, and the one which requires no extra expenditure on supplies, is the hand-sewn closure. The opening left for turning when the pillow top and back are sewed together is simply sewed shut with hand stitches. Remember when stitching the seam that holds the top and back together to backstitch securely at either side of the opening. Turn pillow cover right side out, insert form or stuffing, and sew the opening closed with one of the following stitches:

Whipstitch: Turn the seam allowances on pillow top and back to the inside of the pillow and pin so that the folded edges are even with one another and the stitched edge of the pillow. Working from right to left, stitch as shown across the entire opening, making stitches as short as possible so they won't show. (See fig. 77.)

Slipstitch: This stitch is more invisible than the whipstitch. Fold seam allowances to inside of pillow. Working from right to left, slip the needle through a portion of the fold, first on one side, then on the other. Make the stitches about ¼″ (6mm) long in the folds. Continue across opening; fasten off thread. (See fig. 78.)

ZIPPERS

There are three kinds of zipper applications that work well for pillows: the centered application, meaning that the zipper is centered over a seam and sewed in place; the lapped application; and the invisible application. The centered and the lapped applications use a conventional zipper; the invisible zipper is a very desirable closure because it is the most unobtrusive of any of the closures except hand-stitching. (See fig. 79.) Follow package instructions for the invisible zipper; make certain you have the proper zipper foot for the zipper, or you cannot sew the zipper in.

Centered zipper: 1. Measure the zipper and the length of the seam into which it will be sewed. Allow at least ½'' (1.3cm) at top and bottom of zipper for sewing into the side seams of the pillow. Stitch seam closed, using regular length stitches at the excess above and below zipper and machine basting stitches down the seam where the zipper will actually be sewed. (See fig. 80.) Snip stitches at beginning and end of basting for easy removal later. Press seam open.

2. On wrong side, center closed zipper face down over seam. Match the teeth of the zipper to the seam. Pin in place through seam allowances only.

3. Extend one seam allowance and machine-baste from top to bottom the entire length of the zipper tape. (See fig. 81.)

4. Repeat with the other side of the zipper and the remaining seam allowance. (See fig. 82.)

5. Turn work right side up and

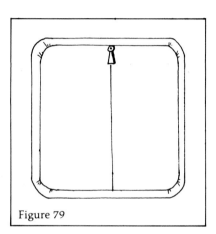

Figure 79

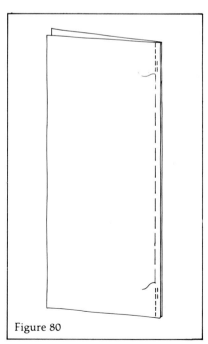

Figure 80

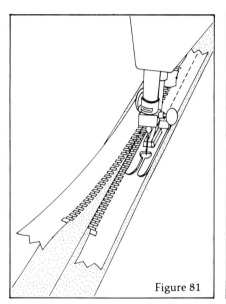

Figure 81

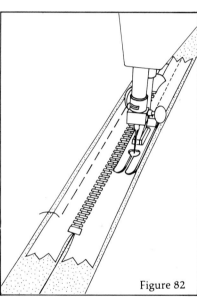

Figure 82

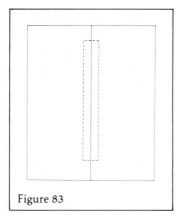

Figure 83

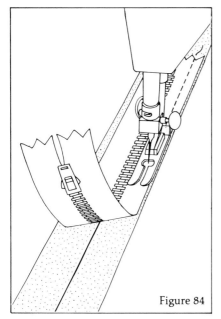

Figure 84

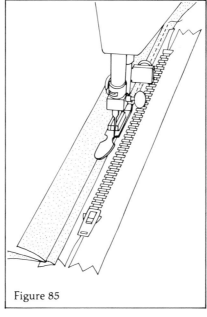

Figure 85

smooth fabric flat over zipper. Topstitch through all layers, making an even number of stitches across top and bottom of zipper. (See fig. 83.) Remove basting in seam.

Lapped zipper: 1. Stitch seam closed as in Step 1 of the centered zipper.
2. Working on the wrong side, extend one seam allowance. Position zipper on this seam allowance so that the full width of the zipper teeth or coil is on the seam allowance. Machine-baste through zipper tape and seam allowance. (See fig. 84.)
3. Turn zipper face up and fold seam allowance so the fold is just next to the zipper teeth or coil. Set machine for a regular stitch length and stitch through fold the entire length of the zipper. (See fig. 85.)
4. Open fabric out flat. Turn zipper face down over the other seam allowance, forming small pleats at each end of zipper in the side already stitched. Hand-baste zipper in place through tape, seam allowance, and fabric. (See fig. 86.)
5. Turn work right side up and topstitch zipper across the top, down the side, and across the bottom. (See fig. 87.) Pull thread ends to the wrong side of the work and tie off. Remove all basting.

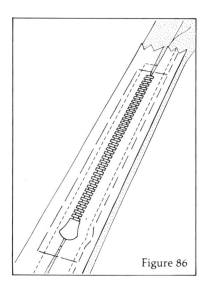

Figure 86

Zipper in a corded edge:

The zipper is put into the pillow while the back and front are still separate. The back and front are sewed together after the zipper has been put in.

1. Choose a zipper that is the same length as one side of the pillow. Open zipper and place it face down on the right side of the pillow top, aligning the teeth or coil of the zipper with the cording of the pillow top. (See fig. 88.) Stitch close to the teeth, trying, if possible, to place stitching over the stitching that holds the cording to the pillow top.

2. Close zipper and fold seam allowance and tape under pillow top so zipper is right side up. Fold under ½" (1.3cm) along the corresponding edge of the pillow back. Lap this edge of pillow back over free zipper tape, placing fold of fabric over the zipper teeth or coil. Pin in place and stitch. (See fig. 89.)

3. The zipper is now sewed in. To complete the other seams of the pillow, place right sides of back and top together, matching corners and raw edges, and stitch the remaining three sides of the pillow. Turn right side out and insert pillow form. (See fig. 76 for finished appearance.)

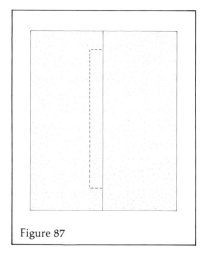

Figure 87

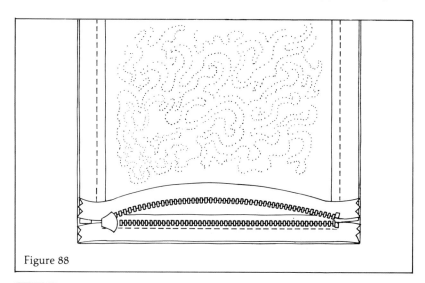

Figure 88

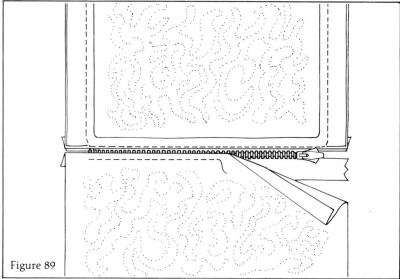

Figure 89

TAPE FASTENERS

Tape fasteners are available by the yard from fabric shops. They are convenient, inexpensive, and easy to use. Hook and eye and snap tape consists of a woven tape to which either hooks and eyes or snaps have been affixed at regular spaces. It is a good idea to preshrink these tapes before use by swishing them around in some hot water in the sink and allowing to dry. Nylon tape does not need preshrinking.

The three kinds of tape fasteners—hook and eye, snap, and nylon—all require that the seam into which they are to be set have a double seam allowance slightly greater than the width of the tape itself. Snap tape and nylon tape must be put in with a lapped application; hook and eye tape requires a centered application. All three types of tape fasteners should be put into boxing if possible. Cut the strips into which you will sew the fastener tape wider than you think you will need; sew the tapes in place, then cut strips down to size.

Lapped applications: Plan

for the socket side of snap tape or the hook side of nylon tape to be on the bottom when the tape is fastened. Press a full seam allowance to the *right* side of the fabric, lap the tape over it, and topstitch in place (See figs. 90 & 91.) This way no raw edge will show. Press seam allowance on remaining piece of fabric to the wrong side, lap the ball part of the snap tape or the fuzzy side of nylon tape over the pressed-under seam allowance and topstitch in place.

Centered application: As

is necessary with hook and eye tape, press the seam allowances on both pieces of fabric to the wrong side. Place tapes in position on the seam allowances, making certain the hooks are aligned with the eyes. Topstitch, stitching around the ends of the hooks and eyes. (See fig. 92.)

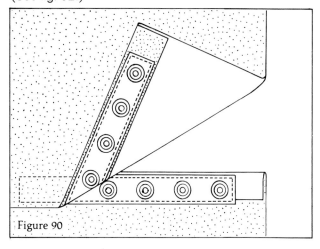

Figure 90

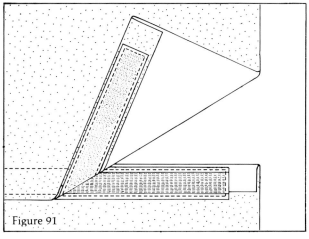

Figure 91

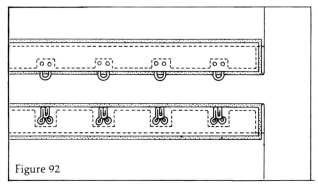

Figure 92

BABY PILLOW, OR ENVELOPE, CLOSURE

This is a very convenient and quick closure for a pillow that requires no zipper or snap tape. The pillow form can easily be slipped in and out, making this particularly appropriate for pillows that soil easily.

1. Cut pillow back in two pieces, allowing for a 3" (7.6cm) overlap on one end of both pieces, plus 1" (2.5cm) hem allowance and ½" (1.3cm) seam allowances. (See fig. 93.)

2. Hem the end of the overlaps by turning under ½" (1.3cm) twice and edge-stitching.

3. Overlap the pieces by the 3" (7.6cm) so that the back measures the same as the pillow top. Stitch along the sides of the overlap to hold pieces in place. Pin the back to the pillow top, right sides together, and stitch around all sides. (See fig. 94.) There is no need to leave an opening for turning. Turn the top right side out through the closure.

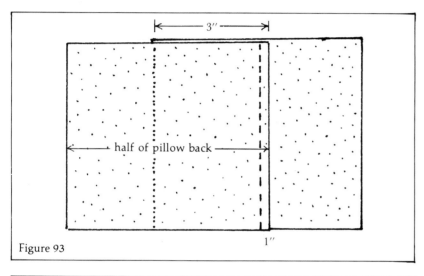

Figure 93

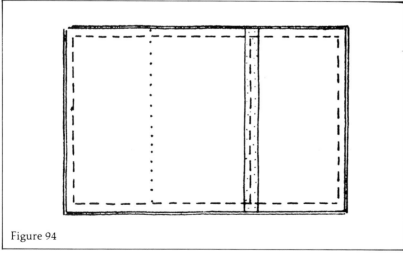

Figure 94

STUFFINGS

It is amazing how many choices are available for stuffing your pillow project. It is fun to think that what you put inside can be as much of a creative expression as the outside of the pillow, especially if you choose an aromatic stuffing or one from nature. Of course, the single most important thing to consider is that the stuffing must complement the intended use of the completed pillow. If the pillow is meant to be firm and solid, the stuffing should be chosen to carry out that objective. If the pillow is to be soft and snuggly, choose a stuffing accordingly. Keep in mind that the stuffing also defines the final shape of the pillow.

You can purchase stuffing that has been made into pillow forms or buy loose stuffing in bulk. Keep in mind that any loose stuffing can be put into a muslin cover to make a pillow form. (Instructions for making your own pillow form come at the end of this section.) Following are descriptions of some of the different stuffings you might choose for your pillow projects.

PILLOW FORMS

Pillow forms or inner pillows are desirable when the pillow must be laundered or cleaned often, as might be the case with much-used pillows made in a light colored fabric. There are two kinds of pillow forms available commercially: those made from a loose stuffing packed into a muslin cover, and rigid foam rubber forms. The filler in commercially produced pillow forms usually is either kapok (which is a cellulose-based product) or polyester fiber fill. Both types of pillow forms are available in a wide range of sizes and shapes. Both come in knife-edged as well as boxed styles. The foam rubber forms are springier and do not pack down with use as do the forms made with loose stuffing, but they are more expensive and the foam rubber tends to harden and become crumbly with the passage of time. Buy molded foam rubber forms in exactly the size desired for the finished pillow; buy the forms made with loose stuffing 1″ (2.5cm) larger all around than the size desired for the finished pillow. For example, if you want a finished pillow that measures 14″ (35.6cm) square, purchase a pillow form of loose stuffing that measures 16″ (40.6cm) square. This will ensure a firmly packed, smooth pillow.

LOOSE STUFFINGS

The list of loose stuffings can go on and on. We begin with some of the more ordinary materials, then go to some that are fairly exotic.

Polyester fiber fill: By far the most popular and readily available stuffing for pillows, fiber fill is non-allergenic, does not shift around in the pillow, and is fairly inexpensive, especially when compared to ready-made pillow forms. Polyester fiber fill can be stuffed directly into the finished pillow cover, thus allowing the corners to be filled really well, and it is easily taken out and put back when the time comes to clean the pillow cover. It is best not to use a hand-stitched closure when using loose polyester fiber fill as a stuffing as the little fibers tend to stick out between the stitches, making a "beard" on that edge.

Kapok: This filler is much favored by upholsterers and others who make pillows commercially; in fact, the best place to try to buy it is from an upholsterer. It is not easy to find, but it is a wonderful stuffing; it holds the shape of the pillow exceedingly well. If you can find it, be prepared to buy it by the pound in big quantities. The disadvantage of this filler is that it may aggravate allergies in very sensitive people. It has a tendency to make dust when the pillow is plumped up. It is also difficult to work with, as the little fibers are so light that they float around with almost no provocation. The best idea is to work outside with it (also a good idea when working with shredded foam) and to wear a coverall apron. Always make a separate pillow form when working with kapok; do not stuff it loose into your pillow cover.

Shredded foam: Purchased by the bag fairly inexpensively, shredded foam is readily available in variety stores as well as fabric shops. This type of stuffing does not get into corners or hold its shape in the pillow as well as some of the other fillers. It is also messy to work with and hardens with time.

Discarded nylon pantyhose and stockings: These make good stuffings. Wash them, then cut off all elastic and cut them into small pieces before stuffing the pillows. They are resilient and lightweight, and if the outside is washable, the whole pillow, stuffing and all, can be tossed into the washer. Good idea for children's pillows!

Fabric scraps: Cut the scraps into strips of about equal size and stuff the pillow quite firmly with the strips. Fabric scraps do have a tendency to shift, so stuff the pillow firmly.

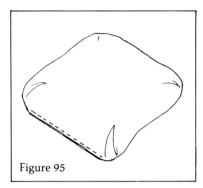

Figure 95

Quilt batting: Polyester quilt batting is a good filler when stacked in layers until the desired thickness is achieved. This provides a custom-made stuffing that won't shift. It is particularly appropriate for making chair pads. Quilt batting is also perfect for wrapping around a molded foam form when you want to soften the shape but keep the firmness of the rigid form.

Sheet foam rubber: Not really a "loose" stuffing, it is nonetheless another material that can be cut and stacked to just exactly the desired size and shape. Sheet foam rubber is usually sold by the foot and comes in many different thicknesses. You can, however, glue layers of it together with rubber cement to get just the height you want. You can also mark the foam rubber with a pen, then cut it to any shape you want. An electric carving knife is by far the best tool for cutting this material.

Feathers and down: The most luxurious stuffings you can choose for your pillows, feathers and down are certainly the most expensive. Down is the term used for the soft feathers that grow on the breast of the goose or duck from which it is taken. It can be distinguished from feathers in that down has no quill, or hard center. While duck

and goose are the "top of the line" as far as feathers and down are concerned, the feathers from other birds such as chickens and guineas make perfectly fine pillows.

Feathers and down that come straight from the bird must be washed before they are used. The old-fashioned way is to boil the feathers in strong soap, then spread them out in the sun between two layers of screening to dry. Admittedly, this may be unrealistic for most of us. A better way to handle fresh feathers is to sew them into a large bag made of sturdy fabric such as mattress ticking, put them several times through the washing machine with hot water and strong detergent. Spread the bag out in the sun to dry, if possible, then put the bag in the dryer on the fluff cycle for a while.

If you are fortunate enough to have some old down or feather pillows that need freshening before they can be used, you can put them in your clothes dryer (one at a time) with a heavy damp towel and tumble on a cool setting for about 20 minutes. This will remove dust and fluff the pillow. (This also works well for pillows stuffed with other materials.) If the pillow cover is mildewed or in sad shape otherwise, check with your local dry cleaner to see what kind of service he provides on feather pillows. Many dry cleaners will clean feathers, put on a new ticking made to the size you specify, and even replenish feathers when there are not enough.

To replace the ticking on a feather pillow yourself, choose a firmly-woven, "feather-proof" fabric. Feathers have a funny way of working themselves out of fabric. Cut the new ticking 1" (2.5cm) larger all around than the size desired for the finished

pillow. Sew up three sides of the pillow, using a ½" (1.3cm) seam. Open up one end of the old pillow, place the open end into the new ticking, and shake the contents into the new ticking. Fold in the raw edges on open end of ticking and machine-stitch with a short stitch to secure. (See fig. 95.)

Sachets, potpourris, and dried pine and balsam needles: These wonderfully fragrant fillings for small pillows, when placed in drawers and closets, perfume clothing and linens with a subtle scent. Balsam and pine are also said to keep moths away. (If you are not sure about their potency, you might try purchased moth crystals or moth balls in their place.) You will enjoy making your own scented stuffings, and you can also look forward to finding potpourris of a great variety of scents in bath shops and wherever crafts are sold.

Here is a recipe for cured rose petals, which may be used by itself as a filling for a dainty pillow or used in the recipe for potpourri that follows.

Gather rose petals early in the morning. Choose the most fragrant roses you can find; add a few rose leaves also, as they give the fragrance of apples when they are dried. Bring petals inside and place them on a spread of newspapers. Sprinkle the petals with salt to discourage insects. Turn the petals gently each day until they are dry. When they are dry to the touch, place them in a half-gallon jar and add 1 tablespoon of glycerin for each quart of petals. Stir gently with your fingers, coating the petals lightly. Add a few drops of your favorite perfume for immediate fragrance. As the fragrance of the perfume fades, the petals will furnish their own fragrance.

Potpourri requires the following: cured rose petals; dried flowers and herbs, such as jasmine, heliotrope, leaves or blossoms of peppermint, rosemary, marjoram, lavender; dried balsam needles or moss rose petals; salt for sprinkling petals; a few cloves; 2 or more nutmegs; small amount ground mace; 1 tablespoon cinnamon; 2 tablespoons glycerine; 1 tablespoon brandy; few drops of your favorite perfume.

Dry the flowers and herbs such as jasmine, heliotrope, peppermint leaves or blossoms, rosemary, marjoram, lavender, or other blossoms by placing between the leaves of a magazine until cured.

Some old formulas say to use a few balsam needles, but if moss rose petals are used, they smell like these needles. Add dried flower petals to cured rose petals in a half-gallon jar. Sprinkle with more salt; add spices. Stir gently with your fingers. Add 2 tablespoons glycerin, 1 tablespoon brandy and a few drops of your favorite perfume; stir gently again with fingers. Close jar tightly with lid and do not disturb mixture for several days. Mixture should be lightly coated, but not sticky, when ready to use.

Bath salts: Another delightful-smelling stuffing for pillows, the salts may be dropped into the bathwater or slipped into the stacks of towels and sheets in the linen closet.

Hair combings: At one time such combings were saved in special receptacles on the dresser to be used as stuffing for pincushions. The natural oil in the hair prevents pins and needles from rusting.

Vermiculite and cat litter: These rather heavy, chipped clay materials are good stuffings for pincushions and floor pillows, as they provide enough weight to keep the pillows from slipping around. They are the perfect choice for a pillow that should be firm and heavy, such as a hassock or ottoman. Take care not to get pillows stuffed with either of these materials wet.

Spanish moss: A familiar sight to residents of the Deep South, Spanish moss was also well known as a stuffing for mattresses and pillows of long ago. To cure Spanish moss (to chase the bugs out) bake it in the oven on a low temperature with a large-sized sweet potato until the sweet potato is soft. The Spanish moss will then be ready to use. Clean all the twigs and leaves out of it and cut it up into small lengths, and you have a wonderful, free pillow stuffing!

Sawdust and sand: Other alternatives for firm, heavy stuffings, sawdust and sand are both ideal for filling firm pincushions and doorstops. Since they can be obtained free or at little cost, they are perfect for big furniture cushions. Make sure the sawdust or sand is thoroughly dry before putting it into a pillow.

HOW TO STUFF A PILLOW

Hold the pillow with the opening up, and begin by stuffing the lower corners firmly. Small handfuls of stuffing work better than large amounts. As you add a new handful of stuffing to the pillow, blend the new with what is already there to prevent lumps. When the lower corners are stuffed, fill in across the lower seam stuffing very firmly. Then go to the side seams, and from there into the center of the pillow. Finally come up to the top corners, then fill in across the open seam.

If you use quilt batting, cut the sheets of the batting 1″ (2.5cm) larger all around than the pillow top and carefully place them in the pillow. For a rounder effect, some loose stuffing may be pushed between the layers.

MAKING YOUR OWN PILLOW FORM

Choose a fabric for your pillow form that is closely woven, such as muslin or sheeting fabric. Cut the fabric to the desired size and shape, adding ½″ (1.3cm) all around for seam allowances. Sew around outer edge of form with a ½″ (1.3cm) seam, turn right side out, and stuff firmly as described above. The opening may be closed with machine stitching by folding the seam allowances of the opening to the inside and edge-stitching with a short machine stitch across opening. (See fig. 95.)

If you need a boxed pillow form, it is not necessary to sew in an extra boxing strip. The fabric for the top and bottom can be cut to include the boxing. For example, if you want a 16″ (40.6cm) pillow with a 2″ (5.1cm) boxing, cut a square for both the top and bottom that measures 21″ (53.3cm) square—16″ (40.6cm) for the top plus 2″ (5.1cm) for the boxing plus ½″ (1.3cm) seam allowances all around. Sew these two pieces together with a ½″ (1.3cm) seam allowance, stitching around all corners, and leaving an opening on one side. Still working on the wrong side, fold each corner so the seams meet and stitch across the corner far enough in to make a 2″ (5.1cm) seam. (See fig. 70). When the square is turned right side out, a mock boxing will have been formed. Stuff form firmly. A slab of solid foam rubber works well.

TUFTING

You may find on occasion that tufting a pillow will add a special dimension to the overall design. Sewing a button into the center of a pillow is a form of tufting. Tufting also has the advantage of holding the stuffing in the pillow in proper place, which is a great advantage on cushions for chair seats and backs. If the pillow is to be reversible, plan to make the tufts identical on both sides of the pillow.

Use a long upholsterer's needle and waxed thread if a button is to be added to the tuft. Make one stitch with the needle, down, and back up through all the layers, pulling through all the yarn except a 2″ (5.1 cm) end on the top. Clip thread off at the needle end, leaving another 2″ (5.1 cm) tail. Tie the two tails together in a secure double knot. (See fig. 96.)

To add a button, bow, or other trim of your liking to the tufts, go down through the fabric with the needle, come up and place the button in the stitch before going into the fabric again. In fact, you may wish to make several stitches through the button for added strength. This is an especially good idea if you are sewing buttons to both sides of the pillow at the same time. Tie the ends of the thread in place over the top of the button. (See fig. 97.) For a shank button, tie thread ends close to fabric.

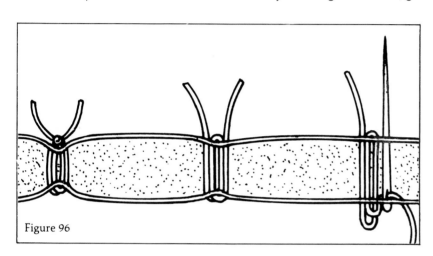

Figure 96

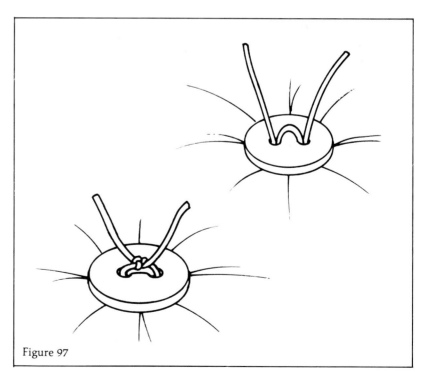

Figure 97

TIES

Ties are necessary to hold in place loose cushions on chair seats such as those in a dining room or kitchen. You may put ties on the back of the cushion only, or on both the front and back.

Ties may be made of ribbon, cord, or straight pieces of fabric that have been either hemmed or faced. The length of the ties depends on how you plan to fasten them. You may tie perky bows (See fig. 98), or snap them unobtrusively underneath the cushion. Decide this when you plan the pillow.

To sew ties onto the pillow, plan to incorporate them into the seam that joins pillow back to pillow front. If wide ties are being used, place one of each pair of ties to either side of the corner. Fold the end of the tie into a pleat at the pillow seamline to make for easier bow-tying. (See fig. 99.)

If you plan unobtrusive narrow ties, measure from the chair seat around back brace and add 1″ (2.5cm). Cut a strip 2″ (5.1cm) wide in a length to equal that needed for all the chair ties. Fold both long edges to the center of the strip, then fold strip in half. (See fig. 100.) Topstitch on both long edges. Cut strip into equal lengths, and sew one end into pillow seam. Sew one side of a snap to the other end, and sew matching side of snap to pillow. Place pillow on chair and snap tie around chair back support. (See fig. 101.)

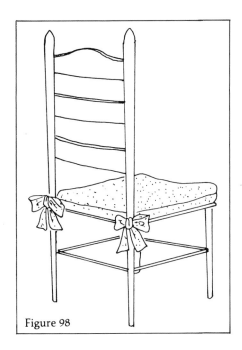

Figure 98

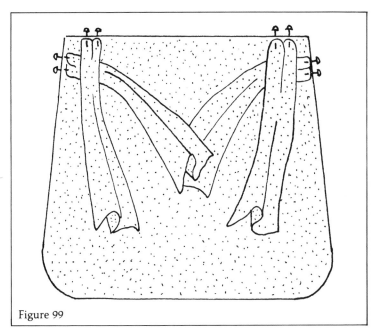

Figure 99

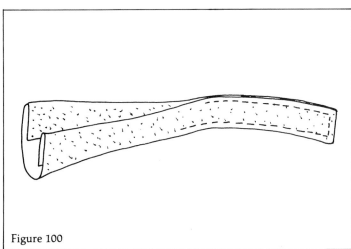

Figure 100

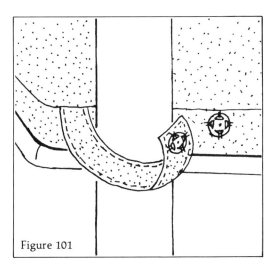

Figure 101

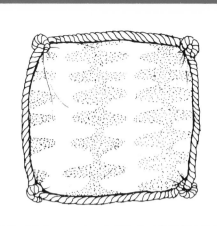

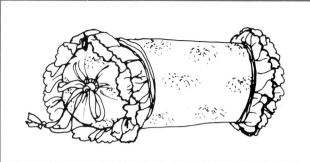

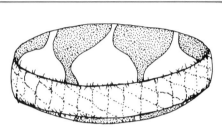

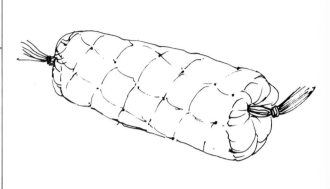

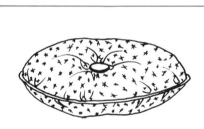

DESIGNER'S
WORKBOOK

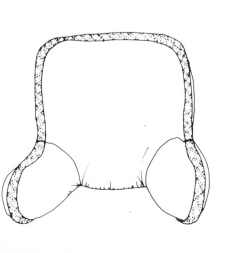

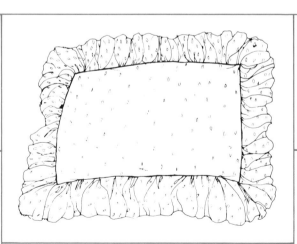

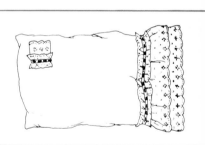

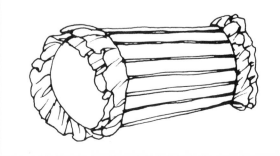

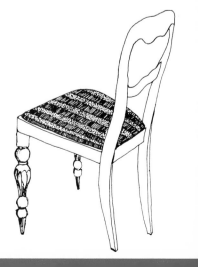

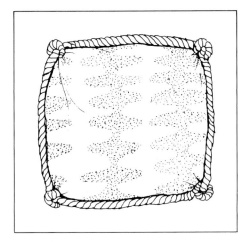

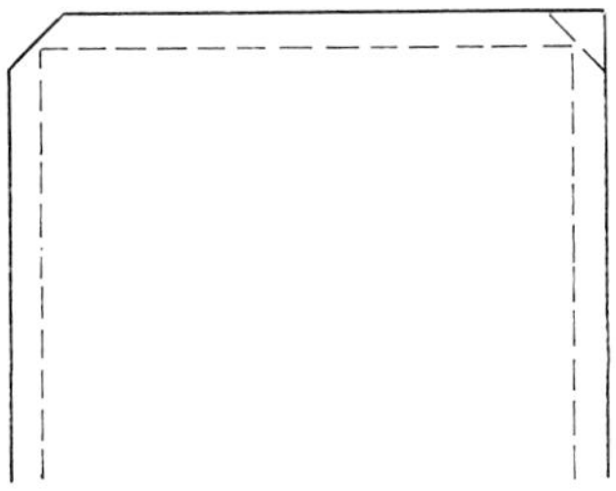

Figure 1

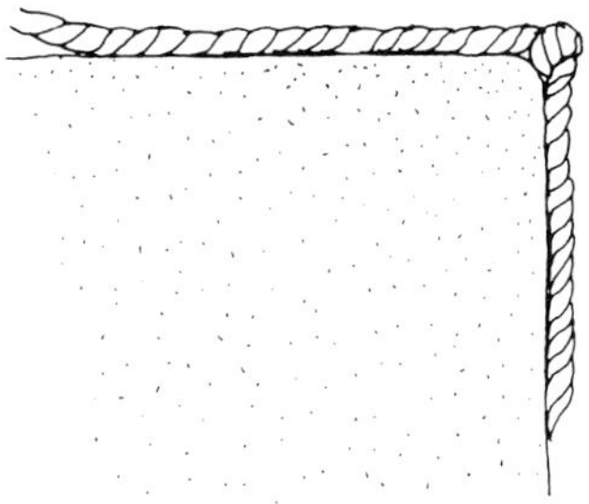

Figure 2

KNIFE-EDGED SQUARE PILLOW TRIMMED WITH SILK CORD

MATERIALS

The materials and directions given are for an 18″ (45.7cm) square pillow.

- ¾ yard (68.6cm) medium- to heavyweight fabric, 42″ to 45″ (106.7cm to 114.3cm) wide
- polyester fiber fill
- 2½ yards (2.3m) purchased silk cording, ¼″ (6mm) thick

METHOD

Step 1: Measure, mark with tailor's chalk, and cut out two 19″ (48.3cm) squares of fabric.

Place right sides together. Using ½″ (1.3cm) seams, pin-baste; then stitch squares in place leaving a 6″ (15.2cm) opening in the center of one side for turning and stuffing.

Step 2: Trim corners. (See fig. 1.) Turn pillow right side out, press, and stuff firmly with polyester fiber fill.

Turn in raw edges and slip-stitch opening closed.

Step 3: To trim pillow, sew purchased silk cording by hand directly on top of seam. As you come to a corner, poke it into the pillow a bit, tie a knot in the cord, and sew it in place. (See fig. 2.) This gives the pillow a more rounded effect.

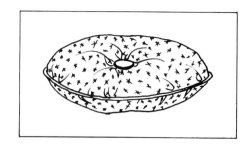

KNIFE-EDGED ROUND PILLOW WITH CORDING

MATERIALS

The materials and directions given are for a 16″ (40.6cm) round pillow.

- 1 yard (91.4cm) light- to medium-weight fabric, 44″ (111.8cm) wide
- 2 cards (1.8m) cable cord, ¼″ (6mm) thick polyurethane pillow form, 16″ (40.6cm) in diameter
- 2 buttons to be covered, each 1½″ (3.8cm) in diameter (if desired)
- fishing line

METHOD

Step 1: Measure, mark with tailor's chalk, and cut out two 20″ (50.8cm) squares of fabric.

Step 2: Fold each square into quarters and press. Measure and mark an arc 9″ (22.9cm) from the folded point. Cut along arc to make an 18″ (45.7cm) circle. (See fig. 1.)

From remaining fabric prepare 2 yards (1.8m) bias strip 2½″ (6.4cm) wide. Cover cable cord with the bias strip as directed on page 45 to make cording.

Step 3: Pin-baste cording to the right side of one circle 1″ (2.5cm) in from outer edge with the raw edges of cording even with the raw edge of circle. (See fig. 2.) Using a zipper foot

attachment, stitch cording in place as close to the cord as possible.

For a smooth finish where ends of the cording overlap, pull cord out of covering and clip it so that the cut ends of both sides meet. Stitch ends in place.

Step 4: With right sides together, place remaining circle on top of corded circle. Pin-baste together, and using a zipper foot attachment, stitch in place exactly on top of cording stitching, leaving a 12″ (30.5cm) opening for turning and stuffing.

Trim seam allowances to ¼″ (6mm) and clip as necessary to release fullness. Turn right side out. Insert pillow form. Turn in raw edges and slip-stitch opening closed.

Step 5: (Optional) Cover buttons following directions on the button package.

Thread a large needle with a double strand of fishing line. Double-knot end. Locate and mark with tailor's chalk the center of the pillow, draw fishing line through it and pull tightly. Repeat this procedure several times to secure fishing line and to pull both sides of the pillow together in the center.

Pass fishing line through one button and then through center. Pass fishing line through second button on the opposite side. Wind fishing line around both buttons to secure.

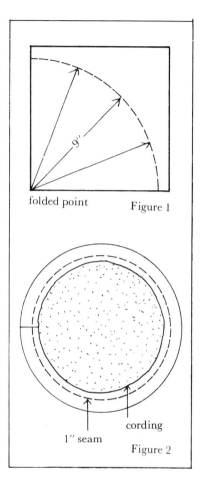

folded point   Figure 1

1″ seam   cording

Figure 2

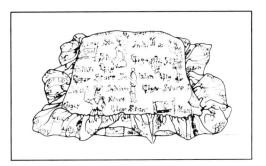

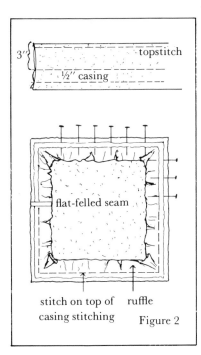

3" topstitch

½" casing

flat-felled seam

stitch on top of   ruffle
casing stitching   Figure 2

RUFFLED-EDGE RECTANGULAR PILLOW

MATERIALS
The materials and directions given are for a 16" (40.6cm) square pillow.
- 1½ yards (1.4m) light- to medium-weight fabric, 44" (111.8cm) wide
- 2 yards (1.8m) cable cord, ¼" (6mm) thick
- polyurethane pillow form, 16" (40.6cm) square

METHOD
Step 1: Measure, mark with tailor's chalk, and cut out four strips of fabric, each 8" x 44" (20.3cm x 111.8cm).

Step 2: Place strips end to end, right sides together. Using ½" (1.3cm) seams, pin-baste, then stitch strip ends together. Press seams open. Fold joined strips in half lengthwise, right sides out, and press.

Step 3: Topstitch along edge of fold. Measure, mark, and stitch a ½" (1.3cm) casing 3" (7.6cm) in from fold. (See fig. 1.)

Attach cord to a safety pin and thread it through the casing. Gather fabric to make a ruffle 64" (162.6cm) long.

Step 4: With remaining fabric, measure, mark with tailor's chalk, and cut out two 18" (45.7cm) squares.

Beginning in the middle of one side, pin-baste the ruffle to the right side of one square with the raw edges of the ruffle even with the raw edges of the fabric square. (See fig. 2.) Continue pin-basting until both ends of the ruffle meet. Seam ends of ruffle together as directed on page 50.

Stitch on top of both sides of the casing stitching to attach ruffle around the entire square. Remove cord from casing.

Step 5: With right sides facing, place remaining fabric square on top of ruffled square. Pin-baste and stitch in place exactly on top of the inside ruffle stitching, leaving a 12" (30.5cm) opening in the center of one side for turning and stuffing.

Trim seam allowances to ¼" (6mm) and clip as necessary to release fullness. Turn right side out and press.

Insert pillow form. Turn in raw edges and slip-stitch opening closed.

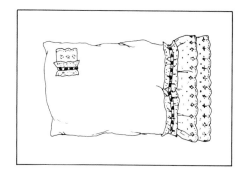

TOOTH FAIRY PILLOWCASE

The Tooth Fairy Pillowcase has a pocket small enough to hold a lost tooth and large enough for the Tooth Fairy to drop in a coin or two.

MATERIALS
The case is designed to fit over an 18″ x 13″ (45.7cm x 33 cm) boudoir pillow.

- ½ yard (45.7cm) light- to medium-weight washable fabric, any width
- 2 yards (1.8m) eyelet trim, 5″ (12.7cm) wide
- 1 yard (.9m) narrow, ribbon-threaded, double-edge eyelet trim, 2″ (5cm) wide

METHOD
Step 1: Measure, mark with tailor's chalk, and cut out two sections of fabric, each 19″ x 15″ (48.3cm x 38cm).

Step 2: Place right sides of fabric together. Using a ½″ (1.3cm) seam allowance, pin-baste, then stitch around three sides leaving one 15″ (38.1cm) side open.

Trim seam allowances and excess fabric from corners. (See fig. 1.) Turn right side out.

Step 3: Cut the 5″ (12.7cm) wide eyelet trim into two equal lengths. Place right sides of trim and fabric together. Using a ½″ (1.3cm) seam, pin-baste one length around the open end of the pillowcase. Cut off any excess trim. Stitch trim in place. (See fig. 2.)

Step 4: Join ends of trim together with small whipstitches, turning raw edges to the inside. Turn the eyelet so that the ruffle extends away from the pillowcase. (See fig. 3.)

For a little boy, you may replace the ruffles with regimental striped ribbon or piping.

Step 5: Fasten the second row of eyelet 1½″ (3.8cm) below the bottom of the first row of trim, and repeat procedure in Steps 3 and 4. (See fig. 3.)

Step 6: Attach the ribbon-threaded, double-edge eyelet trim to the pillowcase directly on top of the bottom edge of the second row of eyelet. (See fig. 4.) Pin-baste; then stitch in place. Turn ends under.

Step 7: Make a 3½″ x 5″ (8.9cm x 12.7cm) pocket out of remaining scraps of 5″(12.7cm) wide trim. Turn raw side edges under, and stitch in place.

Attach a remaining scrap of ribbon-threaded eyelet to the bottom of the larger eyelet, and stitch in place. (See fig. 5.) Turn raw edges under, and pin in place.

Step 8: Pin pocket in position in the upper left-hand corner of the pillowcase, 2″ (5cm) in from the side edge and 1½″ (3.8cm) in from the top edge. Topstitch around sides and bottom edges.

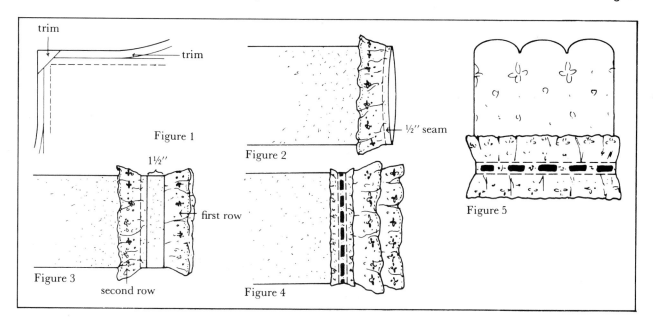

Figure 1

Figure 2

Figure 3

Figure 4

Figure 5

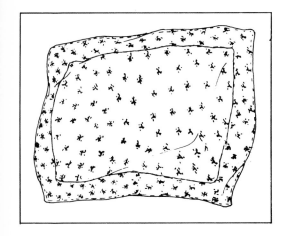

TAILORED PILLOW SHAM

MATERIALS
- 1 yard (91.4cm) medium- to heavyweight fabric, 42" to 45" (106.7cm to 114.3cm) wide

METHOD

Step 1: Carefully measure the pillow you plan to cover. Measure, mark with tailor's chalk, and cut out a section of fabric 2 times the length of the pillow plus 20" (50.8cm), and the width of the pillow plus 7" (17.8cm).

Step 2: Hem the short sides of the fabric section by measuring and turning raw edges under ½" (1.3cm), then under 1½" (3.8cm). Press; then stitch in place.

Fold fabric wrong side out so that side hems are centered with edges overlapping to form a tube 6" (15.2cm) longer than the length of your pillow. (See fig. 1.)

Step 3: Measure, mark, and stitch ½" (1.3cm) seams along each open end of the tube. Trim excess at each corner. (See fig. 2.)

Turn tube right side out and press. Edge-stitch around the entire perimeter of the pillow sham. Form a border by measuring, marking, and stitching 3" (7.6cm) in from the outside edge. (See fig. 3.)

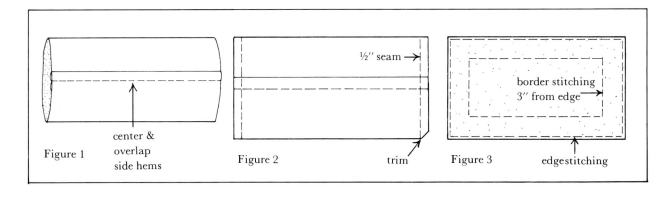

Figure 1 — center & overlap side hems

Figure 2 — ½" seam — trim

Figure 3 — border stitching 3" from edge — edgestitching

RUFFLED PILLOW SHAM

MATERIALS

The materials and directions given are for a sham to fit a 20" x 30" (50.8cm x 76.2cm) pillow.
- 1½ yards (1.4m) fabric for the cover, 44" (111.8cm) wide
- 1½ yards (1.4m) fabric for the ruffle, 44" (111.8cm) wide
- 5 yards (4.6m) cable cord, ¼" (6mm) thick

METHOD

Step 1: Measure, mark with tailor's chalk, and cut out a 20" x 30" (50.8cm x 76.2cm) rectangle from the cover fabric.

Step 2: From the ruffle fabric, prepare 8 yards (7.3m) of continuous bias, 8" (20.3cm) wide.

Fold the bias in half lengthwise, right side out, and make a ½" wide (1.3cm) casing 2½" (6.4cm) in from the fold. (See fig. 1.)

Attach cable cord to safety pin and thread it through the casing. (See fig. 2.) Gather fabric to make a ruffle long enough to fit around the perimeter of the front of the pillow sham.

Step 3: Beginning in the middle of one side, distribute ruffle fullness evenly and pin-baste the ruffle around the pillow sham top, with the ruffle towards the inside. (See fig. 3.) Remove cording from casing. Seam ends of ruffle together as directed on page 50.

Attach ruffle to pillow sham top with a wide zig-zag stitch, sewing between the stitching lines that formed the ruffle casing. (See fig. 3.)

Step 4: From remaining cover fabric, measure, mark, and cut out two 22" x 20" (55.9cm x 50.8cm) rectangles for the back of the pillow sham.

Place the two pieces of fabric on a flat surface, overlapping each at the center, forming a 31" x 20" (78.7cm x 50.8cm) rectangle.

To make double 2" (5cm) hems on the overlapping ends,

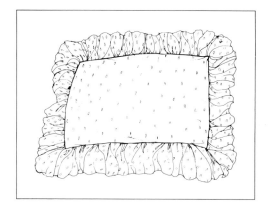

turn raw edges under 2" (5cm) and press. Turn under 2" (5cm) again and press. Stitch in place and press. (See fig. 4.)

Pin-baste the overlap in place. (See fig. 5.)

Step 5: With right sides together, position sham back on top of the front, with ruffle section in between.

Using ½" (1.3cm) seams, stitch around entire pillow sham to attach back to front.

Trim and notch ruffle section to within ¼" (6mm) of the stitching line. Trim corners of the pillow sham front and back to remove excess fabric. (See fig. 6.)

Turn right side out and press. Slip a standard-size bed pillow inside.

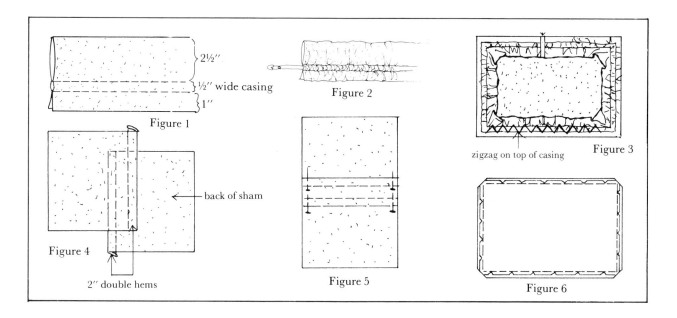

2½"

½" wide casing

1"

Figure 1

Figure 2

zigzag on top of casing

Figure 3

back of sham

Figure 4

2" double hems

Figure 5

Figure 6

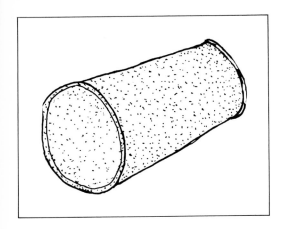

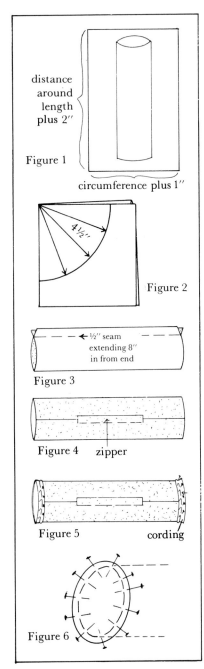

distance
around
length
plus 2″

Figure 1

circumference plus 1″

4½″

Figure 2

½″ seam
extending 8″
in from end

Figure 3

Figure 4   zipper

Figure 5   cording

Figure 6

ROUND BOLSTER

MATERIALS
The materials and directions given are for a 36″ x 8″ (91.4cm x 20.3cm) bolster.
- 1 polyurethane foam bolster, 36″ x 8″ (91.4cm x 20.3cm)
- 1¾ yards (1.6m) medium- to heavyweight fabric, 42″ to 45″ (106.7cm to 114.3cm) wide
- one 20″ to 22″ (50.8cm x 55.9cm) zipper
- 2 yards (1.8m) cable cord, ¼″ (6mm) thick

METHOD
Step 1: Measure the circumference and the length of the bolster. Then measure, mark, and cut out a rectangle of fabric 1″ (2.5cm) more than the circumference and 2″ (5cm) more than the length of the bolster. (See fig. 1.)

From the remaining fabric, measure, mark with tailor's chalk, and cut out two 12″ (30.5cm) squares. Fold each square into quarters and press. Measure and mark an arc 4½″ (11.4cm) from the folded points. (See fig. 2.) Cut along the arcs to make two 9″ (22.9cm) circles.

Step 2: Fold the rectangle of fabric wrong side out with long sides together. Measure, mark, and pin-baste ½″ (1.3cm) seams extending 8″ (20.3cm) in from each end. (See fig. 3.) Press seams open.

Turn tube right side out. Pin-baste zipper in position in center opening, then stitch. (See fig. 4.)

Step 3: From remaining fabric, prepare 2 yards (1.8m) continuous bias strip 1¾″ (4.4cm) wide. (See Techniques, Bias Trim.) Cover cable cord with bias.

Keeping fabric right side out, slip tube over foam bolster. Close zipper. Pin-baste cording around bolster edges so that the raw edges of the cording are even with raw edges of the fabric tube. (See fig. 5.)

Carefully remove fabric tube from bolster, and stitch cording in place using zipper foot attachment. Trim and notch seam allowances to remove excess fabric.

Step 4: Turn fabric tube wrong side out.

Position fabric circles, wrong side out, on each end of the tube. Pin-baste in place so that the ½″ (1.3cm) seam allowances of the circles extend just a bit beyond the stitching line attaching the cording to the tube. (See fig. 6.)

Using a zipper foot attachment, stitch circles to ends of tube by sewing directly on top of stitching line which attaches cording to tube.

Notch seam allowances around circles to make cover fit smoothly.

Turn cover right side out, press, and insert bolster.

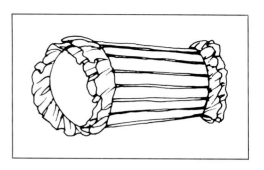

BOUDOIR PILLOW
WITH RUFFLED COVER

MATERIALS FOR PILLOW
The materials and directions given are for an 18″ x 13″ (45.7cm x 33cm) pillow and a 22½″ x 13″ (57.2cm x 33cm) ruffled cover.
- 1 yard (91.4cm) lightweight fabric, 45″ (114.3cm) wide
- polyester fiber fill

MATERIALS FOR COVER
- 2½ yards (2.3m) lightweight fabric, 42″ to 45″ (106.7cm x 114.3cm) wide
- 1½ yards (1.4m) double-edge ruffle trim, 2″ (5cm) wide
- 1½ yards (1.4m) narrow ribbon-threaded eyelet trim, ¼″ (6mm) wide
- 6 yards (5.5m) cable cord, ¼″ (6mm) thick

METHOD FOR PILLOW
Step 1: Measure, mark with tailor's chalk, and cut out a 19″ x 27″ (48.3cm x 68.6cm) rectangle.

Fold the rectangle, wrong side out, to measure 19″ x 13½″ (48.3cm x 34.3cm). Pin-baste and stitch a ½″ (1.3cm) seam down one side, across the bottom, and halfway up the other side.

Turn rectangle right side out and press.

Step 2: Stuff pillow with polyester fiber fill, packing corners firmly. Turn in raw edges and slip-stitch opening closed.

METHOD FOR COVER
Step 3: Measure, mark with tailor's chalk, and cut out a 27″ (68.6cm) square of fabric.

Fold the square in half, right side out. Make a French seam along the side opposite the fold by stitching ⅛″ (3mm) in from the raw edge. Trim as close as possible to the stitching line, and turn fabric so that right sides are together. Stitch to enclose first seam.

Turn raw edges at both ends onto the wrong side of the fabric to form 2″ (5cm) hems with ½″ (1.3cm) seams. (See fig. 1.) Pin-baste; then stitch in place.

Step 4: From remaining fabric, cut bias strips 5½″ (14cm) wide. Join strips together, end to end, with French seams to make two 52″ (132cm) bias strips.

Edgestitch along one long side of each bias strip. Trim as close as possible to stitching line, and make a very narrow rolled hem.

Form a casing on the remaining long side of each bias strip by turning under raw edge ½″ (1.3cm) and stitching in place. (See fig. 2.)

Attach cable cord to a safety pin, and thread it through the casings. Gather fabric evenly to make a ruffle.

Cut additional bias strips, each 3¾″ (9.5cm) wide. Join strips together, end to end, with French seams to make two additional 52″ (132cm) bias strips.

Repeat procedure in Step 4.

Step 5: When all four ruffle sections are complete, pin-baste ruffles 2″ (5cm) in from side openings of pillow cover, with the narrow ruffle on top of the large ruffle. (See fig. 3.) Stitch

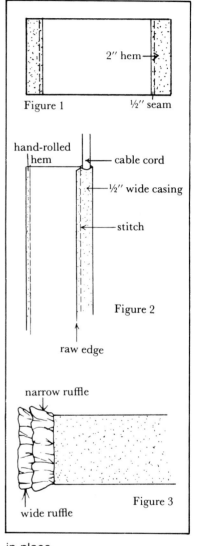

Figure 1   2″ hem→   ½″ seam

hand-rolled hem — cable cord — ½″ wide casing — stitch — Figure 2 — raw edge

narrow ruffle — wide ruffle — Figure 3

in place.

As an optional finishing touch, pin-baste, then stitch the 2″ (5cm) wide double-edge eyelet trim at the base of the ruffles, and attach ribbon to center of eyelet.

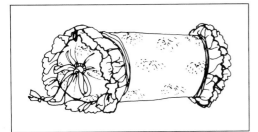

NECKROLL PILLOW WITH RUFFLED COVER

MATERIALS FOR PILLOW
The materials and directions given are for a 12½″ x 6″ (31.8cm x 15.2cm) pillow and cover.
- 1 yard (91.4cm) lightweight fabric, 45″ (114.3cm) wide
- 1 polyurethane foam bolster, 6″ (15.2cm) in diameter

MATERIALS FOR COVER
- 1 yard (91.4cm) lightweight fabric, 42″ to 45″ (106.7cm to 114.3cm) wide
- 1½ yards (1.4m) double-edge ruffle trim, 2″ (5cm) wide
- 5 yards (4.6m) cable cord, ⅛″ (3mm) thick
- 1½ yards (1.4m) narrow ribbon, ¼″ (6mm) wide (optional)

METHOD FOR PILLOW
Step 1: Using a serrated knife, cut a 12½″ (31.8cm) long section from the polyurethane foam bolster.

Step 2: Measure, mark with tailor's chalk, and cut out a 13″

x 20″ (33cm x 50.8cm) rectangle. Fold rectangle in half horizontally, wrong side out, and stitch a ¼″ (6mm) seam along the horizontal raw edges to form a tube. Press seam open.

Turn tube right side out, and slip over foam bolster.

Step 3: Measure, mark, and cut out two 7″ (17.8cm) diameter circles from remaining fabric.

Place circles over ends of bolster, and tuck raw edges inside fabric tube. Fold raw edges of fabric tube inside, and slip-stitch both circles and tube together to complete the pillow. (See fig. 1.)

METHOD FOR COVER
Step 4: Measure, mark with tailor's chalk, and cut out a 20″ (50.8cm) square.

Fold square in half, right side out. Make a French seam along the side opposite the fold by stitching ⅛″ (3mm) in from the raw edges. Trim as close as possible to stitching line, and turn fabric so that right sides are together. Stitch to enclose first seam.

Step 5: Fold in raw edges of both sides of tube to form two ½″ (1.3cm) wide casings. (See fig. 2.) Pin-baste; then stitch casings, leaving a 1″ (2.5cm)

opening for the cable cord.

Cut cable cord into two equal lengths, attach to a safety pin, and thread through casings.

Step 6: From remaining fabric, cut bias strips, each 5¼″ (13.3cm) wide. Join strips together, end to end, with French seams to make two lengths, each 40″ (101.6cm) long. This will be your ruffle trim.

Edgestitch along one long side of each bias strip. Trim as close as possible to the stitching line and make a very narrow hand-rolled hem.

Form a casing on remaining long side of each bias strip by turning under raw edge ½″ (1.3cm) twice and stitching in place. (See fig. 3.)

Step 7: Attach cording to a safety pin, and thread it through casings. Gather fabric to make a ruffle.

Pin-baste ruffles 5″ (12.7cm) in from each end of pillow cover and topstitch in place. (See fig.4.)

Pin-baste and stitch 2″ (5cm) wide ruffle trim on top of stitching line of first ruffle. Stitch ribbon to center of trim, if desired.

Pull cover over pillow, tighten draw strings at each end, tie in place, and tuck cable cord ends inside.

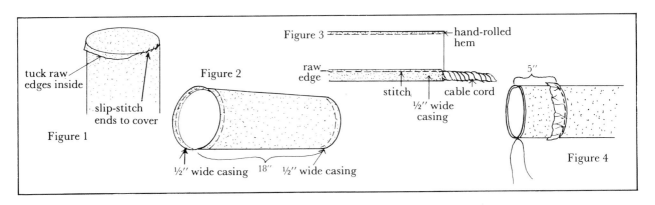

Figure 1 — tuck raw edges inside / slip-stitch ends to cover

Figure 2 — ½″ wide casing / 18″ / ½″ wide casing

Figure 3 — hand-rolled hem / raw edge / stitch / ½″ wide casing / cable cord

Figure 4 — 5″

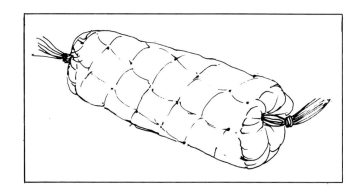

QUILTED BOLSTER COVER

MATERIALS
The materials and directions given are for a 36″ x 8″ (91.4cm x 20.3cm) bolster.
- 2 yards (1.8m) lightweight fabric, 42″ to 45″ (106.7cm to 114.3cm) wide
- 1 yard (91.4cm) polyester batting
- 1 polyurethane foam bolster, 36″ x 8″ (91.4cm x 20.3cm)
- dental floss

METHOD
Step 1: Measure and cut fabric into two 1-yard (91.4cm) pieces. Layer the two pieces of fabric, right sides out, with polyester batting in the middle.
Quilt the layers.

Step 2: Wrap quilted fabric, wrong sides out, around bolster form. (See fig. 1.)
Measure ½″ (1.3cm) seams, and stitch one-third of the way in from each end, leaving a 12″ (30.5cm) opening in the center. Tie each end very tightly with dental floss. (See fig. 1.)

Step 3: Remove cover from bolster form, and trim seam allowances. Turn cover right side out, and press gently.
Reinsert bolster form, and slip-stitch opening closed.
Add a tassel to each end, if desired.

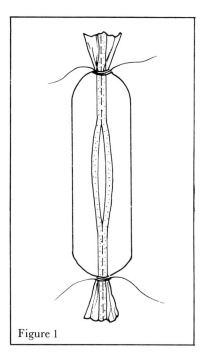

Figure 1

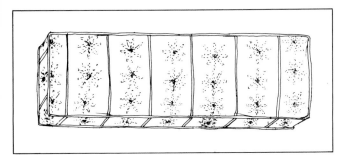

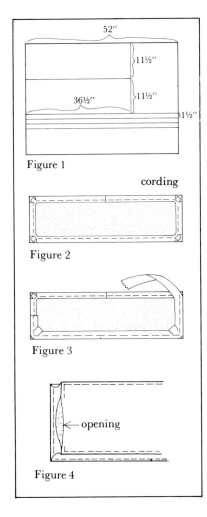

Figure 1

cording

Figure 2

Figure 3

opening

Figure 4

RECTANGULAR PILLOW WITH BOXING

MATERIALS

The materials and directions given are for a 36″ x 11″ x 1″ (91.4cm x 27.9cm x 2.5cm) rectangular pillow.

- polyurethane foam pad, 36″ x 11″ x 1″ (91.4cm x 27.9cm x 2.5cm)
- 1 yard (91.4cm) light- to medium-weight fabric, 44″ to 52″ (111.8cm to 132cm) wide
- 6 yards (5.5m) commercial cording in an accent color, ¼″ (6mm) thick

METHOD

Step 1: Measure, mark with tailor's chalk, and cut out two 36½″ x 11½″ (92.7cm x 29.2cm) rectangles of fabric. (See fig. 1.)

From remaining fabric, measure, mark, and cut out three strips, each the full width of the fabric and 1½″ (3.8cm) wide. (See fig. 1.)

Using ½″ (1.3cm) seams and with right sides together, join strips end to end to make one strip 100″ (2.5m) long.

Step 2: Using a zipper foot attachment and ¼″ (6mm) seams, pin-baste, then stitch commercial cording to pillow top, right side to right side, making sure rounded edge of cording faces in toward the center of the Pillow. (See fig. 2.)

Step 3: Using ¼″ (6mm) seams and with right sides together, pin-baste, then stitch boxing strip to pillow top, starting and ending in the center of one short side. Stitch with pillow side up, using first row of stitching as a guide. (See fig. 3.) Stitch boxing strip ends together and press.

With right sides together, pin-baste, then stitch remaining cording onto boxing strip. Then pin pillow bottom in place and stitch, leaving an opening in the center of one short side for turning and stuffing. (See fig. 4.)

Turn cover right side out and press. Insert foam pad and slip-stitch opening closed.

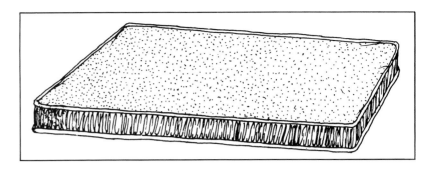

RECTANGULAR PILLOW WITH SHIRRED BOXING.

MATERIALS
The materials and directions given are for any size cushion.
- medium-weight fabric
- polyurethane foam pad
- cording in accent color, ¼" (6mm) thick

METHOD
Step 1: Measure, mark with tailor's chalk, and cut out two sections of fabric 1" (2.5cm) longer and wider than the desired finished measurements of the cushion.

Step 2: From the remaining fabric, measure, mark, and cut out enough 2" (5cm) wide strips to equal 2½ times the distance around the cushion.

With right sides of strips together and using ½" (1.3cm) seams, join ends of strips to make one long strip. Measure and press raw edges under ½" (1.3cm) on long sides.

Run basting threads along each fold line of the fabric strip and pull threads to gather. (See fig. 1.) Distribute gathers evenly to make fabric strip 1" (2.5cm) longer than the distance around the foam cushion.

Step 3: Using a zipper foot attachment and ½" (1.3cm) seams, pin-baste and stitch cording to pillow top, right side up, making sure rounded edge of cording faces in toward center of pillow. (See fig. 2.) Press.

Using ½" (1.3cm) seams, pin-baste; then stitch shirred boxing strip to pillow top, right sides together, starting and ending in the center of one short side. Stitch with pillow top up and use first row of stitching as a guide. (See fig. 3.) Stitch boxing strip ends together and press.

Pin-baste; then stitch remaining cording to shirred boxing strip, right sides together, making sure rounded edge of cording is toward center of boxing. Pin pillow bottom in place, then stitch with boxing side up so first stitching is a guide. Leave an opening in the center of one short side for turning and stuffing.

Step 4: Turn cover right side out and press. Insert foam pad and slip-stitch opening closed.

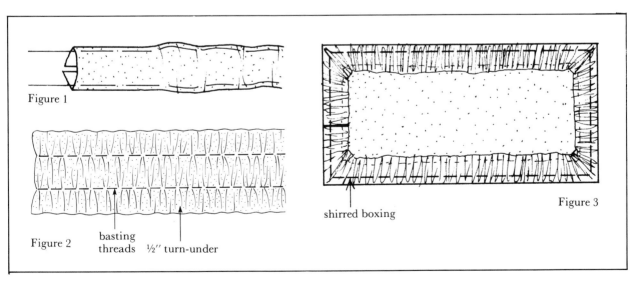

Figure 1

Figure 2

basting threads   ½" turn-under

shirred boxing

Figure 3

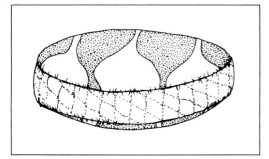

ROUND PILLOW WITH QUILTED BOXING

MATERIALS

The materials and directions given are for one 16″ (40.6cm) round pillow with a quilted boxing.

- 1½ yards (1.4m) light- to medium-weight fabric, 42″ to 45″ (106.7cm to 114.3cm) wide
- ½ yard (45.7cm) polyester fleece padding
- polyester fiber fill

METHOD

Step 1: Measure, mark with tailor's chalk, and cut a bias strip 4″ (10.2cm) wide by 54″ (137.2cm) long. (See fig. 1.)

Measure, mark with tailor's chalk, and cut two strips of fleece padding 4″ (10.2cm) wide by 55″ (139.7cm) long. Overlap two short ends 1″ (2.5cm) and zigzag stitch in place, making a single long strip 4″ wide and 109″ long (10.2cm x 276.9cm). Trim excess on either side of the stitching line.

Pin-baste fabric bias strip to the fleece padding strip and machine-quilt the piece by stitching horizontal and diagonal lines 1″ (2.5cm) apart. (See fig. 2.)

Step 2: From remaining fabric, measure, mark with tailor's chalk, and cut out two 19″ (48.3cm) squares. Fold each square into quarters and press.

Mark an arc 8½″ (21.6cm) from the folded center of each square. Cut along the markings to make a 17″ (43.2cm) circle from each square. (See fig. 3.)

Step 3: Place right sides of one circle and quilted boxing together and stitch ½″ (1.3cm) in from the outer edge. (See fig. 4.) Repeat procedure to attach the remaining circle to quilted boxing, leaving a 4″ (10.2cm) opening for turning and stuffing. (See fig. 5.)

Trim gusset to ⅛″ (3mm). Notch seam allowances of pillow top and bottom.

Turn pillow right side out and stuff firmly with polyester fiber fill.

Turn in raw edges and slip-stitch opening closed.

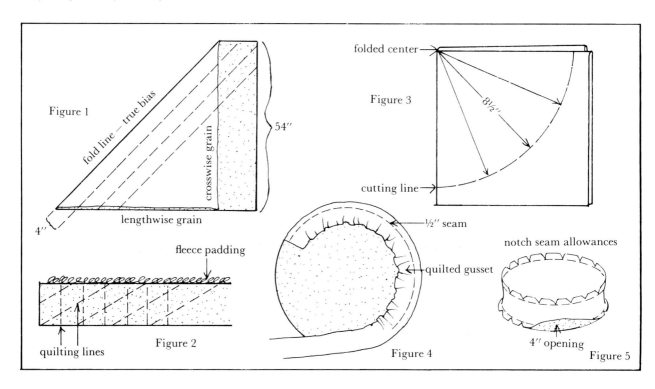

Figure 1

fold line — true bias

crosswise grain

lengthwise grain

54″

4″

fleece padding

quilting lines

Figure 2

folded center

Figure 3

8½″

cutting line

½″ seam

quilted gusset

Figure 4

notch seam allowances

4″ opening

Figure 5

WEDGE-SHAPED BOLSTER

MATERIALS
The materials and directions given are for a bolster approximately 36″ (91.4cm) wide, 16″ (40.6cm) high, and 12″ (30.5cm) deep at the base.
- 1 polyurethane foam bolster, 36″ x 16″ x 12″ (91.4cm x 40.6cm x 30.5cm)
- 2½ yards (2.3m) medium- to heavyweight fabric, 44″ (111.8cm) or wider
- 6 yards (5.5m) cable cord, ¼″ (6mm) thick
- upholstery zipper (optional)

METHOD
Step 1: Measure, mark with tailor's chalk, and cut out all five fabric sections, each approximately 2″ (5cm) larger than the bolster dimensions. (see figs. 1 & 2.)

If you want to be able to remove the cover for cleaning, cut the bottom section 2″ to 3″ (5cm to 7.6cm) wider than the bolster dimensions in order to attach a zipper. Insert upholstery zipper with a lapped or centered application in the middle of the bottom panel of bolster cover.

Step 2: Prepare 6 yards (5.5m)

of continuous bias, 1½″ (3.8cm) wide. Cover cable cord with the bias strip.

Position one of the 38″ x 18″ (96.5cm x 45.7cm) rectangles on the bolster front. Pin-baste cording across top edge of the fabric with rounded edge facing toward the bolster front. Cording should extend 1″ (2.5cm) beyond the cut edge of the fabric on either side. (See fig. 3.)

Following the same procedure, pin-baste a row of cording along bottom edge of bolster front fabric. (See fig. 3.)

Remove fabric from bolster and, using a zipper foot stitch cording in place.

Step 3: With right sides facing and using ½″ (1.3cm) seams, pin-baste the second large rectangle to rectangle with cording attached. Using a zipper foot attachment, stitch along the cording at the top edge.

Turn cover right side out and place on bolster. Firmly smooth into position.

Following the procedure outlined in Step 2, pin-baste a row of cording along the bottom of back section. Remove fabric from bolster and stitch in place.

Step 4: Replace cover on bolster. Position bottom section,

turn under raw edges and pin-baste in place. When cover is pinned to fit snugly, remove it from bolster and replace pins to the inside. Using a zipper foot attachment, stitch along bottom rows of the cording to attach bolster cover bottom.

Step 5: Slip cover onto bolster. Pin-baste cording around side edges of bolster ends so that the rounded part of cord faces toward center of side panel.

Remove cover from bolster and using a zipper foot attachment, stitch cording in place.

Replace cover on bolster. Position side panels and trim to triangular shape. Turn under raw edges, and pin-baste in position following the same techniques as you used to attach the bottom section to the cover in Step 4.

When cover is pinned to fit snugly, remove from bolster by opening zipper or pins in the bottom. Using a zipper foot attachment, stitch along the base of the cording to attach the side sections.

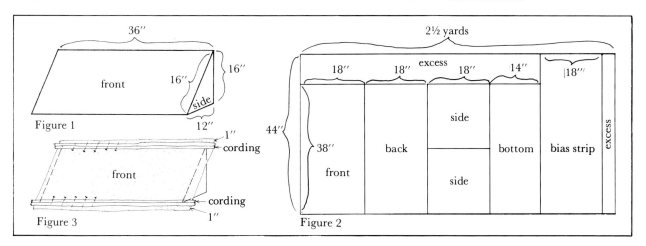

Figure 1

Figure 3

Figure 2

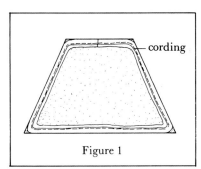

Figure 1

CHAIR SEAT CUSHIONS

MATERIALS
The materials and directions given apply to any size chair seat.
- light- to medium-weight fabric
- polyurethane foam pad, ½" (1.3cm) thick
- cable cord
- 2 yards (1.8m) grosgrain ribbon, ½" (1.3cm) wide

METHOD
Step 1: Measure seat of chair, and cut out a pattern with these measurements from brown wrapping paper. Using the paper pattern, cut out a piece of foam to fit on the chair seat.

Step 2: Using paper pattern, measure, mark with tailor's chalk, and cut two pieces of fabric, allowing for ½" (1.3cm) seams on all sides.

Step 3: From the remaining fabric, prepare a continuous bias strip 2½" (6.4cm) wide and slightly longer than the perimeter of the cover. Cover cable cord with the bias strip to make cording.

Pin-baste cording to right side of one fabric section, ½" (1.3cm) in from the outer edge with raw edge of cording even with raw edge of fabric. (See fig. 1.) Using a zipper foot attachment, stitch cording in place.

For a smooth finish where ends of the cording overlap, pull cord out of covering and clip it so that the cut ends of both sides meet. Stitch ends in place.

Step 4: With right sides together, place remaining fabric piece on top of corded fabric piece; pin-baste. Using a zipper foot attachment, stitch in place exactly on top of corded stitching, leaving back side open for turning and stuffing.

Trim seam allowances to ¼" (6mm), and clip as necessary to release fullness. Turn right side out. Insert foam cushion.

Step 5: Cut ribbon into four equal lengths. Stitch lengths in place on top and bottom of back seam. Make sure they tie around chair frame.

Slip-stitch back opening closed.

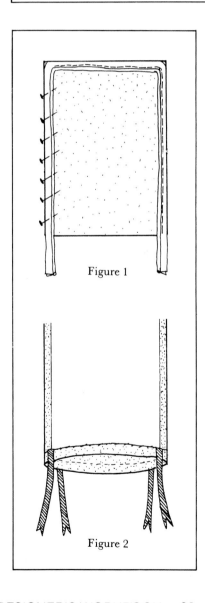

CHAIR BACK COVERS

MATERIALS
- light- to medium-weight fabric
- cable cord or commercial piping
- 2 yards (1.8m) grosgrain ribbon, ½" (1.3cm) wide (optional)

METHOD

Step 1: Trace the chair back onto brown wrapping paper, making the outline 1" (2.5cm) larger on all sides than the chair. (These covers look their best when the finished length reaches the seat of the chair.) To ensure a very snug fit, measure carefully. Following the wrapping paper pattern, cut out front and back sections of the chair cover.

Step 2: If you choose not to use commercial cording, from the remaining fabric prepare a continuous bias strip 2½" (6.4cm) wide and slightly longer than the perimeter of the cover. Cover the cable cord with the bias strip as directed to make cording.

Pin-baste cording to right side of one fabric section, ½" (1.3cm) in from outside edge with raw edge of piping even with raw edge of fabric. Using a zipper foot attachment, stitch in place, leaving one end uncorded. (See fig. 1.)

Step 3: With right sides together, place remaining fabric section on top of piped fabric; pin-baste. Try cover on chair, and make any necessary seam adjustments. Using a zipper foot attachment, stitch in place exactly on top of cording stitching, leaving uncorded end open for turning.

Clip seam allowances to release fullness.

Step 4: To hem the bottom, turn up raw edges ¼" (6mm), then ¼" to ½" (6mm to 1.3cm) again. Press; then stitch in place. (See fig. 2.)

Step 5: (optional) Cut grosgrain ribbon into four equal lengths. Pin lengths in place on front and back of wrong side of cover, positioned so that they will tie around the chair back frame. (See fig. 2.)

Try cover on chair to check positioning of ribbons. Remove cover from chair, and tack ribbons in place.

Press cover.

Figure 1

Figure 2

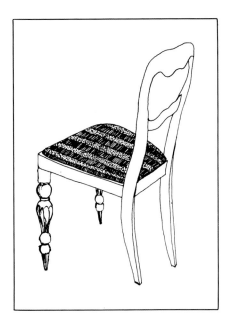

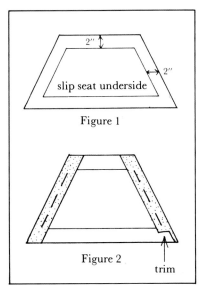

2"

2"

slip seat underside

Figure 1

Figure 2

trim

FABRIC-COVERED SLIP SEAT

A slip seat is the removable, upholstered wooden seat that slips into the framework of a chair.

MATERIALS
The materials and directions given are for four 17″ x 20″ (43.2cm x 50.8cm) slip seats.
- 1¼ yards (1.1m) fabric, 54″ (137.2cm) wide
- tape measure
- fabric shears
- staple gun and staples

METHOD
Step 1: Remove slip seats from chairs. Remove old fabric from seats only if there is a muslin covering underneath. If not, do not remove the old fabric, but cover it with the new material.

Step 2: Working with one seat at a time, place it upside down on top of the wrong side of the fabric. If the fabric has a design, make sure each seat is centered over the design. Cut fabric 2″ larger on all sides than the seat area. (See fig. 1.)

Holding fabric to the slip seat, flip it right side up to make sure the pattern is centered. Return to upside down position.

Step 3: Wrap fabric around side edges of slip seat and staple in place. Trim excess fabric from corners. (See fig. 2.)

Wrap fabric around front and back edges of slip seat making sure corners are neatly square. Staple in place. Trim off excess fabric and replace slip seat in chair.

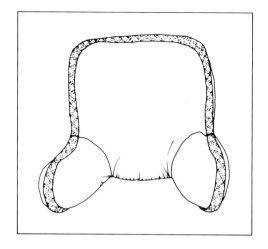

BACK REST PILLOW WITH ARMS

MATERIALS

- 2 yards (1.8m) medium- to heavyweight fabric, 48″ (121.9cm) or wider
- one 16-ounce (448g) package polyester fiber fill
- three 16-ounce (448g) packages polyester fiber fill graff paper

METHOD

Step 1: Enlarge and transfer the outline of the shaped pillow sections, including the front, back, and sides, to square ruled paper. (See fig. 1.)

Step 2: Press fabric and place it on top of a large, flat working surface.

Fold up one corner of the fabric so that the cut end rests exactly on the selvage. Press along this diagonal fold to locate the true bias.

Use the true bias fold as a guide to cut two strips of bias, each 5″ (12.7cm) wide. Attach these strips, end to end, to make a strip of bias approximately 2½ yards (2.3m) long and 5″ (12.7cm) wide. This will be used for the large cording around the back of the pillow.

Cut along the same diagonal edge to prepare another bias strip 4½″ (11.4cm) wide and 1 yard (91.4cm) long. This strip will be used for the cording along the armrests.

Step 3: Position pattern pieces for the front, back, sides and pockets on the remaining fabric, following fig. 1. Cut out the pieces.

Step 4: From a double layer of polyester batting, cut strips 6″ (15.2cm) wide and the exact length of the two bias strips

prepared in Step 2.

Roll the 6″ (15.2cm) batting strips lengthwise to form two smooth tight tubes of polyester. Using a zipper foot attachment, cover each tube with the bias strips to make cording. (See fig. 2.)

Pin-baste the thicker cording made from the 5″ (12.7cm) wide bias strip around the raw edges of the pillow back. Make sure raw edges of the cording face in the same direction as fabric section's raw edges. (See fig. 3.)

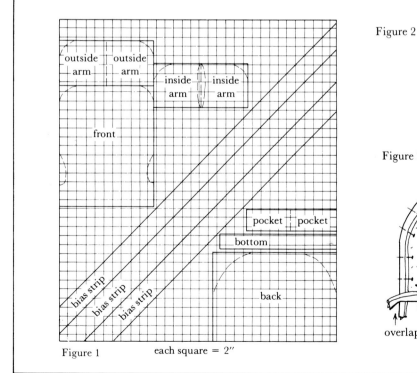

Figure 1   each square = 2″

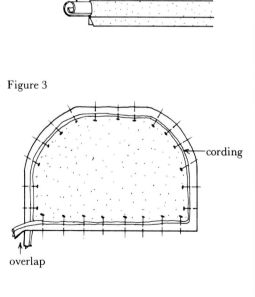

Figure 2

rolled batting

Figure 3

cording

overlap

Using ½″ (1.3cm) seams and a zipper foot attachment, stitch cording in place. Where cording meets, pull batting out of its covering about ½″ (1.3cm) on each end, and clip. Overlap the covering ends at the lower corner of the pillow. (See fig. 3.)

Step 9: With right sides together, pin-baste; then stitch the narrow bottom strip along the wider bottom edge of the cushion. Stitch directly on top of the stitching line which attached the thick cording to the pillow back.

Step 10: Place the pillow front, with the completed arm sections on top of the pillow back so that the right sides are together.

Pin-baste along the cording. Where cording overlaps, clip excess polyester batting, and fold the ends of the cording so that they meet for a finished effect with a minimum of bulk.

Starting at one lower corner, stitch the front and back pieces together, stitching around the outer edge to the opposite lower corner.

Trim seam allowances as necessary, and turn cover right side out.

Step 11: Stuff polyester fiber fill into the pillow, being careful to fill the armrests and back areas evenly and firmly. (If filling compresses when used over a long period of time, open pillow and add more fiber fill.)

Pin-baste the bottom edge of the pillow, and slip-stitch the opening closed. Be careful to spread the ease of this bottom strip across the entire width of the pillow. This will create a shirred, full effect.

Step 5: To hem the outside arm pockets, turn under ½″ (1.3cm), then turn under a ½″ (1.3cm) hem. Stitch in place.

Stitch pockets in place, right sides up, ¼″ (6mm) in from the side and bottom edges of the outer armrest sections. (See fig. 4.)

Step 6: Pin-baste the narrower cording made from the 4½″ (11.4cm) bias strip around the curved edge of the outer arm section. (See fig. 5.) Raw edge of cording should face the same direction as raw edges of fabric.

Stitch in place using a zipper foot attachment and ½″ (1.3cm) seams. Repeat Step 6 to attach cording to the second armrest.

Step 7: Pin-baste the inside section of the armrest to the outside section which has the cording attached. The sections should be right sides together with the cording resting in between them.

Using a zipper foot attachment, stitch along the base of the cording to attach the two armrest sections. Repeat this procedure to complete the second armrest. Turn both armrests right side out.

Step 8: With right sides facing, pin the armrests to the inside front of the pillow on each side. The curved seams at the base of the armrests fit exactly into the curved seams on the inside back pillow section. (See fig. 6.) Stitch.

With right sides together, stitch ½″ (1.3cm) seams directly underneath the outer pockets to finish the bottom of the armrests and form the base of the cushion.

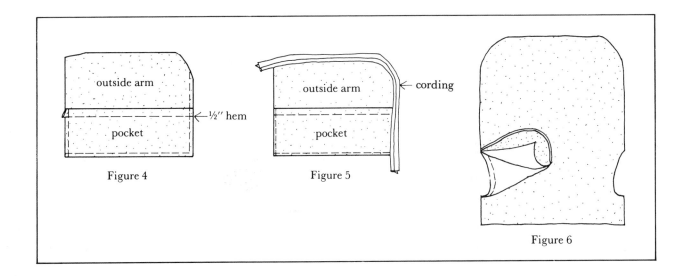

Figure 4

Figure 5

Figure 6

SPECIAL PILLOW PROJECTS

ALEX'S ANIMALS

Turtle

MATERIALS
- 1 standard-size pillowcase
- 1 white terry bath towel
- 3 (1-pound) packages polyester fiber fill
- fusible bonding web

METHOD
Step 1: Enlarge pattern on page 156. (See Appendix for enlarging instructions.) Cut eyes, mouth, and body pieces from pillowcase. Cut all other shapes from the white terry bath towel. Cut eyes and mouth from fusible bonding web.

Step 2: Pin all pieces, right sides together, and stitch, leaving an opening 4″ (10.2cm) long for stuffing. Clip seams, turn, and stuff with fiber fill. Before stuffing head, iron on eyes and mouth with fusible bonding web. Stitch openings closed.

Swan

MATERIALS
- 1 standard-size pillowcase
- 1 peach terry hand towel
- 2 (1-pound) packages polyester fiber fill
- fusible bonding web

METHOD
Step 1: Enlarge pattern on page 156. (See Appendix for enlarging instructions.) Cut body from pillowcase; cut all other pieces from towel.

Step 2: Cut out eye and iron on to right side of head with fusible bonding web.

Step 3: Pin all pieces right sides together and stitch, leaving a 4″

(10.2cm) opening for stuffing. Clip seams, turn, and stuff with fiber fill. Stitch openings closed.

Step 4: Stuff the beak; then stitch around the opening and gather it tightly closed. Slipstitch the beak to the head.

Fat Cat

MATERIALS
- 2 standard-size pillowcases in two different blue patterns
- 1 blue terry hand towel
- fusible bonding web
- 3 (1-pound) packages polyester fiber fill
- green embroidery floss
- embroidery needle, size 6

METHOD
Step 1: Enlarge patterns on page 156. (See Appendix for enlarging instructions.) Cut head and legs from one patterned pillowcase, body and ears from other pillowcase, and ear lining and tail from blue terry hand towel.

Step 2: Follow instructions for making the Easter Bunny, except in step 3 do not use fusible bonding web or stuffing in the ears.

Easter Bunny

MATERIALS
- 2 standard-size pillowcases in two different pink patterns
- 1 pink terry hand towel
- fusible bonding web
- 3 (1-pound) packages polyester fiber fill
- 6 sew-on snap fasteners
- green embroidery floss
- embroidery needle, size 6

METHOD
Step 1: Enlarge pattern on page 156. (See Appendix for

enlarging instructions.) Cut head and body from one patterned pillowcase. Cut arms, legs, and one pair of ears from other pillowcase. Cut another pair of ears from pink terry towel. Cut one pair of ear tips from fusible bonding web, making them half as long as the ears.

Step 2: Pin all fabric pieces except head right sides together

and stitch, using ½" (1.3cm) seams. Leave a 4" (10.2cm) opening for stuffing. Clip seams and turn all pieces right side out.

Step 3: Slip fusible bonding web into the tips of the ears and press. Stuff the bottom half of the ears with fiber fill. Lay the ears on right side of back of head, terry side up. Baste with ½" (1.3cm) seams.

Step 4: Cut eyes and nose/mouth from terry towel and from fusible bonding web. Iron shapes to right side of face with fusible bonding web.

Step 5: Place face on top of ears, right side down, and pin all around edges to back of head. Stitch, leaving a 4" (10.2cm) opening at the top for stuffing. Clip seams and turn.

Stuff head, and hand-stitch opening closed.

Step 6: Stuff the body, arms and legs with fiber fill; stitch openings closed.

Step 7: Line up the legs and head against the body and mark the spots for snaps.

Step 8: Embroider eyelashes and whiskers on face.

strips 3″ x 13″ (7.6cm x 33cm) and 2 strips 3″ x 19″ (7.6cm x 48.3cm)
- 10½″ x 3½ yards (26.7cm x 3.2m) strip of fabric for ruffle
- 1½″ x 2 yards (3.8cm x 1.8m) strip of fabric cut on bias for cording
- 19″ (48.3cm) square of fabric for pillow back
- square of batting for quilting (size of square plus border gives size of batting needed)
- polyester fiber fill for stuffing
- approximately 2 yards (1.8m) of ⅛″ (3mm) cording
- 19″ (48.3cm) square muslin to back quilting
  All measurements include ¼″ (6mm) seam allowance

METHOD

Step 1: For border: On opposite sides of quilt square, sew 13″ (33cm) long strips of fabric. Press seams. Sew remaining two borders to 19″ (48.3cm) sides.

Step 2: For quilting: With quilt square on top, batting in the center, and muslin square on bottom, quilt, joining all three layers. These three layers may be stretched on a small frame (embroidery frame will also work) or quilted in the lap. Baste through the three layers to hold squares together while quilting. This pillow is quilted by the piece—that is, the quilting outlines the existing design. However, any quilting design will work.

Step 3: Make and attach cording and ruffle according to directions in The Portfolio of Pillow Techniques.

Step 4: Finish your pillow with your choice of the methods described in The Portfolio of Pillow Techniques.

QUILT BLOCK PILLOW

Do you have just one quilt block that you have stitched up to see how a pattern worked, or have you found an old quilt block or two tucked away with some family treasures? Here's a good idea for using those single blocks. Notice that the fabrics of the borders and the ruffle are similar in scale to the fabrics used in the antique quilt block. The block shown dates back to 1875.

MATERIALS
- 13″ (33cm) square quilt block
- 4 strips of fabric for border: 2

CALICO ANGEL

Not only wonderful as a Christmas decoration, this calico angel, when sewed up in a non-seasonal color scheme, can be kept out and loved all year. To make a pair of angels that fly toward each other, cut out and sew up the angel with the body, wing, and arm patterns right side up, then turn these pattern pieces wrong side up to cut out the second angel.

MATERIALS
- assorted gingham fabrics
- white fabric (such as sheeting)
- braid
- ribbon
- ruffled eyelet and rickrack trim
- polyester fiber fill for stuffing
- yarn for hair
- large needle for yarn
- embroidery thread or felt-tip markers for facial features

METHOD

Step 1: Trace and enlarge pattern for angel on page 157, allowing ¼'' (6mm) for seams. (See Appendix for enlarging instructions.) Trace pattern onto fabric. Paint or embroider facial features on face, then stitch the two small circles together, leaving a small opening for stuffing. Turn right side out, stuff, whipstitch opening closed. Thread needle with yarn and sew loops of hair to top of circle.

Step 2: Stitch ruffled eyelet trim to arm for sleeve, then stitch braid, ribbon, rickrack, and ruffled eyelet trim to body of angel. Sew body, wing, and arm parts together, leaving small openings for stuffing. Turn to right side and sew, then attach arm and head. Stuff, then whipstitch openings closed.

Step 3: Use tacking stitch to attach rickrack around circle for halo; then seam, leaving small opening for stuffing. Stuff, and whipstitch opening closed. Place halo on back of head and stitch in place. (Note: You may choose to make a star instead of a halo for your angel. We show this alternative in the close-up photograph.)

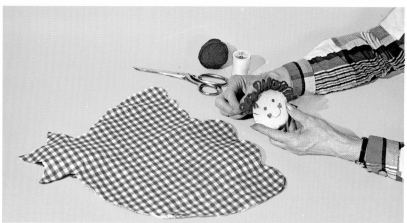

BARGELLO PILLOW

This project is designed to teach the basic flame stitch, one of the most well-known bargello stitches. Flame stitch patterns are formed from zigzag design lines. The heights of the peaks and valleys may vary from pattern to pattern or within a single pattern. Once the first design line is established, it is repeated in different colors to form the pattern of the piece. Most bargello patterns have a set color scheme and a repeating color sequence. But historic pieces in museums show clearly that needleworkers of the past used any color yarn they had in any sequence they pleased. In addition to being thrifty, using yarn scraps provides a good way to learn about color harmony and makes the piece even more interesting to work. Experimentation will show that sharply contrasting colors make the pattern stand out and that related colors used together give a softer look.

The method for working the basic flame stitch is shown in the photographic sequence. This is the English "to-and-fro" method, the best way to work bargello. Remember that when you do your own bargello designs, you may make the peaks and valleys any height you want; the more stitches or "steps" the higher the peak. The materials and directions are for an 8'' (20.3cm) square pillow.

MATERIALS
- 11'' (27.9cm) square of 14 mono canvas
- tapestry yarn or Persian yarn (two 32'' (81.3cm) lengths per

row, approximately 28 rows)
• tapestry needle, size 18 or 20

METHOD
Step 1: Start first row, your pattern row, 1½'' (3.8cm) from right edge of canvas. In basic flame stitch, each stitch encloses four threads of the canvas. The next stitch starts at the halfway point of the first stitch and overlaps the first stitch by two threads. Always make your stitches straight; never slant over a vertical thread as in basic needlepoint.

Step 2: When you take several stitches in this way, you will see that you are creating a slanted line of stitches—the ''up'' side of the peak. The number of stitches or ''steps'' you take determines the height of the peak. In this particular pattern, peaks that are five stitches high are alternated with peaks that are seven stitches high.

Step 3: When you are ready to come ''down'' the peak, count *down* four threads. Remember that when working *up* a peak, count *up* four threads of canvas; when working *down* a peak, count *down* four threads of canvas. The stitch on the back of the canvas always covers only two threads. Complete the pattern line across the canvas following the sample, alternating the height of the peaks as shown.

Step 4: Follow the pattern line you have established to complete the subsequent rows in the colors of your choice.

Step 5: Block work, if necessary, and finish your pillow with your choice of the methods described in The Portfolio of Pillow Techniques.

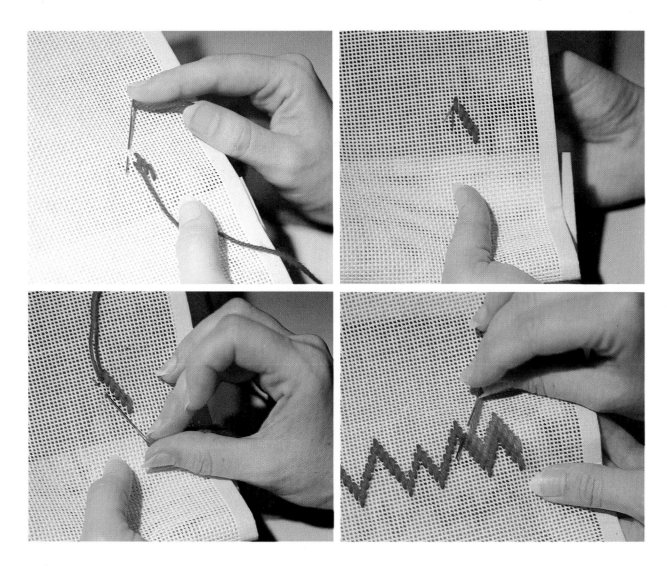

NOAH'S ARK

In any language, Noah's Ark
represents the great flood and
God's help to those who believe
in him; the rainbow symbolizes
God's love and protection. This
charming rendering of Noah's
famous craft is worked on Aida
cloth in cross stitch. The colors
chosen seem just right for the
small pillow, but you may wish
to alter the background color to
match a particular room's decor.

Pair this design with Noah's
Animals found on page 113 for
stunning additions to a child's
room. Or you might want to
work both designs into kneeling
pads for the children's chapel at
your house of worship.

Working from a charted
design is easy to learn and has
several advantages over working
on a painted canvas. For one
thing, all danger of colors
bleeding during blocking is
eliminated. Refer to the
Appendix for instructions on

how to work from a charted
design and for easy-to-follow
diagrams for working the cross
stitch.

Finish your pillow with your
choice of the methods given in
The Portfolio of Pillow
Techniques.

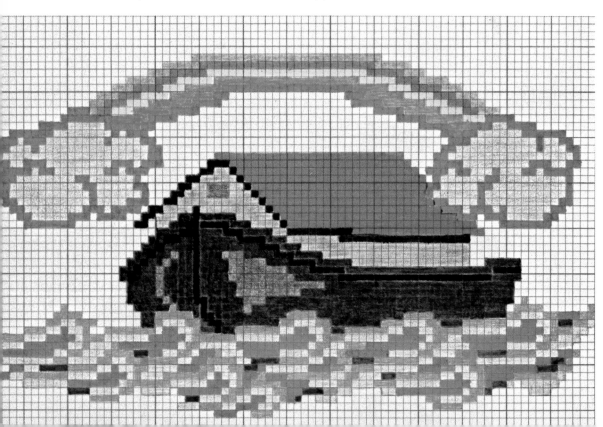

RINGBEARER'S PILLOW

The seven gifts of the Holy Spirit—power, riches, wisdom, strength, honor, glory, and blessing—are represented by the Columbine on this beautiful needlepoint pillow. We call it a ringbearer's pillow to be used on generations of special wedding days. What a treasured present for a bride-to-be—a gift of promised gifts!

Instructions for working from a charted design and diagrams for the basketweave stitch appear in the Appendix.

Finish your pillow with your choice of the methods given in The Portfolio of Pillow Techniques.

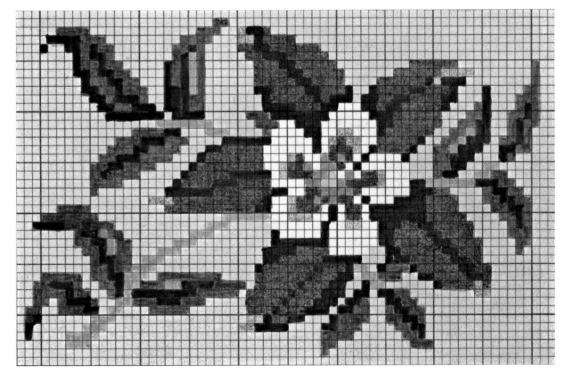

LION

Majesty, power, and strength—a
lion symbolizes all three even
when he's staring at you from a
needlepoint pillow. The eyes are
a mesmerizing focal point in the
tangled wave of brown tones,
and the touches of white under
his eyes and around his whiskers
accent his intense expression.
He will be the piece de résistance
in any pillow grouping.

Diagrams for working the
basketweave stitch are found in
the Appendix as are the
instructions for working from a
charted design.
Finish your pillow with your
choice of the methods given in
The Portfolio of Pillow
Techniques. If you choose to
adapt this design to make a
circular pillow, as shown above,
remember that a round pillow
must be boxed to prevent the
edges from rippling.

BLACKWORK PILLOW

Blackwork basically is a type of counted-thread embroidery done with black thread and is sometimes highlighted with gold. The design area on the pillow measures 9'' x 10'' (22.9cm x 25.4cm), and the finished pillow size is 15'' (38.1cm) square. Refer to the Appendix for any embroidery stitches not illustrated with the chart for design on page 158.

MATERIALS
- 18'' (45.7cm) square evenweave linen, 18 threads per inch
- dressmaker's carbon paper
- 1 ball #5 black pearl cotton
- 1 ball #8 black pearl cotton
- fine gold thread
- tapestry needle, size 22 or 24
- crewel needle, size 3

METHOD
Step 1: To keep the fabric from unraveling, turn over the raw edges of the linen ½'' (1.3cm) and baste down or tape with masking tape. Enlarge the pattern on page 158 to the desired size and trace the design onto your fabric using dressmaker's carbon paper.

Step 2: Thread the crewel needle with #5 black pearl cotton. Using the chain stitch, outline outside edge of design.

Step 3: With the crewel needle and #5 pearl cotton, outline the tulip-shaped area with coral stitch.

Step 4: Outline the remaining pattern areas 1 through 6 with the stem stitch using the crewel needle and #5 pearl cotton.

Step 5: Thread the tapestry needle with #8 pearl cotton. Work each of the patterns in turn. Consult photo to see how to properly center patterns 3 and 6. The other patterns do not need to be centered in any way.

Step 6: Work the whipped spider in the circle below the tulip-shaped area. Thread the tapestry needle with #5 pearl cotton. The stitch should be done with a continuous piece of thread so start with a fresh piece about 18'' (45.7cm) long. Anchor thread securely on back of work by running it under previous stitching. Come up in the hole in the fabric nearest the center of the circle. Go down in the first hole beyond the line at the top center of the circle as shown by 1 in the illustration. Come back up in the center hole and down at 3. Continue in this manner until all the spokes are formed. Come back up in the center and you are ready to weave. The weaving is done around the spokes on top of the fabric. Do not go back into the fabric again until the weaving is complete. Go under spokes 1 and 13 and come up. Go under spoke 13 again and under 7 and come up. Go under spoke 7 again and under spoke 11. Continue in this manner around the circle until none of the traced outer line is showing; then do two more rows for security.

Step 7: With the crewel needle and the fine gold thread, sew a row of back stitches around the outer edge of the chain stitches. Come up in the center of the second link and down in the first, up in the third and down in the second link, etc. all the way around.

Step 8: Thread the tapestry needle with the fine gold thread and come up on the left side of the whipped spider. Go under and around and under the black thread without going into the linen; the needle should follow the row of stem stitches that encloses pattern 6. Make the interval between stitches about every ¼'' (6mm).

Step 9: Finish pillow with The Portfolio of Pillow Techniques.

LOG CABIN PILLOW TOP

All log cabin quilts are composed of blocks of narrow strips of fabric, usually half light and half dark. The way the quilt blocks are set together determines the final design of the overall quilt. The one shown here is called "light and dark." One of the best-loved and most famous of all pieced quilt designs, the log cabin is adaptable to many color arrangements, subtle or bold.

MATERIALS
- printed fabric in light and dark colors
- fabric for quilt backing
- batting

METHOD
Step 1: See diagram and cut fabric strips as indicated, adding ¼″ for seams to all sides of log. Accuracy in cutting and pressing is essential. As you work, push seams to one side, rather than pressing them open.

Step 2: Begin piecing in the center (see photo 1) with first log to the right side and continue to piece clockwise, two light and two dark. See photo 2 for how squares should be sewn together. Note that the 2″ (5cm) square center block is red in each square.

Step 3: Join four completed squares to form a block with the light-colored strips meeting at the center. To "quilt as you go," cut a square for backing ¼″ (6mm) larger all around than the block. Cut a piece of batting ¼″ (6mm) smaller all around than finished block. Baste these three layers together through center to

each side and from corner to corner.

Step 4: Quilt from center to outside. Do not quilt closer to the edge than ¼″ (6mm).

Step 5: When quilting is complete, make quilt block into a pillow, using desired techniques from The Portfolio of Pillow Techniques.

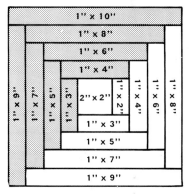

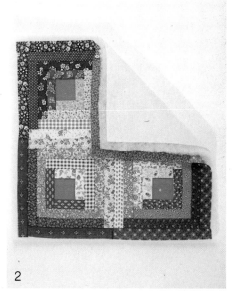

YARN-PUNCHED PILLOWS FROM INDIAN INSPIRATION

The method is traditional to rug-making. To adapt it to pillow-making, take a square or rectangle of burlap, punch a design with rug yarn, back it with velveteen, and stuff it with fiber fill. The effect is fresh, and so are the colors. These Indian-inspired designs are lavish in their use of brilliant hues.

MATERIALS
- 18″ x 20″ (45.7cm x 50.8cm) piece of white or beige burlap
- dressmaker's carbon paper
- no. 6 rug punch
- 4 skeins turquoise rug yarn
- 1 skein black rug yarn
- 1 skein white rug yarn
- 1 skein shocking pink rug yarn
- 2 skeins red rug yarn

- 2 (16-ounce) bags polyester fiber fill
- liquid adhesive
- 18" x 20" (45.7cm x 50.8cm) piece of turquoise velveteen

METHOD

Step 1: Enlarge pattern from page 160 or 161 to desired size and trace onto burlap with dressmaker's carbon paper, leaving a 1" (2.5cm) seam allowance on each side. (See Appendix for enlarging instructions.) Bind edges of fabric either with zigzag stitching or masking tape.

Step 2: Thread the rug punch according to instructions that come with it. Punch the black outline first, then fill in the inside areas. Finish by punching the turquoise background.

Push the punch from the wrong side to the right side of the burlap. Pull punch back through the same hole, leaving a ½" (1.3cm) loop on the right side. Make the punches close together so that the pile is thick and the burlap does not show. After punching is completed, rubber backing may be applied, if desired, with liquid adhesive.

Step 3: Using the velveteen as a backing, finish your pillow with your choice of the methods described in The Portfolio of Pillow Techniques.

Step 4: Make tassels for corners using a mixture of yarn colors. (See "Tassels" in the Portfolio of Pillow Techniques.)

Right side of work.

Wrong side of work.

SILK-SCREENED ANIMALS

During the early 1890s, there appeared in the toy stores of America a Tabby Cat, printed in colors on calico, to be cut out, sewn together and stuffed. He was a solemn, dignified creature, irresistably catlike. He quickly became the rage, and his sober face must be among the earliest memories of many of our older citizens. He is important in the history of American childhood because, although not quite the first cutout rag toy to be produced commercially, he was the first to achieve nationwide fame, and he paved the way for a long procession of the cuddly animals that are our first and most important toys.

The toy was first sold at Christmas in 1892 and was distributed from Maine to California. The Tabby Cat was a wildfire success, starting a craze for rag toys that continued unabated until World War I and after. This craze produced, among others, the famous advertising dolls that many of us remember: "Sunny Jim" and "Aunt Jemima." From the rag toys evolved the more elaborate, jointed plush toys.

The Tabby Cat was quickly followed by "her" kittens, which at first sight were simply a reduced version of the original design.

This "family" was displayed at the World's Fair in Chicago in 1893. In Philadelphia, Wanamakers had one of their main show windows filled with them. References to the Tabby Cat can be found in newspapers and periodicals of the time from all over the world. A great part of their attraction was that the cats had a remarkable lifelike quality when made up; again and again there are stories of people and even animals deceived into thinking that a Tabby Cat was alive. Farmers in Lincoln County, Maine, used them as bird scarers in their fruit trees!

. . . Excerpted from the original by John Noble, Curator of The Toy Collection, Museum of the City of New York

Editor's Note: To obtain a price sheet for the animals pictured above, write to The Toy Works, Department OH, Middle Falls, New York 12848. You can purchase the printed fabric to make your own, or you can buy the animals completely made up.

NOAH'S ANIMALS

A parade of pairs! Noah's charges march across the canvas in subtle, natural colors to make a stunning needlepoint pillow. Even the tiniest shapes turn into creatures with a second careful look. This design would make a nice complement to the cross stitch of Noah's Ark found on page 104.

The chart for this charming design is given on page 159.

Working from a charted design is easy; beginners need not be wary. Refer to the Appendix for instructions and for a diagram of the basketweave stitch.

Finish your pillow with your choice of the methods given in The Portfolio of Pillow Techniques.

RIBBONPOINT™ PILLOW

Ribbonpoint™ is an exciting new needle art that is much like needlepoint, except that it is worked with tiny ribbon. It takes one-third the time of needlepoint, and the finished design is given a beautiful, damask, mosaic effect.

Follow the pattern according to the color chart on the adjoining page. (Note that the French blue area has been left white.) The floral border is worked in the basic Ribbonpoint™ stitch, outlined below. The center design is worked in the herringbone stitch (almost the same as basic Ribbonpoint™), also outlined below. The inside yellow border is worked in two stitches: the outside row is basic Ribbonpoint,™ the inside row is the running stitch, outlined below.

MATERIALS
- 16" (40.6cm) square wooden frame
- 16" (40.6cm) square No. 7

mono canvas (Note: This must be worked on No. 7 mono canvas. No other will do.)
- tapestry needle, Size 20
- rug needle, Size 13
- ⅛" (3mm) wide double-faced satin ribbon precut in 19" (48.3cm) lengths in the following colors:
Parrot Green: 40 yards
Coral: 30 yards
Dusty Rose: 20 yards
French Blue: 120 yards
Cinnamon: 30 yards
Bright Yellow: 20 yards (160 yards extra, for tassels)
If ribbon is not available locally, you may order it from: Patricia Mabry Enterprises, P.O. Box 523, Fairfield, Alabama 35064   Ribbonpoint™ is U.S. PAT. 4,075962

Notes: To begin each ribbon: Thread tapestry needle with one length of satin ribbon. Fold long end of ribbon back ¾" (1.9cm) and cut a ⅛" (3mm) long vertical slit using very sharp scissors. (See fig. 1.)

To lock the first stitch of any

pattern, run the threaded needle through the tiny slit and pull tightly so the slit is on the wrong side of the canvas. A knot will be formed. (See fig. 2.)

Each ribbon seems to twist (this is especially true when the ribbon gets shorter). Use the rug needle to hold the ribbon flat on right side of the canvas as you pull through to the other side of canvas. As you pull the twisted ribbon to the wrong side of the canvas, the ribbon should lie flat on the front of the canvas with no wrinkles.

If the ribbon frays while in work, snip off a tiny end. If, when making a stitch, the ribbon is pulled too tightly, slip the needle under the stitch and loosen slightly.

METHOD
Basic Ribbonpoint™ Stitch:
Step 1: Make the first stitch going from left to right across the top right-hand corner of your design. Hold the ribbon between the thumb and forefinger of your left hand. Pull the twisted ribbon to the back of the canvas *before* you let go with your thumb and forefinger. Do not try to untwist the ribbon. The ribbon should lie flat across the space with no wrinkles.

Step 2: The second stitch will fall in a straight line immediately below the first stitch. Skip the hole immediately below Stitch 1 and bring the ribbon up from the bottom to the top across this space. Hold the ribbon securely with your left hand thumb and forefinger. Slide the needle under the ribbon of the first stitch to the back of the canvas. (See fig. 3.) Pull all the twisted ribbon through to the back of the canvas *before* you let go of the ribbon with your left hand.

Figure 1

Figure 2

Figure 3

Figure 4

Figure 5

Figure 6

Step 3: Bring the needle up in the middle of the space directly to the left of your second stitch. Hold the ribbon securely with your thumb and forefinger of your left hand. Cover the space directly to the left of your first stitch. This stitch will also go up and down like the second stitch.

Step 4: Skip a space to the left of the third stitch. Bring your needle up. Cover the skipped space with a ribbon going from left to right, as in your first stitch. Slide the needle under the ribbon of the third stitch. (See fig. 4.) Continue to hold the ribbon securely with your left hand until all of the twists in the ribbon are pulled to the back of the canvas.

Step 5: Come up in the center of the space directly below Stitch 4. Hold the ribbon securely with the left hand and cover the space from left to right below Stitch 3. (See fig. 5.) Continue to work the ribbon in the same manner with each succeeding stitch.

Step 6: Bring the needle up in the space directly below Stitch 5. Cover the space directly below Stitch 3 moving the ribbon from left to right. All stitches going down the diagonal row will cover the space from left to right. All stitches going up the diagonal row will cover the space from bottom to top. (See fig. 6.) To finish off each ribbon, make two loop knots, then run the ribbon under several stitches as you would in canvas embroidery.

Work the floral border in the basic Ribbonpoint™ stitch, changing colors as necessary to follow the pattern. Then work one solid row of the yellow band

at the inside edge of the border in basic Ribbonpoint™ stitch. The yellow band will consist of two rows side by side: one row in basic Ribbonpoint™ stitch and the second row in a running stitch. Complete the running stitch of the yellow border after the center design is worked in the herringbone stitch.

Step 7: To make the tassels: Tassels can vary in size but the ones shown require four packages of yellow ribbon per tassel. Lay the ribbon out side by side in a straight line. Find the middle of the ribbon length. Take away two strips of ribbon for each tassel. Lay one strip across the center of the four packages of ribbon. Fold the ribbon across the one piece of ribbon and wind the second strip around all of the folded ribbon about 1'' to 1½'' (2.5cm to 3.8cm) from the crease. Tie or sew securely. Make sure all the ends are trimmed bluntly.

Herringbone Stitch: Thread needle and slit and knot ribbon as for basic Ribbonpoint™
Step 1: Count up two stitches and over two stitches from the inside right-hand bottom corner of the first yellow row. This point will determine your first herringbone stitch. Bring the threaded needle up in the middle of this determined space. Count up over three spaces. Bring the needle down in the fourth space.

Step 2: The ribbon should go up and down for this stitch. Bring the needle up in the space directly to the left of the first space of the preceeding stitch. Count up and over three spaces. Bring the needle to the back of the canvas in the fourth space.

Remember to hold the ribbon between the thumb and forefinger and allow the twisted ribbon to pull to the back of the canvas before letting go.

Repeat Step 2 all of the way up the row. Stop at the last full stitch closest to yellow border.

To go down the row, count three spaces to the left of the bottom space of any of your up and down stitches. Bring the needle up in the fourth space.

Running Stitch: Thread needle, slit and knot ribbon as for basic ribbon point.

Step 1: Begin at the right-hand bottom corner of the yellow band. Count up along the right side of the canvas until you come to three stitches running from left to right of the herringbone stitch. Move one space to the right. Come up in the hole below the last space; count up and over three spaces and bring your needle to the back of the canvas in the fourth space. Be sure and hold the ribbon in your left hand with your thumb and forefinger until all the twisted ribbon is on the back of the canvas. This stitch will run up and down and should go across the three left to right stitches of the herringbone. The ribbon should lie flat across the three spaces.

Step 2: The next stitch should go from left to right across one space above the last stitch. The next stitch should go from bottom to top across the second space. The ribbon should go from left to right across the third space. This completes the basic running stitch.
Be sure to do the sides of the band first and make the corners fit following the graphed design.

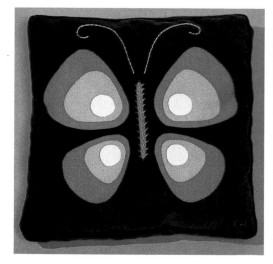

REVERSE APPLIQUÉ BUTTERFLY

The finest examples of reverse appliqué are found in the *molas* created by the Cuna Indians of the San Blas Islands off the Atlantic coast of Panama. Their designs are completely covered with cut out areas of every imaginable shape, some designs more intricate than others.

The butterfly mola shown here is a relatively simple pattern, but since the reverse appliqué technique is so unique itself, even the simplest design will be distinctive. The finished pillow measures 15″ (38.1cm) square.

MATERIALS
- four 16″ (40.6cm) squares lightweight fabric in four contrasting colors
- dressmaker's carbon paper
- embroidery scissors
- thread colors to match fabric squares
- 16″ (40.6cm) square fabric for back
- polyester fiber fill for stuffing

METHOD
Step 1: Place the four fabric squares directly on top of each other in whatever order you desire. Baste layers together.

Step 2: Enlarge pattern on page 162. (See Appendix for enlarging instructions.) Using dressmaker's carbon paper, trace the outline of the *largest* areas to be cut out on the top layer of fabric. Be sure to center the design on the fabric square.

Step 3: Using embroidery scissors, cut along the marked lines, making sure to cut only through the top layer of fabric. It is wise to cut a small area at a time and stitch it down before cutting more so your work doesn't shift and become distorted.

Step 4: Turn under the raw edge of the cut out areas about ¼″ (6mm). Using a thread to match the top layer, stitch the turned edges to the second fabric layer with a tiny slipstitch. Clip corners and curves to help them turn under smoothly.

Step 5: When the top layer is completely cut and sewn, trace the outline of the next smaller size areas on the exposed portions of the second layer of fabric. Cut out these areas to reveal the third layer color, turn under raw edges ¼″ (6mm), and stitch.

Step 6: When the second layer is completely cut and sewn, trace the outline of the third smallest size areas on the third layer of cloth. Cut, turn edges under, and stitch. If you are working with four layers of fabric, you cut patterns into three layers only; never cut any holes in the bottom layer of fabric.

Step 7: When the entire pattern has been cut and stitched, remove the basting stitches. You may wish to add an embroidered detail such as the antenna on the butterfly or accent stitches on the body.

Step 8: Finish your pillow with your choice of the methods described in The Portfolio of Pillow Techniques.

SPRING PROMISE

A dainty reminder of spring never fails to soothe winter-weary spirits. The delicate design here is worked in counted cross stitch on Aida cloth. The subtle shadings of the flowers and their leaves make the arrangement almost life-like.

Refer to the Appendix for easy directions for working from a charted design and for instructions on the cross stitch. Then finish your pillow with your choice of the methods given in The Portfolio of Pillow Techniques. The pillow shown is accented with distinctive double ruffles—one of lace, the other of fabric—similar to the ones used on the Lace Ruffled Pillows, page 153.

MESSAGE PILLOWS

Happy Birthday

MATERIALS
- two 6″ x 8″ (15.2cm x 20.3cm) pieces printed cotton
- 30″ (76.2cm) length 1″ (2.5cm) wide plain white ruffle
- 1 yard (91.4cm) rickrack
- 4″ (10.2cm) square cotton
- polyester fiber fill for stuffing

METHOD
Step 1: Stitch rickrack to outside edge of white ruffle. With right sides facing and raw edges together, stitch ruffle to one rectangle of fabric.

Step 2: Arrange 4″ (10.2cm) square on second piece of cotton, angling bottom into a point. Turn edges under ¼″ (6mm), press, and topstitch pocket to fabric along three sides. Trim with rickrack.

Step 3: With right sides facing and raw edges of ruffle and fabric together, stitch two pieces of fabric together using ½″ (1.3cm) seams. Leave a small opening for turning. Turn, stuff lightly with polyester fiber fill, and slipstitch opening closed.

Heart Throb

MATERIALS
- two 6″ x 8″ (15.2cm x 20.3cm) pieces silver-colored fabric—metallic, satin, or velvet

- 30″ (76.2cm) length wide lace
- two 6″ (15.2cm) squares red satin
- white embroidery floss
- 1 yard (91.4cm) ribbon
- polyester fiber fill for stuffing

METHOD
Step 1: With raw edges together and using ¼″ (6mm) seams, stitch lace ruffle around right side of one piece of fabric.

Step 2: With right sides facing and raw edges of fabric and ruffle together, stitch two pieces of fabric together using ½″ (1.3cm) seams. Leave a small opening for turning. Turn, stuff lightly with polyester fiber fill, and slipstitch opening closed.

Step 3: Cut two identical heart shapes out of the squares of red satin. Embroider message with a chain stitch on one heart shape. With right sides facing, stitch two heart shapes together using ¼″ (6mm) seams. Leave a small opening for turning. Turn, stuff lightly with polyester fiber fill, and slipstitch opening closed. Tack heart to one side of pillow.

Step 4: Make a bow with satin ribbon and tack securely to top of pillow.

Have a Nice Day

MATERIALS
- four 6″ x 8″ (15.2cm x 20.3cm) pieces printed cotton [two in one print (A), two in

complementing print (B)]
- 1¾ yards (1.6m) of 1″ (2.5cm) wide white eyelet ruffle
- 2 yards (1.8m) ribbon
- white embroidery floss
- polyester fiber fill for stuffing

METHOD
Step 1: With raw edges together and using ¼″ (6mm) seams, stitch eyelet ruffle around right side of both pieces of A.

Step 2: On the remaining two pieces of cotton (B), use embroidery floss in a chain stitch to write out your message or symbol, such as a heart. (See Appendix for stitch diagrams.)

Step 3: With right sides facing and raw edges of fabric and ruffle together, stitch one piece of A and one piece of B together using ½″ (1.3cm) seams. Leave a small opening for turning. Turn, stuff lightly with polyester fiber fill, and slipstitch opening closed. Repeat Step 3 for remaining pieces of A and B.

Step 4: Cut satin ribbon into six 12″ (30.5cm) lengths, three for each pillow. Stack pillows with message in center and A sides out, as a book would appear. Align and tack two lengths of ribbon to each pillow at the left side of the pillow/book. Center and tack one length of ribbon to each pillow at the right side of the pillow/book. Tie pillows together with bows.

VICTORIAN HOUSE CLUSTER

You might want to think of this intriguing house sculpture more as a delightful wall hanging than as a pillow. After you try this style, why not design a companion pillow that looks like your own home?

MATERIALS
- 15″ x 20″ (38.1cm x 50.8cm) piece pintucked fabric or similar design for section A
- 20″ x 7″ (50.8cm x 17.8cm) piece fabric for section B
- 6″ x 8″ (15.2cm x 20.3cm) piece fabric, same color as house section B
- assorted scraps for details
- ½ yard (45.7cm) flat lace for curtains, ¾″ or 1″ (1.9cm or 2.5cm) wide
- 12″ (30.5cm) long piece narrow lace or crochet for round window trim
- 14″ (35.6cm) long piece braid (or scraps) for shutters, ½″ (1.3cm) wide
- 3″ (7.6cm) eyelet or flower print scrap for flowers
- 8″ x 7″ (20.3cm x 17.8cm) piece muslin for roof section A
- 20″ x 6″ (50.8cm x 15.2cm) piece muslin for roof section B
- 12″ x 20″ (30.5cm x 50.8cm) piece muslin for shingle backs
- 29″ x 30″ (73.7cm x 76.2cm) piece pintucked or solid color fabric for backs
- 9″ x 2″ (22.9cm x 5.1cm) piece velvet
- small button for doorknob
- polyester fiber fill for stuffing

METHOD
Step 1: Following patterns on page 164-165, cut out house sections A and B, lining up edges and/or seam lines with pintucking.

Step 2: Draw 1¾″ x 3″ (4.4cm x 7.6cm) window on a 3″ x 4″ (7.6cm x 10.2cm) piece of fabric that is the same color as the house section B pintucking. Place over window position on *right* side of house fabric. Stitch. Cut diagonally across from corner to corner. Turn to inside and press.

Step 3: Make the window box by stitching two pieces of fabric together along all seam lines. Make a small slit in back. Trim, turn, and press.

Step 4: Place windowpane fabric and lace curtains in position under the window opening. Pin or baste, fastening a curtain tieback at same time, if desired.

Step 5: Shutters are made by the same process as the window box. If you're using braid, turn the ends under so that the shutters are about ⅛″ (3mm) longer than the window at both ends. Press and pin in place.

Step 6: Make lace "flowers" by finishing edges of 1½″ (3.8cm) long piece of eyelet with the satin stitch or by using a flower print fabric.

Step 7: Pin or baste window box in place, positioning the lace flowers at the same time so that the eyelet is gathered slightly. Topstitch or sew by hand around window, shutter, and window box close to the edges. Repeat Steps 2 through 7 for second window.

Step 8: Make front door by first cutting bottom door fabric (c) 3″ x 4″ (7.6cm x 10.2cm). Then on top door fabric (d), topstitch around door panel lines. Cut insides of door panels out to within ⅛″ (3mm) of stitching. Fold back to stitching, clipping where necessary, and press. Also, press under edges of door. Pin or baste in place (over c) in middle of house section A approximately 1″ (2.5cm) from bottom. Topstitch. Attach button for doorknob.

(Continued on page 165.)

KNITTED NATURAL SQUARE AND TRIANGLE

The unusual textures on this pair of knitted pillows make them an interesting addition to any room. The subtle, natural coloring shown here is only one way to make the pillows; use your imagination and whip up three or four in this design using brighter, complementary colors. The square measures 15" (38.1cm). Each side of the triangle is 16" (40.6cm).

Square

MATERIALS
- 4 (50 gr.) balls bulky gray yarn (A)
- 4 (50 gr.) balls textured white yarn (B)
- knitting needles, size 11
- crochet hook, size I
- 45" x 15" (114.3cm x 28.1cm) piece polyester batting
- 5" (12.7cm) square piece polyester batting
  Gauge: 5 st to 2" (5.1cm)
  3 rows to 1" (2.5cm)

METHOD
Front Section (make 4): With A, cast on 1 st
Row 1: K 1, P 1, K 1 in cast on st.
Row 2 (wrong side): P all sts.
Row 3: Increasing in first and last st, knit across.
Row 4: P.
Rows 5-10: Repeat rows 3 and 4 until there are 11 sts on needle, ending with a P row. Cut A, join B.
Row 11: Repeat row 3.

Row 12: Insert needle into first st as if to purl, yarn over twice, pull needle through. Do not drop loops from needle. Repeat across. Cut B, join A.

Row 13: Inserting needle in loop behind each stitch and increasing 1 st in first and last st, pick up a st in each loop across (15 sts).

Row 14: P across.

Rows 15-20: Repeat rows 3 and 4, ending with row 4 (21 sts). Cut A, join B.

Row 21: Repeat row 3.

Row 22: Repeat row 12. Cut B, join A.

Row 23: Repeat row 13.

Row 24: Repeat row 4.

Rows 25-32: Repeat rows 3 and 4, ending with row 4 (33 sts). Cut A, join B.

Row 33: Repeat row 3.

Row 34: Repeat row 12. Cut B, join A.

Row 35: Repeat row 13, but do not increase (35 sts).

Row 36: P across. Bind off all stitches.

Back: Cast on 35 sts. Knit each row until there are 28 ridges. Bind off.

Finishing: Block back to measure 15'' (38.1cm) square. With right sides together, sew front and back sections together with backstitch and matching yarn, being careful to keep loops free.

Gather 5'' (12.7cm) square of batting into a ball and place in center of pillow front from wrong side. Adjust knit fabric around batting to form a "knob" and wind firmly with a 36'' (91.4cm) piece of A, doubled. Tie securely; leave ends free.

With I crochet hook and A, sc around back, making 3 sts in each corner and spacing 33 sc on each side. Join and cut yarn. Sc around front in same manner;

do not cut yarn. Place front, right side up, on back. Matching corners, reverse sc (that is, crochet from *left* to *right*) around three sides.

Fold large piece of batting into thirds and insert into pillow, adjusting fullness. Finish reverse sc on fourth side. Join and end off. With long darning needle, tuft through pillow with yarn ends, ending on front side. Tie securely and fasten yarn.

Tassels (make 4): Wind B 20 times around a piece of 3'' (7.6cm) cardboard. Tie at one end with an 18'' (45.7cm) length of A. Cut other end. Wind tassel with another length of A and fasten off. Attach one tassel at each corner.

Triangle

MATERIALS

- 3 (50 gr.) balls bulky off-white yarn (A)
- 2 (50 gr.) balls textured brown yarn (B)
- knitting needles, size 11
- crochet hook, size I
- 45'' x 15'' (114.3cm x 38.1cm) piece polyester batting

Gauge: 4 st to 1'' (2.5cm)
3 rows to 1'' (2.5cm)

METHOD

Front Section (make 3): Cast on 39 sts.

Row 1: K across, decreasing 1 st at each end.

Row 2: Repeat row 1.

Row 3: Decreasing 1 st at each end of row, K each st, yarning over twice before pulling the st through.

Row 4: K first 2 sts together, dropping extra yo, *K into back of second st from needle dropping extra loop, K into the front of the first st on needle

dropping extra loop, * repeat across to last 3 sts, K in back of third st from needle dropping extra loop, knit two sts together dropping extra loops.

Repeat these 4 rows twice more, then continue in garter st (K each row), decreasing 1 st at each end of row until 3 sts remain. K 3 sts together, end off.

Back: Cast on 39 sts.

K each row and dec 1 st at each end of every third row until 3 sts remain.

K 3 sts together, end off.

Finishing: Block back to measure 16'' (40.6cm) on each side. Matching rows, sew front sections together (keep cast-on edges free). Cut approximately 100 6'' (15.2cm) lengths of B. Working on garter st rows in center of front only, *insert crochet hook in loop of garter st ridge, catch loop of 6'' (15.2cm) length of B folded in half, draw through, yo and catch and pull through both ends of yarn (1 fringe made).* Tighten if necessary.

Repeat until center garter st rows are fringed, 1 fringe per st. Repeat fringe detail up each of the three seams. Fold batting into thirds, cut through all three layers to form a triangle 16'' (40.6cm) on each side. Sc around back piece, making 3 sts in each corner and spacing 37 sc on each side. End off.

Repeat sc around front edges in same manner. Do not end off. Working in reverse sc (from *left* to *right*) join front to back, matching corners, along two sides. Insert batting through third side, adjusting fullness. Continue reverse sc along third side. Join and end off.

Tassels (make 3): Make tassels from B as for square pillow and attach at corners.

BEAN BAGS

Stuff a tiny, brightly colored pillow with dried beans and you've created a safe, educational plaything for your youngster. Especially welcome for long hours on a rainy afternoon, bean bags can be used to emphasize color awareness, to improve counting skills, and to encourage physical dexterity. You might want to appliqué large felt numbers or letters on the bean bags to make your child's games even more instructive. These durable, 5" x 7" (12.7cm x 17.8cm) bags are just the right size and weight to be easily grasped by young hands.

MATERIALS
- medium-weight, pinwale corduroy in several bright colors
- dried beans

METHOD
Step 1: For each bag, cut four 6" x 8" (15.2cm x 20.3cm) rectangles of corduroy. (Two layers are used for each side to ensure durability.)

Step 2: Sandwich all four layers of corduroy together, right sides facing in. Using ½" (1.3cm) seams, stitch around outside edge, leaving a small opening for turning.

Step 3: Turn bag right side out and fill *loosely* with dried beans—about ¾ cup. Do not fill so full that the bags cannot be easily clutched by a small hand. Slipstitch opening closed.

Step 4: Topstitch two rows around outside edges about ¼" (6mm) apart.

PERSONALITY DOLLS

Personable and charming, these dolls can be tailor-made to suit special personalities you know. The bride doll was made for a radical women's libber who did a complete about-face when she decided to marry; the ballerina belongs to the company manager of a city ballet; the French Madam emerged from a beginning of lace collar and gold earrings. Other personalities include a school teacher, an Indian maiden, a pioneer lady, a freckle-faced girl with cat, a baseball player. You will find that the most fun of making these pillow-like dolls is seeing each individual personality develop according to the kind of fabrics you choose and the special details such as jewelry that you add. Recycle your old costume jewelry, or haunt variety stores for little accessories.

MATERIALS
- assorted fabric scraps, bits of lace, ribbon, etc. as desired
- muslin for face and hands
- yarn for hair
- jewelry and accessories as desired
- polyester fiber fill for stuffing
- polyester fleece

METHOD
Step 1: Using the patterns on pages 166-167, cut out fabrics for doll front (Sections 1, 2, 3, and 4) and doll back (Section 5). For special garments such as the ballerina's halter top, you may want to draw a pattern piece, then cut out the fabric and lay it over the body of the doll.

Step 2: Cut hands out of muslin and sew in place on section 3 of doll body with a short, narrow zigzag stitch. Hands may be positioned as on the madam, or as on the bride. The bride's fingers are formed by zigzag stitching lines.

Step 3: Pin and stitch together all the pieces for the front of the doll.

Step 4: Cut the face out of muslin, then stitch the two halves of the face together down center front with a 1/8'' (3mm) seam. Open face out and press seam allowance to one side. Draw eyes and mouth lightly with a pencil onto right side of face, spacing the eyes equidistant from the nose. Cut a circle of polyester fleece and a circle of muslin the same size as the face. Stack face, fleece, and muslin circle together with fleece in the middle; pin. Working from the face side, stitch eyes and mouth with a short, narrow zigzag stitch, through all three layers, changing thread colors as necessary. Cheeks are made with a dab of lipstick.

Step 5: Place face on section 1 of doll body, overlapping section 2 slightly. Zigzag face in place.

Step 6: Form hair out of yarn by making several long loops of the same size, then tying a topknot in the center. Place hair in position around doll's face and zigzag across hair to make a ''part'' on either side of doll's face. Tack underneath topknot.

Step 7: Place front and back of doll right sides together, making certain hair is not caught in seamline at top of doll. Stitch around outside, leaving bottom open for turning.

Step 8: Turn doll right side out, stuff until she is nice and huggable, then slipstitch bottom seam closed. By now you're hooked, so start on your next personality!

BROOMSTICK LACE
BOUDOIR PILLOW

You may remember first seeing a
piece of broomstick lace at
Grandmother's house, but its
unusual charm makes this
pillow-top design an exciting
conversation piece in any
generation.

MATERIALS
- 2 (2-ounce) (56.6 grams)
  skeins baby pompadour yarn,
  white
- knitting needle, size 50
- crochet hook, size H
- 1½ yards (1.4m) satin
- 42'' x 63'' (106.7cm x 160cm)
  piece quilt batting

Gauge: 1 pattern round to 1¼''
(3.2cm) blocked. Finished size
14'' x 21'' (35.6cm x 53.3cm)
not including ruffle

METHOD
Broomstick Lace: ch desired
number of sts.
Row 1: Holding knitting needle
in your left hand with foundation
ch to your right, draw out loop
of last ch and slip onto knitting
needle. * Insert hook into next
ch, yo, draw through and slip
loop onto knitting needle.*
Repeat from * to * desired

number of times. Do not fasten
Row 2: Row is sc worked over
groups of loops. Refer to
directions for specifics.
Pillow Top
Pattern Round One
Row 1: Chain 56. Work
broomstick lace st in each ch
across (56 loops). Do not fasten.
Row 2: Slip off first 5 loops from
knitting needle, keeping twist
intact. Insert hook into center of
loops, yo, draw through, yo,
draw through both loops on
hook (sc made), 4 sc in same
loop, * slip off next 5 loops, 5 sc
over loops* 4 times, * 5 sc in
next loop* 3 times, * 5 sc over
next 5 loop group* 5 times, * 5
sc in next loop* 3 times (80 sts).
End off.
Joining row: (All joining rows are
worked in reverse sc, that is,
from left to right.) Join yarn in
55th st of foundation chain,
insert hook in 54th st, yo, draw
through, insert hook in 56th st,
yo draw through, yo, draw
through 3 loops on hook.
Matching sts on each side and
working through both edges at
one time, reverse sc to within
last 3 ch. S1 st in middle ch of
last 3 ch. End off.
Pattern Round Two
Row 1: Chain 80. Broomstick
lace st in each chain across (80

loops).
Row 2: ** *5 sc over next 5-
loop group* 5 times, *5 sc over
next 2-loop group* 3 times, *5
sc over next loop* 3 times, *5
sc over next 2-loop group* 3
times, ** repeat once (120 sts).
Joining row: Matching the 5
groups of 5 loops of this row to
the 5 groups of 5 loops in the
previous pattern round, and
working through both the
foundation chain of this pattern
round and the sc of the previous
pattern round, wrong sides
facing, 1 reverse sc in each st
around. Join and fasten off.
Pattern Round Three
Pattern Round Three
Row 1: Chain 120 sts.
Broomstick lace st in each chain
across (120 loops).
Row 2: ** *5 sc over next 5-
loop group * 5 times, *5 sc over
next 3-loop group, 5 sc over
next 4-loop group* 5 times,**
repeat once (150 sts).
Joining row: Repeat joining row
of Pattern Round Two.
Pattern Round Four
Pattern Round Four
Row 1: Chain 150. Broomstick
lace st in each ch across (150
loops).
Row 2: ** *5 sc over next 5-
loop group* 5 times, *5 sc over
next 3-loop group, 5 sc over
next 2-loop group* ten times, **
repeat once (250 sts). Join end.
Joining row: Repeat joining row
of Pattern Round Two.
Finishing: Run in all yarn ends.
Block lace to size indicated on
pattern on page 163. Pin and sl
st lace to one piece of satin.
Fold batting into thirds and cut
batting same size as satin.

Finish pillow with a double
ruffle. Use the three layers of
batting as stuffing. Fold pillow in
half across center and tack
together around ruffled edge.

CUTWORK PILLOW

This lovely boudoir pillow combines an old and well-loved needlework technique with a new color approach. Instead of the white embroidery so traditional with cutwork, a mixture of lovely peaches and greens has been used to outline the cut areas. The finished pillow, including border, measures 11″ (27.9cm) square. See Appendix for diagrams of embroidery stitches.

MATERIALS
- 15″ (38.1cm) square piece of white dress-weight linen (or cotton and polyester blend that looks like linen)
- dressmaker's carbon paper
- two 15″ (38.1cm) square pieces pale peach cotton batiste or similar fabric
- 2 skeins (8.7 yards (8m) each) dark green floss
- 1 skein medium green floss
- 1 skein dark peach floss
- 1 skein medium peach floss
- 1 skein light peach floss
- embroidery needle, size 5 approximately

METHOD
Step 1: Turn over and baste the raw edges of the white fabric to keep it from unraveling as you work. Enlarge the pattern on page 163 to desired size. (See Appendix for enlarging instructions.)

Step 2: Trace the design on the fabric with blue dressmaker's carbon paper. The lines should be equidistant to keep the size of the buttonhole stitch uniform throughout. The X marks indicate the parts to be cut away.

Step 3: Work the flower that seems to be in the back of the design with the darkest shade of peach. The middle flower is worked in medium peach and the front flower in light peach. The dots are French knots, and the vein lines are crewel outline stitch worked with three strands of floss. The double lines around the edges of the flowers are worked in the padded buttonhole stitch, using three strands of floss.

Step 4: Work the veins of the leaves with the crewel outline stitch using three strands of medium green floss. Work the leaf edges in padded buttonhole stitch in the same way as the flower petals with the buttonhole stitch ridge on the outside of the leaf.

Step 5: Use the dark green floss for the remaining buttonhole stitch areas. The ridge on the inner circle should be on the inside edge of the circle. The ridge on the outer scalloped edge should be on the outside.

Step 6: At this point, if any blue lines still show or if the work has become soiled, launder the piece in mild soap and block while still wet. If the work is clean and not too full of "puckers" caused by poor tension, it can be readied for the cutting step by merely placing it upside down on top of a bath towel with a damp press cloth between the work and the iron and pressing.

Step 7: Turn the piece over on the back and very carefully cut out the areas marked X on the diagram. If you cut too closely you will cut the buttonhole stitches. Go very slowly and use small, sharp scissors. Finally, cut out the edge of the pillow. Press again and set aside.

Step 8: Using the peach colored fabric, make and stuff tightly a pillow that measures 9½″ (24.1cm) square. (See Techniques.) Baste the cutwork to this pillow. The peach color will show through the holes in the cutwork, adding interest to the design. The edge of the cutwork extends beyond the pillow forming a lacy trim.

DESIGN YOUR OWN NEEDLEPOINT

Creating an original needlepoint canvas gives you almost unlimited options for designs and colors. And it's more economical than a professionally painted canvas. The cost of a professionally painted 12" x 14" (30.5cm x 35.6cm) canvas will usually range from $20 to $30. If you paint your own, the cost of the basic canvas (same size) will run $4 or less, and the initial outlay for paints and brushes or needlepoint markers (a set of six) will be about $7.

Choosing the design. Much of the success of your needlepoint canvas will depend on choosing a design that fits your skills and the graphlike, block form of needlepoint. Our design was taken from nature, then simplified for ease of drawing and needlepointing.

Once you decide on a design, draw or trace it on tracing paper with heavy black ink so that it will show through when placed under the canvas (See fig. 1.)

Choosing the canvas. Take the design you've drawn on tracing paper with you when you go to purchase the canvas and the yarn. A good rule of thumb

Figure 1

in buying the right amount of yarn is to allow 1½ yards (1.4m) for every square inch (centimeter) of canvas to be covered.

One factor to consider in choosing canvas is the amount of detail wanted in the final needlepoint piece. Delicate, detailed designs should be worked on small canvas, such as 14-mesh (14 stitches per inch); bolder, larger designs can be executed on 10- or 12-mesh canvas. The thistle, shown here, was drawn in stylized form; this eliminated intricate detailing, so it was done on 10-mesh canvas.

Transferring design to the canvas. With a 2" (5.1cm) margin on all sides, center the design beneath the canvas. Make sure that any definite vertical and horizontal lines in the design line up with the

Figure 2

vertical and horizontal lines of the canvas; then tape the canvas over the drawing. (See fig. 2.)

To outline and paint the design on the canvas, use either

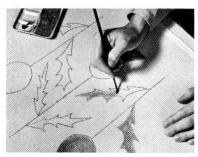

Figure 3

needlepoint markers or acrylic paints. (See fig. 3.) Ideally, the canvas should be painted a tint lighter than the yarn color you plan to use. Acrylic paints allow you to mix colors in exact shades. Thin the paints to a creamy consistency with water; they will dry quickly and be waterproof.

To spread the paints without blocking the holes in the canvas, use a stiff, flat acrylic brush and a small amount of paint. If a few holes are blocked, just blow the paint out of the holes.

If you're not comfortable with paint and brush, you may find markers easier to handle. Be sure to use waterproof markers specified for needlepoint; otherwise, the ink will run when the finished needlepoint is blocked.

MACHINE EMBROIDERED PILLOW

One of the most attractive qualities of machine embroidery is that it allows you to create your own fabric by quickly stitching any design you want. This distinctively Indian-inspired design can be sewed up on a machine that has basic embroidery stitch capabilities—a wonderful way to take advantage of all that your sewing machine offers you. Machine embroidery is one of the quickest of all needlecraft techniques to master and use to accomplish desired design objectives. This finished pillow measures 14½" (36.8cm) square.

MATERIALS
- 1½ yards (137.1cm) rust-colored linen-type fabric
- ½ yard (45.7cm) iron-on interfacing
- white marking pencil
- 65" (165.1cm) length of cable cord
- 14" (35.6cm) zipper
- 2 spools white machine embroidery thread
- 1 spool black machine embroidery thread

METHOD
Step 1: Cut one 15½" (39.3cm) square of fabric for pillow front and a square of iron-on interfacing the same size. Apply interfacing to wrong side of fabric following instructions accompanying interfacing.

Step 2: Working from chart on page 168, mark the design on the right side of fabric with a white marking pencil.

Step 3: Stitch the design, keeping the following points in mind:

a. Lock each row of stitching at beginning and end by moving the stitch length setting to 0;
b. Work from the center of the design out, finishing with the border;
c. Use the maximum width setting for each stitch;
d. Stitch all rows in the same direction unless stitch pattern must be reversed;
e. Write down all settings if you must interrupt your stitching;
f. Use a new needle if possible—preferably a ball-point.

Step 4: Make cording, insert zipper, and finish pillow as instructed in The Portfolio of Pillow Techniques.

Stitch Key
(Refer to chart on page 168 for illustrations of stitches.)
Center: Outline the star and bar shapes with a fine zigzag and fill in with the satin stitch.
Rows 1, 2, and 6: Zigzag at fine stitch length
Row 3: Blind hem at fine stitch length
Row 4: Rick rack stitch
Rows 5 and 7: Icicle stitch in opposite directions
Rows 7-11: Icicle stitch at fine stitch length
Row 12: Zigzag stitch at fine stitch length
Border: Rows 1 and 6: Zigzag at fine stitch length
Rows 2 and 4: Rick rack stitch at fine stitch length
Row 3: Icicle stitch
Row 5: Leave unstitched

"SUBURBIA" NEEDLEPOINT DESIGN

This fresh little design is excellent for using up leftover scraps of yarn. Mix colors as you desire. You might want to make a seasonal "Suburbia" pillow by using fall or spring colors, or even a winter one with shades of white, cream, and gray. Refer to your favorite needlepoint book for directions for specific stitches other than the basketweave, which may be found in the Appendix.

MATERIALS
- canvas (10 mono for beginners, 14 mono for advanced)
- Persian yarn in your choice of colors
- needle according to canvas (size 18 for 10 mono canvas, size 20 for 14 mono canvas)
- waterproof needlepoint marking pen
- acrylic paints (optional)
- masking or other adhesive tape

METHOD
Step 1: Trace and enlarge pattern on page 169; then go over all lines with a felt-tip pen, which will make the pattern easy to see. (See Appendix for enlarging instructions.)

Step 2: Cut your canvas about 2'' (5.1cm) larger than your project. Tape all four sides and mark top and bottom of canvas.

Step 3: To transfer your design onto the canvas, put canvas over your paper. You should be able to see the pattern lines easily. Use a waterproof needlepoint marker and transfer the design from paper to the canvas.

Step 4: A 1'' (2.5cm) border of basketweave finishes the design of decorative stitches. Leave one spot for your initial and put it in before you work that space in basketweave.

Note: Feel free to use the stitches you know best and enjoy doing, and make up your own combinations, or the design can all be done in one stitch, if you wish. Use stitches according to the shape of space. Finish by adding at least three rows (or more) of basketweave in the same color you will use for the pillow backing.

Step 5: Finish your pillow with one of the methods described in Techniques.

DOVE PILLOW

Although numerous valentines designed throughout the years have become collectors' items, nothing you purchase for the occasion can rival the sentiment expressed in a valentine you design and create especially for the recipient.

MATERIALS
- fabrics in these or other colors of your choice: solid green, red and white print, yellow calico, red for hearts, off-white for envelope
- muslin or cotton fabric for quilting backing
- fabric for pillow back
- black and green embroidery thread
- 18'' x 20'' (45.7cm x 50.8cm) piece of polyester batting
- polyester fiber fill for stuffing

METHOD

Step 1: Enlarge pattern from page 169 to desired size. (See Appendix for enlarging instructions.) Cut a 13'' x 15½'' (33cm x 39.4cm) piece from solid green fabric.

Step 2: Cut dove from white fabric and baste to green background, leaving bottom of dove open. Cut envelope from off-white fabric. Slit wing ¼'' (6mm) from tip and insert envelope as shown. Appliqué, then embroider edges with black thread. Cut heart and drops from red fabric. Using pattern for placement, appliqué in place. Finish wing of dove over letter. Embroider eye of dove with black thread. Work stem with green embroidery thread. Cut ribbon and streamer from yellow calico fabric and appliqué in place.

Step 3: Cut four 2½'' (6.4cm) squares from yellow calico. Cut two strips 2½'' (6.4cm) wide and 12½'' (31.8cm) long from red print. Also cut two strips from red print, 2½'' (6.4cm) wide and 15'' (38cm) long. Allow for ¼'' (6mm) for seams on all sides.

Step 4: Join shorter strips to shorter side of green background using ¼'' (6mm) seams. Sew yellow calico squares to each end of longer strip. Join this band to longer side of pillow.

Step 5: Cut an 18'' x 20'' (45.7cm x 50.8cm) piece of cotton fabric and of polyester batting for quilting. Quilt pillow top.

Step 6: Finish your pillow with one of the methods described in Techniques.

CREWEL SAMPLER PILLOW

Every beginner should learn to embroider by practicing the various stitches on a sampler. And what better way to display your new talent than by making this charming crewel sampler pillow! Easy-to-follow stitch diagrams appear in the Appendix. The materials and instructions given are for a 11½″ x 12″ (29.2cm x 30.5cm) design area to be embroidered. The finished pillow measures approximately 12″ (30.5cm) square with a 2″ (5.1cm) wide ruffle.

MATERIALS
- ½ yard (45.7cm) linen
- embroidery crewel yarn (30 yard (27.4m) card): 1 package each of the following colors:
  light gold
  gold-brown
  medium brown
  light green
  green
  dark green
  red
  yellow
  orange
  blue
  pink
  black
  white
- 1 yard (91.4cm) calico fabric for ruffle
- ½ yard (45.7cm) muslin for inner pillow
- polyester fiber fill for stuffing
- embroidery hoop
- crewel needles
- masking tape
- dressmaker's carbon paper

METHOD
Step 1: Enlarge pattern on page 170. (See Appendix for enlarging instructions.)

Step 2: Cut one 15″ (38.1cm) square from linen. Cover edges of linen with masking tape to prevent fraying. Lay linen on hard surface. Place dressmaker's carbon on fabric, colored side down. Position pattern on top of carbon and pin securely on all four sides.

Trace pattern firmly with ballpoint pen, checking linen occasionally to be certain it is printing on the fabric. Remove the pins and pattern and place fabric in embroidery hoop.

Step 3: Thread needle with black yarn and work buttonhole stitch around each section. Work each section in stitches and colors described below in any order desired, but saving the highly textured stitches for last. (See Appendix for stitch diagrams.)

Step 4: When you have completed the stitches, clean (if needed) and block your crewel piece.

Step 5: Finish pillows as desired from methods in The Portfolio of Pillow Techniques.

CHINESE-INSPIRED CREWEL PILLOW

Oriental blossoms and a dragonfly offer Chinese enchantment for any decor. The lovely coloring and graceful curve of the design provide added interest to this beautiful crewel embroidery pillow. Easy-to-follow stitch diagrams appear in the Appendix. The finished pillow measures approximately 14″ (35.6cm) in diameter.

MATERIALS
- ¾ yard (68.6cm) crewel linen,
- dressmaker's carbon paper
- crewel yard in the following quantities and colors:
  8 yards (7.3m) dark brown
  18 yards (16.5m) medium brown
  14 yards (12.8m) light brown
  25 yards (22.9m) light green
  20 yards (18.3m) medium green
  15 yards (13.7m) dark green
  5 yards (4.6m) light pink
  8 yards (7.3m) medium pink
  8 yards (7.3m) deep pink
  5 yards (4.6m) rose
  1 yard (91.4cm) dark gold
  4 yards (3.7m) medium gold
  2 yards (1.8m) light gold
- embroidery needle, size 3
- embroidery hoop, 5″ to 8″ (12.7cm to 20.3cm) diameter
- 1¾ yards (1.6m) gold cording
- polyester fiber fill for stuffing

METHOD
Step 1: Cut a piece of linen 18″ (45.7cm) square. Bind the edges

with tape or zigzag on the sewing machine to keep the edge from unraveling.

Step 2: Enlarge the pattern on page 171. (See Appendix for enlarging instructions.) Trace the design on the linen with dressmaker's carbon paper.

Step 3: Using the three shades of brown yarn, embroider the main vine with rows of crewel outline stitch. Use the split stitch for the bud stems that hang from the vine.

Step 4: Work the leaves in long and short stitches in shades of green. The leaf stems are worked in the split stitch.

Step 5: Work the flowers and buds in the buttonhole stitch in shades of pink.

Step 6: Work dragonfly wings in the closed fly stitch in shades of gold. Use gold satin stitches for the body with brown satin stitches for the stripes on the body and straight brown stitches for the legs. Work the eyes in the

padded satin stitch in gold outlined with brown back stitches.

Step 7: Block the finished piece of crewel. When the piece is tightly stretched, wet the entire piece with clear, cold water. Allow it to dry completely before taking it off the board.

Step 8: Baste the gold cording to the circular seam line on the pillow front with the raw edges facing out. Cut a piece of linen for the back of the pillow the same size as the front.

Step 9: Cut a piece of linen 4¼″ x 44¼″ (11.4cm x 112.4cm) for boxing. Seam the ends together with a ⅝″ (1.6cm) seam.

Step 10: Sew boxing, pillow top, and pillow back together as directed in Boxing, Portfolio of Pillow Techniques. Leave a 6″ (15.2cm) opening in the back seam.

Step 11: Turn pillow inside out and stuff firmly with fiber fill. Whipstitch opening closed.

BEDTIME STORY

Fascinating designs on sheets and pillowcases may not insure sweet dreams, but that's the message inscribed on these—in French and Italian. And even more wonderful, two humorously portrayed angels seem to occupy the bed. Painted in ordinary acrylics, the bed set is machine washable and suffers almost no loss of brilliance in a year's careful laundering in cold water.

MATERIALS
- white sheet
- pair of white pillowcases
- ½'' (1.3cm) stiff artist brush
- pointed paintbrush
- few tubes of acrylic paint (your choice of colors)
- permanent ink felt-tip marking pen
- paper for tracing pattern and transferring design
- dressmaker's carbon paper

Notes:
Colors and paints: When diluted with water, most acrylic colors are semitransparent; white is not.

Marking pen: The safest thing to do is test your pen on a scrap of fabric. When it has set for a few minutes, try scrubbing it under running water. If it blurs or fades badly, don't use it.

Workspace: The pillowcases will not require a very large workspace, but the bedsheet will. Because of the amount of water involved in painting the sheet, it is best to work on a table that water won't damage, using a stack of newspapers underneath sheets and pillowcases. Place a thick newspaper covering inside pillowcases also to prevent paint from seeping through to the back piece of fabric.

METHOD
Step 1: Insert pillows in pillowcases to determine approximate center of pillow. Mark center of the design here. Be sure the pillowcases are facing in the proper direction—one with opening to the right, the other to the left.

Step 2: Enlarge and transfer the designs from pages 175-177 to pillowcases. Draw the outlines onto the pillowcases with the waterproof marking pen.

Step 3: "Practice" on the sky using a stiff ½'' (1.3cm) paintbrush. Mix a bit of blue paint with a bit of white until you have the sky color desired. Try to paint in long, sweeping, horizontal strokes, dipping tip of brush in water each time you pick up paint and keeping the brush fairly wet. Paint sky on both cases so they will be the same color. Wash brush with water and proceed to another area.

Paint wing area in shades of blue or gray with a long stroke of your large brush, conforming roughly to the black lines.

Blue and ochre were mixed together to get green tones in the male angel, and his skin tone is made up of a little red and ochre mixed with white. Mix enough of one color at one time to complete both faces as well as the lady's torso.

When you have completed the skin areas and while they are still wet, heighten the color of the cheeks by adding a little more red to the paint mixture and working this into cheek areas. Feather the new color out at the edges and scrub it lightly in with the paintbrush. Lips can be done with red straight from the tube.

Color eyes and hair in shades desired. We have used straight tube colors: ochre for gentleman and yellow for lady. The necktie and lady's dress can be any color.

When you have completed both pillowcases, let them dry thoroughly before removing the newspaper stuffing.

Step 4: After transferring your design to the sheet, mix the color for the sky in the bottom of a small jar. Squeeze 2'' or 3'' (5.1cm to 7.6cm) of cerulean blue paint into container, then add an ounce or so of water, a little at a time, stirring and mixing thoroughly so that all the paint is well mixed with water in an inky solution. When this mixture is sufficiently thinned with water, you will have a transparent blue "dye," which will resemble pale blue when it is applied to the white sheet. Since this solution of paint is much wetter than the one you were working with previously, it will have a tendency to run. Begin your painting in an area away from any of the pattern lines until you gauge the distance the solution will spread.

When the sky is completed, paint the birds. Allow material to dry before lifting the sheet from the newspapers.

CROCHET WITH A NEW LOOK

These two pillows artfully combine purchased edgings and braid with the well-loved needle art, crochet. The pillow on the left is made from an old and treasured afghan stitch, also known as the Tunisian stitch. The pillow on the right utilizes the basic single and double crochet stitches. Sizes are approximate; they will vary according to the way you work.

PILLOW WITH FLORAL BRAID INSERT

MATERIALS
- crochet hook, Size H
- 8 ounces (226.7 grams) yarn
- 4 feet (1.2 meters) of 2'' (5cm) wide floral braid

METHOD
Step 1: Make two identical squares as follows.
Ch 22—work single and double crochet alternately across row. Continue in pattern until approximately 8¾'' (22.2cm) long (or until block is approximately square). SC around entire outer edge, join; do not turn.
Ch 1—1 SC in last SC of previous row * 1 SC in next SC to right; repeat from * to end. Fasten off.
Whip 1 edge of trim to entire outer edge of square.

Step 2: Work border as follows:
Row 1: Ch 156 * work single and double crochet pattern across 39 st., ch 2 for corners repeat from * across row ch 1 turn.
Row 3: * work pattern in next 39 st. ch 2 for corners; repeat from

* across row ch 1 turn.
Row 3-5: Repeat row 2. Fasten off.
Step 3: Whip edge without border to outer side of trim.
Step 4: Make an inner pillow as directed in Techniques.
Step 5: SC both sides of pillow together on three sides. Insert pillow and finish crocheting together. Do not turn ch 1.
1 SC in last SC of previous row; * 1 SC in next SC to *right;* repeat from * to end. Fasten off.

PILLOW WITH FLORAL RUFFLE

MATERIALS
- Afghan hook, Size 8
- approximately 8 ounces (226.7 grams) yarn
- 2 yards (1.8 meters) 2'' (5.1cm) wide embroidered ruffle

METHOD
Step 1: Make two identical squares as follows.
Row 1 - First Half: Work basic afghan stitch across row.
Row 1 - Second Half: Work off loops.
Row 2 - First Half: Insert hook under 2nd and 3rd bars and draw up loop * yo, draw up loop under next 2 bars; repeat from * ending yo, draw up loop in last bar.
Row 2 - Second Half: Work off loops.
Row 3 - First Half: Repeat first half of Row 2, inserting hook under vertical bar and slanted stitch.
Row 3 - Second Half: Work off loops.
Repeat rows 2 and 3 for pattern for 16'' (40.6cm).

Step 2: border: SC around

entire outer edge join. Do not turn. Ch 1 - 1 SC in last SC of previous row * 1 SC in next SC to *right;* repeat from * to end. Fasten off.

Step 3: Whip embroidered ruffle to wrong side of one piece and sew 2 pieces together, leaving one side open.

Step 4: Make pillow casing to the same dimensions as the pillow—stuff, insert in pillow—sew opening closed.

Basic Afghan Stitch
Row - First Half: Make chain. Insert hook in 2nd ch. from hook, draw up loop; * insert hook in next ch, draw up loop. Repeat from * across.
Second Half: yo and draw through 1 loop, * yo and draw 2 loops, repeat from * across. (*Note:* the loop remaining on hook always counts as first loop of next row.)

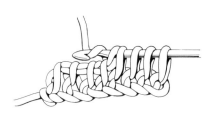

SOFT FRUIT
ORNAMENTS
FOR CHRISTMAS

These easy-to-make and inexpensive little fruit ornaments make most original Christmas tree ornaments and package decorations. The ones shown were made with a type of heat-transferable fabric dye that comes on a sheet of paper. It's the easiest method in the world for coloring fabric according to your own design. Of course, you can use traditional fabric paints and achieve the same beautiful results.

MATERIALS
- white fabric in a 50% cotton, 50% polyester blend
- fabric print kit or poster board and colored inks for stencil
- fine-point felt-tip pens
- polyester fiber fill for stuffing
- ⅜'' (9mm) wide white satin ribbon

METHOD
Step 1: Determine what size fruit ornaments will best fit your tree or package size. Allow for a ¼'' (6mm) white border around all fruit. Trace pattern from page 162 on untreated side of fabric print paper and cut out fruit shape. Follow kit directions for ironing transfer onto white fabric. If using stencil method, trace pattern onto poster paper and cut out stencil with a matte knife. Lay stencil on white fabric. Use a fairly dry bristle brush in colored ink and, with a scrubbing motion, fill in stenciled area.

Step 2: Use fine-point felt-tip pens to dot shadows onto fruit. Cut out shapes, leaving a ¼'' (6mm) border.

Step 3: Lay this shape on white fabric and trace around it, and cut out for the back of the fruit that will remain white. Place back and front right sides together. Leaving top open, stitch around fruit with a ¼'' (6mm) seam. Clip curves, turn, and press. Fill with a small amount of stuffing.

Step 4: Fold a 10'' (25.4cm) length of ribbon in half and insert folded end into top of fruit, turning opening seam allowance under. Pin and slipstitch opening closed, securing ribbon.

Step 5: Tie ribbon in bow and insert wire hanger or thread.

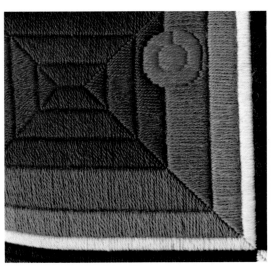

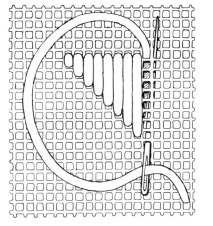

VARIATIONS ON A BARGELLO THEME

This ultra-modern grouping of pillows repeats three themes: pattern, color, and medium. Each of the pillows is made from either a single or multiple of the basic block clearly seen on the pillow at the left on the sofa. The other two pillows feature multiples of the basic block—either four or nine. The color scheme is varied slightly from block to block to create interest—but in each block the same neutral colors of black, white, and gray are used, occasionally with a touch of red. And, of course, all three of the pillows are executed in bargello, the easiest of all needlepoint stitches to work.

This idea is adaptable to many themes. Choose a unit which becomes a building block and repeat in different combinations to achieve a grouping of pillows that has interest as well as a strong feeling of continuity.

The materials needed for each pillow will vary according to how you choose to work it. This is a perfect project to use left-over scraps of yarn, particularly if you go for a patchwork effect. (Think of how lovely this would be worked in primary colors.) Study the close-up photograph to get the beginning of the basic block, then work from there to make the pillow you desire. Notice that the mitered effect at the corners of the design is achieved by shortening each succeeding stitch by one thread of canvas. Also, the more blocks that are used, the smaller the center of each one becomes. The portion illustrated is the center of one of the blocks of the pillow at right.

Work from the center out to accomplish your design, using the stitch illustrated. Then finish pillows with your choice of methods from The Portfolio of Pillow Techniques.

PULLED THREAD PILLOW

Pulled thread is a needlework technique that is gaining in popularity. This interesting grape design uses thread colors that contrast sharply with the canvas color giving the finished piece a bold, dramatic effect; a more subtle effect would be achieved with a thread color that matches the canvas. The design area measures 9½" x 12" (21.4cm x 30.5cm). See the Appendix for any embroidery stitches not shown below.

MATERIALS
- 12½" x 16" (31.8cm x 38.1cm) piece of 17 or 18 mesh mono canvas. Do not use interlocked weave canvas; linen canvas works best.
- four 18" (45.7cm) stretcher strips
- waterproof needlepoint marking pen
- 40 yards (36.6m) rust colored crewel yarn
- 1 skein (8.7 yards (8m)) dark rust embroidery floss
- 2 skeins medium rust floss
- 2 skeins light rust floss
- crewel needle, size 3
- tapestry needle, size 24
- 18" (45.7cm) square fabric for backing
- polyester fiber fill

METHOD
Step 1: Bind the raw edges of the canvas with tape to keep it from unraveling. Enlarge the pattern on page 172 to desired size. (See Appendix for enlarging instructions.)

Step 2: Put the canvas over the design. Square the solid outer border lines to the canvas threads to make sure the design is straight on the canvas. Trace the design onto the canvas with a needlepoint marking pen. Make the line as fine as possible on the canvas so that covering it will be no problem.

Step 3: Put stretcher strips together to make a frame. Staple or thumbtack canvas to stretcher frame as tightly as possible.

Step 4: The most important tip in doing pulled thread work is to start and end each thread carefully. Using one strand of crewel yarn and the crewel needle, stitch the stem and leaves in the chain stitch. Use the coral stitch to work the two tendrils. Each of these stitches may be started by doing a few running stitches in the area to be covered, ending at the place you want to begin the stitch and then working over the running stitches. End your thread by running it under the yarn on the back of the canvas for about ½" (1.3cm).

Step 5: With three strands of light rust floss and the crewel needle, outline the grape with the crewel outline stitch. By outlining the shape of each grape first, you will have an area of worked stitches to anchor your threads to as you do the pulled stitches. Fill the center of grape #1 with the spaced gobelin stitch, using the tapestry needle and six strands of floss.

Step 6: For grapes #2 through #15 the procedure is the same as in Step 5. Use three strands of floss and the crewel needle to outline each grape in the crewel outline stitch. Use six strands of the same color floss and the tapestry needle to work the pattern designated for the inside of that grape. Each grape in the design is labeled with the color of floss and the pattern stitch to be used.

Step 7: Finish pillow with your choice of the methods described in The Portfolio of Pillow Techniques.

Spaced Gobelin: Start at a point in the upper right corner of the area to be covered that will give you the longest diagonal. Anchor your thread on the back in the stitches that outline the grape's edge. Come up at 1 and pull tightly to draw the canvas threads together. Go down at 2 and pull again. Repeat this until you go down at 10. Pull and skip down eight threads and over 1 to 11. Continue in this manner until you reach the other side of the grape. The dark line at the edge of the diagram represents the edge of a grape. If you can't fit in a whole stitch, do as much of the stitch as you can before you run into the edge. Try to pull

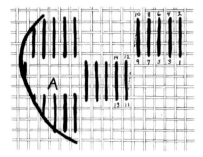

with the same tension for each stitch so that your stitches will be even. The harder you pull, the bigger the holes. If you pull too hard, however, you will break your thread.

Diagonal Cross: Begin this stitch in the lower right-hand corner of the grape. Compensate at the edges of the grape in the same way as mentioned in the instructions for the spaced gobelin stitch. Come up at 1 and pull, down at 2 and pull, etc. until you reach the top left edge of the grape. The pattern is completed as you come back down the row and cross the previously worked stitches.

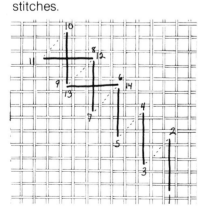

Pyramids: This stitch is *not* pulled. Begin in lower right corner of grape. Come up at 1, down at 2, etc., following pattern.

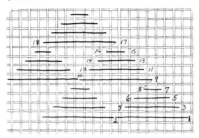

Checkerboard: This is a fairly complicated pattern, so study the chart carefully as you work. Begin in the upper left corner of the grape. Come up at 1 and pull, down at 2 and pull, etc., until column A is complete. Start column B at number 1 and work it in the same manner as column A. Go to letter A and work column C; then go to letter A in column D and work that column.

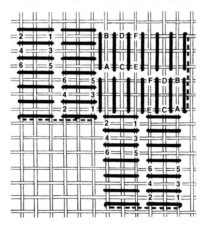

This completes a unit of four columns. Begin the next unit by going from the last stitch in column D to number 1 in column E.

Waffle Stitch Over Two: Begin at the middle of the right-hand side of the grape. Come up at 1 and pull, down at 2 and pull, etc. across the row until you reach the other side. On the return trip

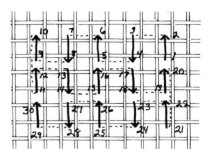

across the grape, go under the same vertical threads. This stitch often confuses people because the stitches are straight in the drawing but the pulling makes them look diagonal.

Half Cushion Stitch: Begin at the lower right-hand corner of the grape. Come up at 1 and pull, down at 2 and pull, etc.

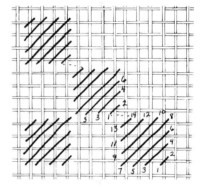

Blockstitch: This stitch is *not* pulled. Begin at the lower right edge of the grape. Come up at 1, down at 2 and pull, etc., following the pattern.

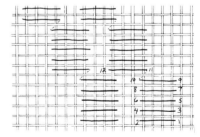

Four Sided Stitch: This stitch is worked in vertical rows with one thread left between rows. Begin at the upper left corner of the (Continued on page 172.)

PARTICULAR PIN PILLOWS

Decorative forms of the pincushion became popular by the early nineteenth century, reaching a peak in the early twentieth century. From about 1900, pincushions were made in fanciful shapes such as fans, shoes, flowers, baskets, wheelbarrows, dolls, animals, and fruit, particularly strawberries. These fabric pillows made in velvet or silk or needlework often had elaborate beadwork on the top and bottom with texts, executed in cross-stitch. Pins were stuck into the sides. The fanciest cushions were mounted on ornate holders of gold, silver, enamel, bone, ivory, mother-of-pearl, wood, or papier-maché.

Our designs offer an interesting assortment of styles and shapes for tiny pin pillows. Some are reminiscent of earlier eras, such as the Victorian beaded purse pillow and the petit point pincushion. And some are so easy to make that a child can join in the fun.

Many of the designs include a loop for hanging since any of the patterns would make striking Christmas ornaments. Try a handful of our designs, then add a few original pin pillows from your own imagination.

Mountain Daisy

MATERIALS
- 5″ (12.7cm) square of 10 mono canvas
- 2-ply needlepoint yarn in deep red, golden yellow, and dark green
- polyester fiber fill for stuffing
- velvet or satin
- small piece velvet or satin ribbon

METHOD
Step 1: Trace pattern on page 178 onto canvas. Work design in petit point in cross stitch.

Step 2: Block and cut out pattern, leaving ⅜″ (1cm) all around for seams.

Step 3: Cut out back piece of velvet or satin. Stitch pattern pieces together, right sides facing, leaving a small opening for turning. Turn cushion right side out, stuff firmly, and slipstitch opening closed. Stitch small loop of ribbon to cushion for hanging.

Aztec Flower in Crewel

MATERIALS
- linen or heavyweight, but loosely woven, cotton
- crewel yarns in orange, green, magenta, and gold
- polyester fiber fill for stuffing
- small piece of velvet ribbon

METHOD
Step 1: Trace pattern on page 179 and embroider as indicated. The cushion shown was worked in the satin stitch but you may vary the stitches as your talents and whims dictate. (See Appendix for stitch diagrams.) Work all the pattern except the outer edge.

Step 2: Cut out pincushion pattern. Stitch pattern pieces together, right sides facing, leaving a small opening for turning. Turn cushion right side out, stuff firmly with polyester fiber fill, and slipstitch opening closed.

Step 3: Complete embroidery design down to seam where top and bottom meet. Stitch small loop of velvet ribbon to cushion for hanging.

Old Glory
MATERIALS
- blue dotted swiss
- bright red cotton
- narrow white rickrack
- polyester fiber fill for stuffing

METHOD
Step 1: Trace pattern on page 180. Cut two pieces of red fabric and one smaller piece out of blue dotted swiss.

Step 2: Sew dotted swiss in upper left corner of one of the red pieces. Stitch the white rickrack in rows onto same piece of red fabric.

Step 3: With right sides facing, sew second piece of red fabric to flag piece, leaving a small opening for turning. Turn, stuff firmly, and slipstitch opening closed.

Victorian Hat
MATERIALS
- green velvet
- narrow red velvet ribbon
- polyester fiber fill for stuffing
- narrow white lace

METHOD
Step 1: Make this pincushion in two separate pieces: the brim

and the crown. Trace patterns on page 180 and cut fabric.

Step 2: Sew two circles together, right sides facing, leaving a small opening for turning. Turn, add just enough fiber fill to give the brim some shape, and slipstitch opening closed. Take a few stitches in center of brim to help keep stuffing in place.

Step 3: Sew two smaller circles and the strip together forming a small drum; leave small opening. Turn, stuff firmly, and slipstitch opening closed.

Step 4: Center drum shape on brim and stitch two parts together. Stitch velvet ribbon arounds top of hat and lace around brim. Make a small flower out of lace and tack in place on hat.

Victorian Beaded Purse
MATERIALS
- velvet
- beads in a size and color to fit your design
- polyester fiber fill for stuffing
- nylon fleece or suede cloth
- bias tape

METHOD
Step 1: Trace pattern on page 179 and cut out fabrics. (A piece of muslin laid over the velvet aids in cutting.)

Step 2: Do beading on velvet before putting pincushion together. Beading is accomplished with a backstitch (see Appendix). Slip a bead onto each stitch before inserting the needle back into the fabric for the succeeding stitch.

Step 3: Sew two pieces together, right side out, leaving a

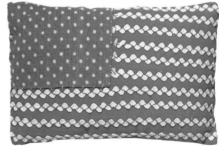

small opening for stuffing. Stuff purse firmly but stuff overhanging flap lightly. Slipstitch opening closed.

Step 4: Line inside part with nylon fleece or suede cloth. Trim edges with bias tape.

Tic Tac Toe
MATERIALS
- small checked blue and white gingham

- red and black embroidery floss
- polyester fiber fill for stuffing
- small piece velvet ribbon

METHOD
Step 1: Trace pattern on page 178 and cut out.

Step 2: Embroider design using straight stitch and cross-stitch. (See Appendix for stitch diagrams.) Use squares on gingham as your guide lines for the embroidery.

Step 3: Cut out back of cushion out of gingham. With right sides facing, stitch the two pieces together, leaving a small opening for turning. Turn right side out, stuff firmly, and slipstitch opening closed. Attach loop of ribbon for hanging.

Calico Heart
MATERIALS
- small-patterned calico
- polyester fiber fill for stuffing
- narrow white and yellow rickrack trim

METHOD
Step 1: Trace pattern on page 179. Cut out heart and 2″ (5.1cm) wide strip for ruffle.

Step 2: Fold strip width in half and gather evenly. Sew ruffle onto right side of heart.

Step 3: With right sides facing, sew two heart pieces together leaving a small opening for turning. Turn, stuff firmly, and slipstitch opening closed.

Step 4: Add rickrack trim around outside edges of heart.

American Star
MATERIALS
- medium-weight cotton in a small print

- ½″ (1.3cm) wide decorative trim
- polyester fiber fill for stuffing

METHOD
Step 1: Trace pattern on page 179 and cut out two star shapes.

Step 2: With right sides facing, sew two stars together, leaving a small opening for turning. Clip corners, turn, and stuff firmly. (A knitting needle is helpful in pushing stuffing into the points of the star.) Slipstitch opening closed.

Step 3: Add decorative trim by placing one edge on the seam and handstitching trim to top side of star. Extend trim beyond last point to form a loop for hanging.

Mouse
MATERIALS
- brown suede cloth
- red suede cloth or velvet
- black embroidery floss
- polyester fiber fill for stuffing

METHOD
Step 1: Trace pattern on page 178 and cut out fabric.

Step 2: Sew the two pieces together on the wrong side of the suede cloth, leaving a small opening. Turn, stuff firmly and slipstitch opening closed.

Step 3: Embroider the nose and eyes using satin stitch. (See Appendix for stitch diagrams.)

Step 4: Cut ears out of brown and linings out of red. Sew wrong sides together so they stand up. Attach them to the head with small stitches. Add a short length of brown floss for a tail.

PAINTED EGYPTIAN CAT PILLOW

This intriguing design is easily executed with liquid embroidery markers. Try this technique with other designs; you can use any design that has been charted. Simply trace it onto your fabric and start painting! (Suggestions for embroidery stitches are included with the chart, as we are sure you will find this design tempting enough to work more than one way!)

MATERIALS
- two 11'' (30.9cm) squares natural canvas
- dressmaker's carbon paper
- liquid embroidery markers in gray, black, turquoise, and dark red

METHOD
Step 1: Using pattern on page 174, enlarge as desired and transfer design to right side of one of the squares of canvas with dressmaker's carbon paper.

Step 2: Outline cat in gray marker. Color in gold, red, and blue areas referring to chart as you work. Allow each color to dry completely before beginning the next color.

Step 3: Finish your pillow with your choice of the methods described in The Portfolio of Pillow Techniques.

SACHETS

Sachets are tiny little pillows filled with fragrant materials that are easily slipped into linen closets and lingerie drawers. Favorite fillings for sachets are potpourris and cured, dried rose petals. (The directions for both may be found in The Portfolio of Pillow Techniques.) However, if the aim is to keep away moths, fill your sachets with dried balsam needles or moth crystals

Strawberry Sachets

Taffeta or satin fabric works best for the fruit, and felt is best for the tops. Using the patterns on page 181, cut out desired number of strawberries. With right sides together, stitch along straight sides with a ⅛″ (3mm) seam allowance. Stitch around top (curved) edge ⅛″ (3mm) from outside edge using a hand running stitch. Stuff strawberry with desired filling and polyester or cotton; then gather up top and stitch back and forth

through gathers and knot thread securely. Glue or hand stitch felt top in place.

Handkerchief Sachets

Choose a handkerchief with the same design in all four corners. Cut handkerchief into four equal parts. If the fabric is thin, line with fabric of the same color. Cut a piece of fabric the same size for the back. With right sides together and outer edges aligned, stitch with a ⅛″ (3mm) seam, leaving an opening for turning. Turn to right side and fill with a combination of polyester fiber fill or cotton and your favorite fragrant filling. Slipstitch opening closed. Whipstitch narrow lace all around.

Embroidered Sachets

These sachets were designed to be worked on pillowcase fabric of different colors. Two layers are used for the front and back to add strength. Enlarge the patterns on page 181 to desired size. (See Appendix for enlarging instructions.) Trace entire enlarged pattern lightly onto pillowcase.

Embroider flowers, working through both layers of the pillowcase. (See Appendix for stitch diagrams.) When embroidery is completed, fold pillowcase in half and cut along outside edge of pattern through all four layers of pillowcase.

With right sides together, pin back to front. Using a ⅛″ (3mm) seam, machine stitch around three sides of the sachet. Clip seams, turn right side out, and press. Fill sachets with a mixture of desired potpourri or rose petals and cotton or polyester fiber fill, and stitch opening closed.

BLUEPRINT PILLOWS FROM NATURE

These unique pillows utilize a very simple technique—blueprinting—and the design comes from interestingly shaped leaves, grasses and flowers. The project is so easily executed and so inexpensive that it is a perfect choice if you need large, furniture-sized pillows. Our directions are for a 9" (22.9cm) square pillow.

MATERIALS
- prewashed and ironed cotton
- 10" (25.4cm) square of cotton
- blueprinting solution
- posterboard
- clean paintbrush

METHOD
Step 1: To make a frame for arranging your design, cut a 12" (30.5cm) square out of posterboard, then cut a 9" (22.9cm) square opening in the center. Put the 10" (25.4cm) square of cotton on a pad of newspapers that has been placed on a board or tray. In a room that is dimly lit, paint the cotton with the chemical solution. Fabric will turn chartreuse.

Step 2: Arrange dried or fresh wild flowers on fabric. (Observe the shadows or silhouettes of the plants. Delicate plants with interesting spaces will produce a more interesting print than heavy masses of leaves.) Place the cardboard frame over the plants to help hold the plants in place and to give perspective to the arrangement. Hold in place with pins or thumbtacks.

Step 3: Carry the print out into direct, bright sunlight. Allow

chemical to dry in the sun. First the chemical turns blue, and as it dries it develops a slight brown haze. During the time it is developing, do not move it. After it has dried, take it inside. Remove frame and plants.

Step 4: Immediately wash the print in clear, cool water until the water runs clear. The undeveloped chemical washes out. The developed chemical is blue. The unexposed fabric (where the plants were placed) remains white.

Do not print in the wind or on an overcast or cloudy day. On a clear, warm day the average print might take ten to fifteen minutes. If it is dark and there is little white remaining, the print is overexposed.

Step 5: Finish pillow with your choice of the methods described in The Portfolio of Pillow Techniques.

How to Prepare Blueprinting Solution

For a price list on the chemicals needed write to Cold Type Supply, Inc., 400 North Beach, Dept. DCI, Fort Worth, Texas 76111.

MATERIALS
- ½ ounce potassium ferricyanide
- 1 ounce ferric ammonium citrate
- 1 cup water
- wide-mouth glass jar
- old spoon
- strainer
- rubber gloves

METHOD
Step 1: Pour one cup water in glass jar. Add ½ ounce potassium ferricyanide and stir until completely dissolved. Add ferric ammonium citrate.

Step 2: Pour solution through strainer into a second glass container to test for undissolved chemical and then return to wide-mouth jar. It is very important to have thoroughly mixed the chemical. Note: Wear rubber gloves while working with chemicals. If the chemical gets on your skin, your skin will develop blue color when exposed to sunlight. The color will fade in a day or two.

PATCHWORK FLOOR PILLOWS

A pair of floor cushions combines a traditional needle art, patchwork, with a non-traditional fabric for the technique, batik. The floor pillow shown at the left is made from the *Oklahoma Trails and Fields* design, using the actual size pattern pieces to result in a central block that measures 11″ (27.9cm) square. Three different borders of varying widths and styles were added to bring the total size up to 19¼″ (48.9cm) square. The pillow on the right is made from the *Wheels* pattern, enlarged to made a central square that measures 21″ x 21″ (53.3cm x 53.3cm). The addition of two borders bring the overall size up to a 34″ (86.4cm) square. The width, number, and design of the borders on your patchwork pillows can vary greatly.

After assembling each of the pillow tops, decide on a quilting pattern that suits your talents and the design. Quilt the tops before finishing the pillows.

The materials given are the same for both patterns. Finish each pillow with your choice of the methods given in The Portfolio of Pillow Techniques.

MATERIALS
- lightweight fabric (three colors for *Oklahoma Trails and Fields;* two colors for *Wheels*)
- sandpaper or stiff cardboard for templates
- backing fabric
- polyester fiber fill for stuffing
- yarn for tassels (optional)

METHOD

Oklahoma Trails and Fields
Step 1: Trace patterns on page 172 and make a template for each.

Step 2: One quilt block is made up of four 5½″ (14cm) squares: two *Fields* and two *Trails.* For one *Trails* block, cut: Pattern A, 4 of first color; Pattern B, 4 of second color. For one *Fields* block, cut: Pattern C, 4 of third color and 5 of first color.

Step 3: Following diagram, piece together two squares of each pattern. Join the four together as shown for a finished block that measures approxi-mately 11″ (27.9cm) square.

Step 4: Frame the block with a 1¾″ (4.4cm) wide border, mitering the corners as shown.

Make up the next border of two rows of alternating colors of Pattern C (80 squares in all).

Attach a 3″ (7.6cm) wide solid color border for the outside edges. Miter the corners as for the inside border.

Wheels
Step 1: Enlarge patterns on page 173. (See Appendix for enlarging instructions.) Make a template for each pattern piece.

Step 2: One quilt block is made up of four identical squares. For each square cut: Pattern A, one of first color and one of second color; Pattern B, one of first color; and Pattern C, one of second color.

Step 3: Following diagram, piece together four squares; join to make block.

Step 4: Frame the block with as many borders as desired. The inside border shown measures 3½″ (8.9cm). The outside border was made of alternating colors of Pattern C.

ART DECO
CREWEL BOLSTER

This brightly-colored bolster has a distinct art deco flavor, derived from the shell shapes of the background and from the traditional art deco color scheme. The bolster form provides a nice contrast to ordinary pillow shapes when used in a grouping and is striking displayed alone.

This crewel pattern is fun to work. The stitch diagrams for the individual stitches appear in the Appendix. The finished bolster is 15″ (38.1cm) long with a 20″ (50.8cm) circumference.

MATERIALS
- ½ yard (45.7cm) crewel linen 45″ to 60″ (114.3cm to 152.4cm) wide
- dressmaker's carbon paper
- crewel yarn as follows:
  28 yards (25.6m) green
  35 yards (32m) blue
  60 yards (54.9m) black
  5 yards (4.6m) dark red
  30 yards (27.4m) light red
  5 yards (4.6m) purple
  13 yards (11.9m) yellow
- embroidery needle, size 3

- embroidery hoop, approximately 8″ (20.3cm) diameter
- 1¼ yards (1.1m) black cording
- 2 covered button forms, size 1⅞″ (4.8cm)
- scrap of black fabric to match cording to cover buttons
- polyester fiber fill for stuffing

METHOD
Step 1: Cut a piece of linen 22″ x 17″ (55.9cm x 43.2cm). Enlarge the pattern on page 182. (See Appendix for enlarging instructions.) Trace the design on the fabric with dressmaker's carbon paper.

Step 2: With the blue and green crewel yarns, embroider the rows of scallops with three rows of chain stitch. Outline each scallop in black thread using the crewel outline stitch.

Step 3: Outline the flower petal edges and center with black thread using the crewel outline stitch. Work the vein lines of each flower petal with two rows of dark red split stitch on each vein line. Make each stitch about ½″ (1.3cm) long. With light red thread, fill in each flower petal

using the split stitch. The stitch direction should follow the vein lines. Make the stitches ½″ (1.3cm) long.

Step 4: Fill the flower center with regular French knots done in yellow yarn. With elongated French knots, fill the areas in the valley between each scallop. Put purple knots in the green valleys and yellow knots in the blue valleys.

Step 5: Block the finished piece of crewel according to the instructions in The Portfolio of Pillow Techniques.

Step 6: Match the top and bottom of the design, folding under one edge. Sew the lengthwise seam by hand; make the stitches as invisible as possible. The idea is to make a continuous design all around the pillow.

Step 7: Finish bolster acccording to the instructions for Bolsters in The Portfolio of Pillow Techniques.

WHITEWORK PILLOW

Whitework is exquisitely beautiful in its simplicity. This design utilizes only 12 different stitches, and the work goes very quickly. The design area is 13" (33cm) in diameter, and the finished pillow is 14" (35.6cm) in diameter. Refer to the Appendix for diagrams of embroidery stitches.

MATERIALS
- ½ yard (45.7cm) heavyweight white linen
- 60 yards (54.9m) white crewel yarn
- embroidery hoop
- crewel needle, size 3

METHOD
Step 1: To keep the fabric from unraveling, turn over the raw edges of the linen ½" (1.3cm) and baste down or tape with masking tape. Enlarge the pattern from page 183 to the desired size and trace the design onto your fabric using dressmaker's carbon paper. (See Appendix for enlarging instructions.) The blue lines will probably all come out, but if any remains it will work like old-fashioned bluing to make the white appear whiter.

Step 2: One strand of crewel yarn is used for all stitches. Begin working the design with the center flower.

Work the four main flower petals with satin stitches that come up on the solid outer line and down on the inner dotted line. The marks on the detail diagram I show the stitch direction.

Fill in the center areas of the four main petals with three rows of coral stitch. Refer to the detail diagram for stitch placement.

Use the chain stitch to outline the outer edge of the four remaining petals. The centers of these petals are filled with seeding.

The center is a whipped spider stitch with a French knot in the center.

Step 3: The interlocking curved bands are all outlined with one row of chain stitch. The V-shaped area in the center of each band is worked in the buttonhole stitch with the ridge on the outer edge.

Step 4: The four outer bands of flowers are worked last.

Work the stems in the crewel outline stitch.

Work the petals of the two small flowers in the buttonhole stitch and fill the centers with French knots.

The leaves are worked in a closed fly stitch.

Work the center flower petals first in the satin stitch. Refer to detail diagram II for stitch direction. Then work a continuous row of stem stitch around the entire flower close to the edges of the petals. Work a continuous row of detached buttonhole stitch on this row of stem stitch.

The center of the large flower is a woven spider stitch.

Step 5: Since this is a round design, a boxed pillow will work best. Refer to The Portfolio of Pillow Techniques for finishing.

SMOCKED CRIB PILLOW

What a wonderful gift this charming crib pillow would be to a precious newborn! It will work up quickly and easily even for the beginner.

MATERIALS
- 1 yard (91.4cm) dotted swiss
- 1 skein each of three different colors of embroidery floss
- crewel needle, size 8

METHOD
Step 1: Cut a rectangle of material 10″ x 24″ (25.4cm x 61cm). Leaving a 1″ (2.5cm) margin around all edges, follow the pattern below and mark off dots you will be "picking up."

Step 2: The first row is done in the cable stitch and goes straight across to secure the upper edge of the pillow. Using first color floss, come up from the back of the material with thread below the needle. Go in right side of next dot and out the left side of it, thus "picking up" the dot. (Fig. 1.) Pull the thread up, bringing the dots together.

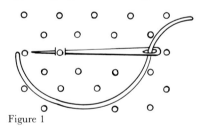

Figure 1

Step 3: With thread above the needle, pick up third dot (Fig. 2). Pull thread down. Continue

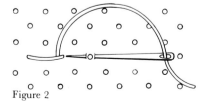

Figure 2

across, following pattern. After completion of cable row, count down five rows and begin design.

Step 4: With thread below needle, pick up first dot as shown in Fig. 3 and pull up. Follow Fig. 4 to complete stitch

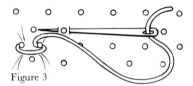

Figure 3

as follows. Go up diagonally with thread below the needle and pick up dot. Pull thread up.

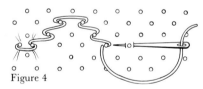

Figure 4

Repeat once. With thread above needle, go straight across to next dot and pick it up. Pull thread down. Come down diagonally with thread above needle and pick up next dot, pulling thread down. Repeat once. With thread below needle, pick up next horizontal dot and pull up.

Step 5: Repeat step 4 across row. Skip a row of dots and work row 2 exactly as first row. Rows

2 and 3 are done exactly as row 1, except in different colors.

Step 6: After completion of the three smocked rows, count down five rows (see pattern) and begin another set of rows. After five sets of rows have been smocked, count down 5 rows and finish with a cable row.

Step 7: Block smocked material by pinning to the ironing board so that the smocked area measures 8″ x 10″ (20.3cm x 25.4cm). Hold steam over smocking for about ten seconds. Let dry completely before removing from ironing board.

Step 8: Make ruffle and finish pillow as described in The Portfolio of Pillow Techniques.

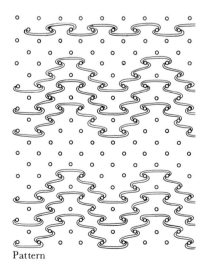

Pattern

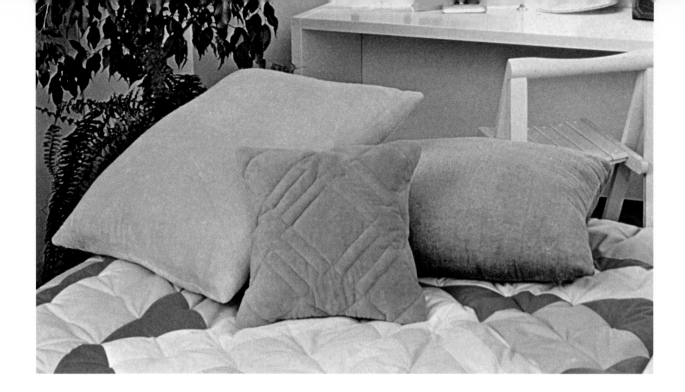

TRAPUNTO PILLOWS

Trapunto is an Italian form of quilting in which the design is stitched to fabric and a backing, and then selected parts of the design are stuffed to achieve a raised effect.

MATERIALS
- 1 sheared terry bath towel
- 1 standard-size solid color pillowcase
- carbon paper
- 2 (1-pound) packages polyester fiber fill
- knitting needle, size 8, 9, or 10
- 2 snap fasteners

METHOD
Step 1: Cut open pillowcase along seam line and folded edge.

Step 2: Enlarge pattern on this page and transfer to pillowcase with carbon paper. (See Appendix for enlarging instructions.) Mark areas to be stuffed on pillowcase.

Step 3: Cut out pillowcase and place right side up on wrong (loopy) side of terry towel. Use center third of towel for this; reserve the bound edges of the towel for the border of the opening on the pillow back. Cut out terry towel, using the pillowcase piece as a guide. Pin to pillowcase piece along edges and at intervals through center of square.

Step 4: Starting at center of square, machine-stitch through all lines of traced pattern.

Step 5: With knitting needle, poke a hole through pillowcase in one of the areas marked for stuffing. Jab a small puff of polyester fiber fill through hole

with needle. Continue stuffing until the area is filled with fiber fill. Repeat technique until all areas to be stuffed have been filled. The holes can be darned closed, if desired.

Step 6: Cut the two remaining sections of terry towel to same width as front. Lay them out with bound edges overlapping by 3'' (7.6cm) and trim to same size as front. Cut linings for each back section from pillowcase.

Step 7: Machine-baste linings to pillow backs on all four sides.

Step 8: Pin backs to trapunto front, right sides together, and overlap the bound edges. Machine-stitch along outer edge. Trim seams, clip corners, and turn right side out.

Step 9: From remaining pillowcase cut two 15'' (38.1cm) squares. Using ½'' (1.3cm) seams, stitch around all four sides, leaving an opening. Clip corners, turn, and stuff. Stitch opening closed. Stuff into trapunto pillow, and snap opening closed.

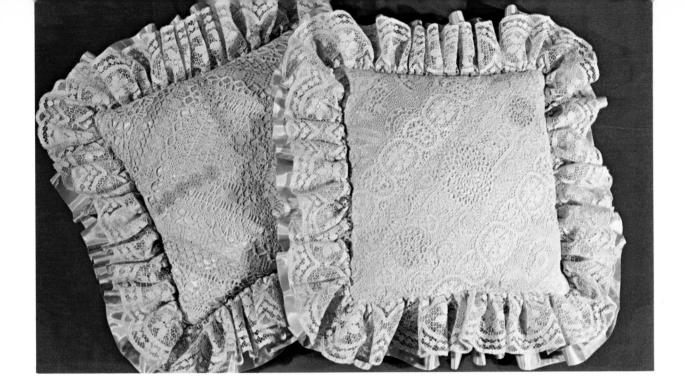

LACE RUFFLED PILLOWS

Taffeta and lace—an extravagant combination for a lady's luxurious boudoir. This beautiful design may be worked on a smaller scale and filled with a potpourri to sweeten closets and drawers. The materials given are for two 12″ (30.5cm) square pillows. Instructions that follow are for the pillow with the diamond-shaped arrangement of lace; the pillow with the diagonal pattern is easily done by following the photograph.

MATERIALS
- 3 yards (2.7m) taffeta
- ½ yard (45.7cm) non-woven interfacing
- 130″ (3.3m) of 3½″ (8.9cm) wide lace for ruffle
- polyester fiber fill or two 12″ (30.5cm) square pillow forms
- purchased lace or lace scraps

METHOD
Step 1: Cut two 13″ (33cm) square pieces from taffeta. Cut one 13″ (33cm) square from interfacing. Baste interfacing to one piece of taffeta.

Step 2: Divide faced square into four equal parts either by basting stitches or by pressing creases into the fabric.

Step 3: Cut strips of lace and blindstitch diagonally across each of the four squares. Arrange all four squares in an identical manner.

Step 4: After all four squares are complete, sew together and cover seams with lace. Sew a medallion in the center of the pillow top. Cut away ends of lace strip from beneath medallion.

Step 5: Divide pillow into four equal parts and divide lace ruffle into fourths. Run a row of gathering thread along ½″ (1.3cm) seam line and another row ¼″ (6mm) inside. Break gathering thread at each of the four markings.

Step 6: Match four ruffle and pillow markings, pull up gathers to fit, allowing extra fullness to go around corners and overlap where joining. Baste lace ruffle in place.

Step 7: The fabric ruffle measures 4″ (10.2cm) wide when finished. Cut ruffle strip 9″ (22.9cm) wide, fold in half lengthwise, and press. Divide strip of ruffle into fourths and gather as for lace ruffle.

Baste fabric ruffle in place, being very careful that no part of the lace ruffle edge is caught when stitching ruffle to pillow. Stitch along ½″ (1.3cm) seam, securing both ruffles to pillow.

Step 8: With right sides facing, stitch back and front together. Leave a small opening for turning. Turn, stuff firmly with polyester fiber fill, and blind stitch opening closed. If a pillow form is used, leave one complete edge open.

SOCK IT TO ME

Here's a super idea for making use of socks that come up without mates after a trip through the laundry. Simply machine-appliqué the odd socks to a fabric backing to make a really unique pillow. You can make just one side with the sock appliqué or, depending on the supply of single socks, make both the front and back out of socks. The brighter and more varied the assortment the better!

MATERIALS
• 2 rectangles of the desired size for finished pillow
• assortment of different socks
• polyester fiber fill or pillow form

METHOD
Step 1: Cut each sock in half, cutting down center front, across center bottom, and up center back, to make two identical halves.

Step 2: Lay out sock halves on one rectangle of fabric with the toes all going in one direction on one row, and going in the opposite direction on the next row. This will enable you to make sure the right side of all the socks is up. Pin socks in place, then baste around outer edges if you wish.

Step 3: Set your sewing machine for a narrow, fine zigzag stitch. Use a bright thread color if you desire. Stitch around outer edges of each sock, stitching over the raw edges to prevent raveling.

Step 4: Zigzag-stitch around all four sides of the rectangle to finish off edges.

Step 5: Finish your pillow with your choice of the methods described in The Portfolio of Pillow Techniques.

PATTERNS FOR
THE PROJECTS

Pattern for Alex's Animals, page 98-99.

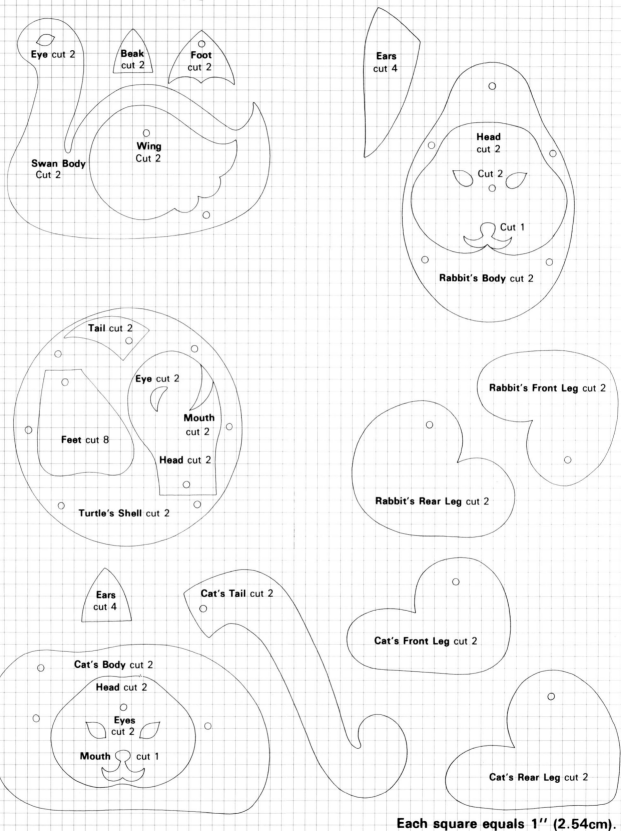

Eye cut 2

Beak cut 2

Foot cut 2

Ears cut 4

Swan Body Cut 2

Wing Cut 2

Head cut 2

Cut 2

Cut 1

Rabbit's Body cut 2

Tail cut 2

Eye cut 2

Mouth cut 2

Feet cut 8

Head cut 2

Turtle's Shell cut 2

Rabbit's Front Leg cut 2

Rabbit's Rear Leg cut 2

Ears cut 4

Cat's Tail cut 2

Cat's Front Leg cut 2

Cat's Body cut 2

Head cut 2

Eyes cut 2

Mouth cut 1

Cat's Rear Leg cut 2

Each square equals 1'' (2.54cm).

Pattern for Calico Angel, page 101.

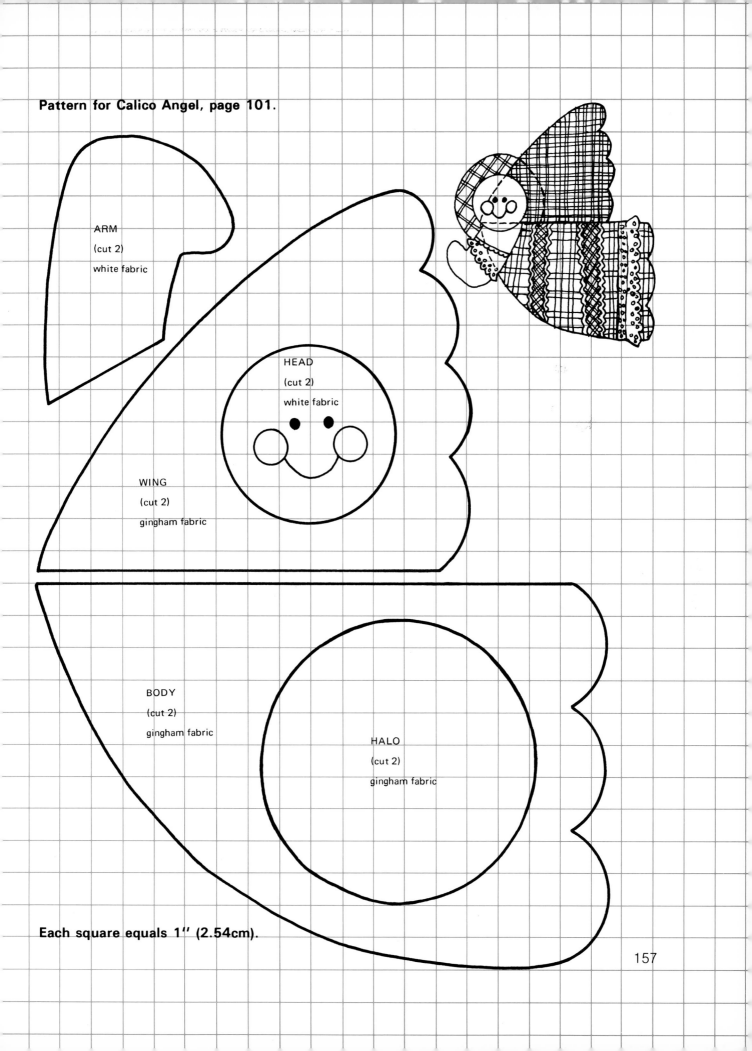

ARM
(cut 2)
white fabric

HEAD
(cut 2)
white fabric

WING
(cut 2)
gingham fabric

BODY
(cut 2)
gingham fabric

HALO
(cut 2)
gingham fabric

Each square equals 1'' (2.54cm).

157

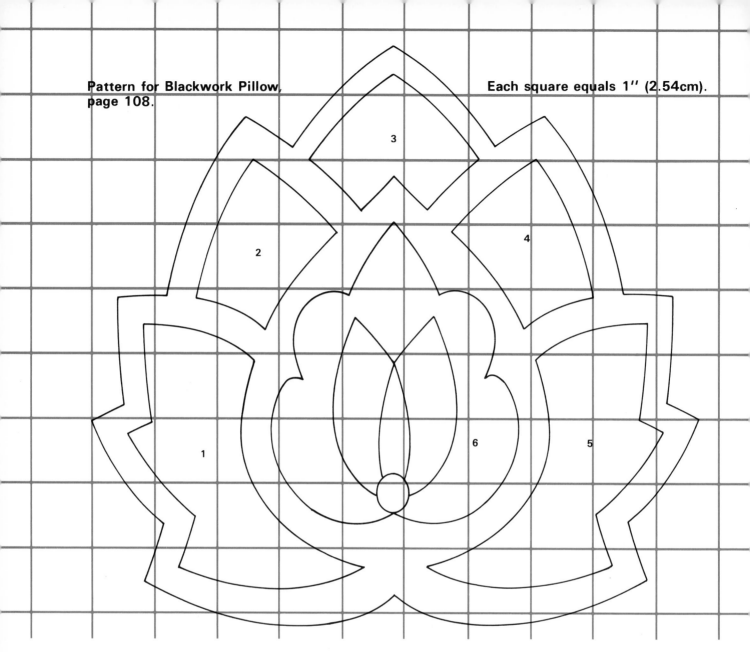

Pattern for Blackwork Pillow, page 108.

Each square equals 1'' (2.54cm).

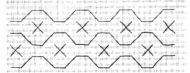

Pattern No. 1

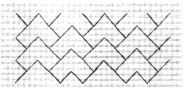

Pattern No. 2

Pattern No. 3

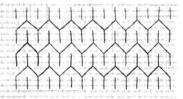

Pattern No. 4

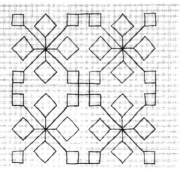

Pattern No. 5

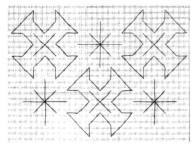

Pattern No. 6

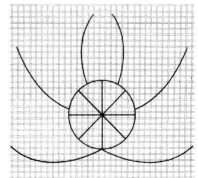

''Spokes'' for Whipped Spider's Web.

Chart for Noah's Animals pillow, page 113.

light color ☒ medium color ◨ dark color ⊡ white or pale color

Each square equals 1'' (2.54cm).

Each square equals 1'' (2.54cm).

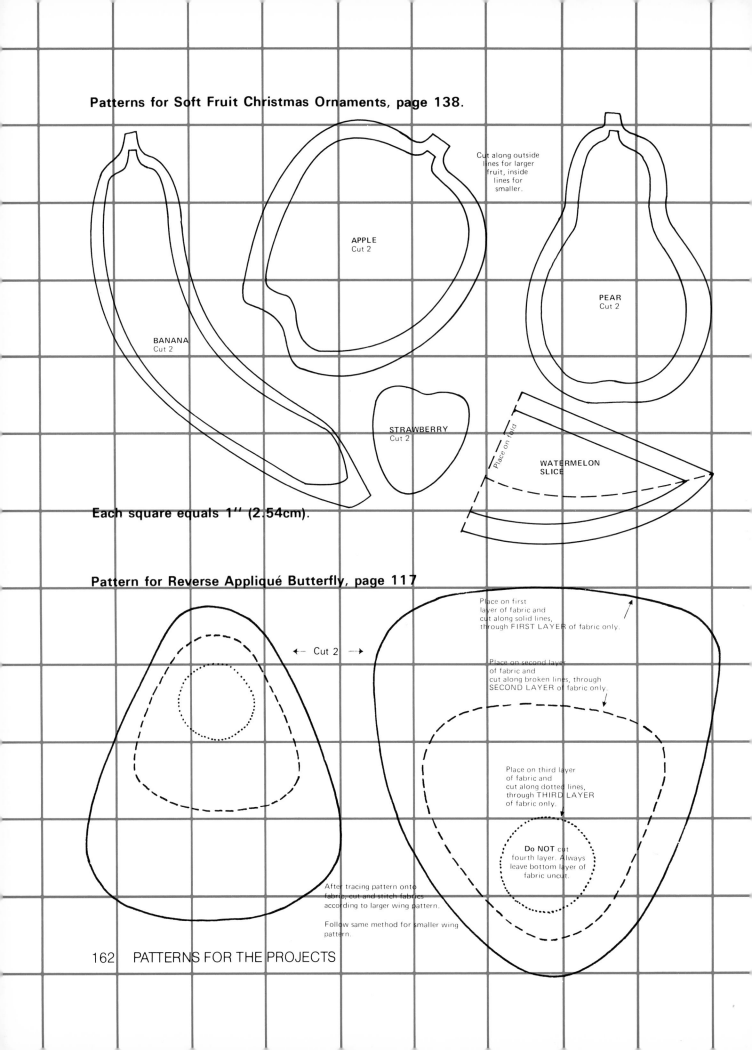

Patterns for Soft Fruit Christmas Ornaments, page 138.

APPLE
Cut 2

Cut along outside
lines for larger
fruit, inside
lines for
smaller.

PEAR
Cut 2

BANANA
Cut 2

STRAWBERRY
Cut 2

Place on fold

WATERMELON
SLICE

Each square equals 1" (2.54cm).

Pattern for Reverse Appliqué Butterfly, page 117

← Cut 2 →

Place on first
layer of fabric and
cut along solid lines,
through FIRST LAYER of fabric only.

Place on second layer
of fabric and
cut along broken lines, through
SECOND LAYER of fabric only.

Place on third layer
of fabric and
cut along dotted lines,
through THIRD LAYER
of fabric only.

Do NOT cut
fourth layer. Always
leave bottom layer of
fabric uncut.

After tracing pattern onto
fabric, cut and stitch fabrics
according to larger wing pattern.

Follow same method for smaller wing
pattern.

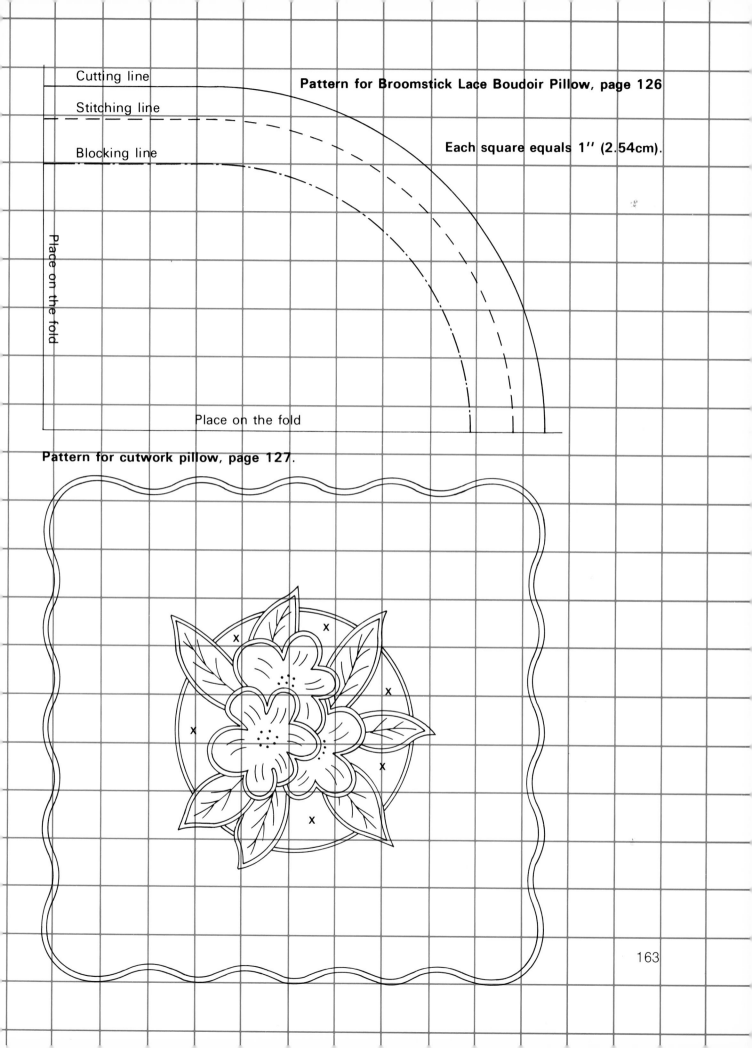

Cutting line

Stitching line

Pattern for Broomstick Lace Boudoir Pillow, page 126

Blocking line

Each square equals 1'' (2.54cm).

Place on the fold

Place on the fold

Pattern for cutwork pillow, page 127.

163

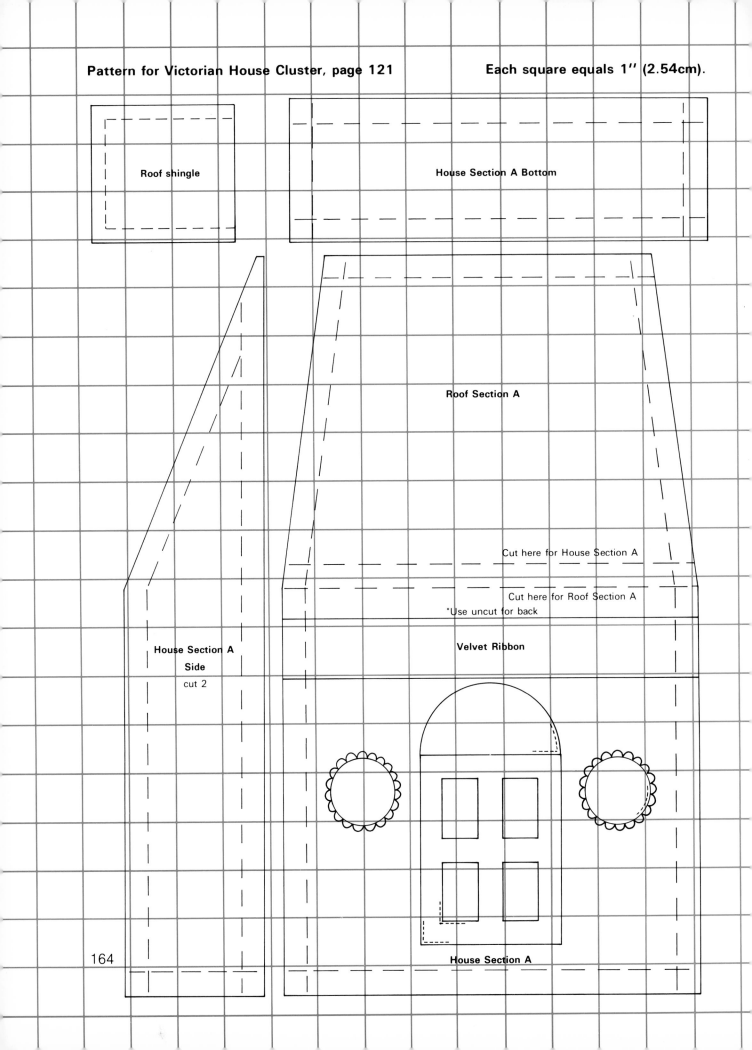

Pattern for Victorian House Cluster, page 121

Each square equals 1″ (2.54cm).

Roof shingle

House Section A Bottom

Roof Section A

Cut here for House Section A

Cut here for Roof Section A

*Use uncut for back

House Section A
Side
cut 2

Velvet Ribbon

House Section A

Each square equals 1'' (2.54cm).

(Continued from page 121.)

Step 9: Make top window using same process as window box (Step 3). Pin and topstitch above door.

Step 10: Cut two 1⅜'' (3.5cm) circles for round windows. Pin ½'' (1.3cm) from door, aligned with top of door. Stitch lace over edges.

Step 11: Sew, trim, and turn roof shingles using scraps for top and muslin (or more scraps) for underside. Cut roof patterns from muslin. Attach shingles in rows, overlapping every other one. Use 12 for house section A and six for each side of house section B. Sew roof sections to corresponding house bottoms, making sure not to sew shingles into bottom seam. Sew velvet strip to center front.

Step 12: Sew house section A sides and bottom to each other to form a strip, then sew to front of house section A. Cut and attach back, leaving an opening at bottom to turn. Trim, turn, stuff firmly, and slipstitch opening closed.

Step 13: Cut and attach back to house section B, leaving an opening to turn. Trim, turn, stuff firmly, and slipstitch opening closed.

Step 14: Sew house section A to house section B by hand using a blind stitch.

Roof Section B

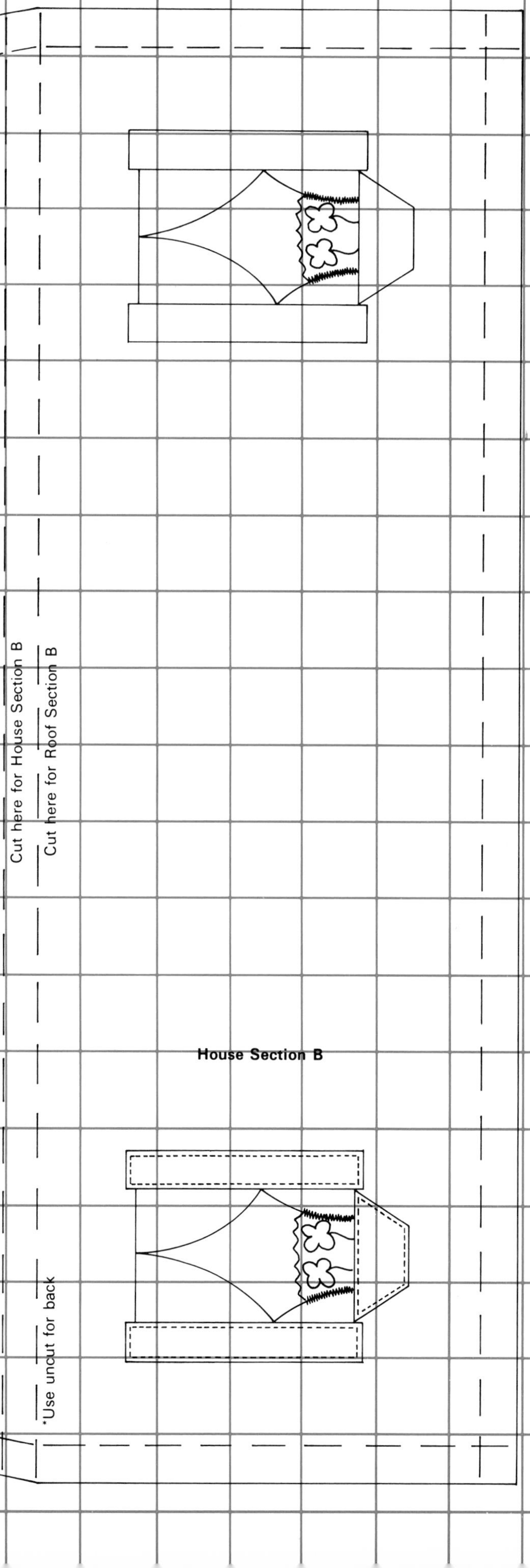

Cut here for House Section B

Cut here for Roof Section B

House Section B

*Use uncut for back

165

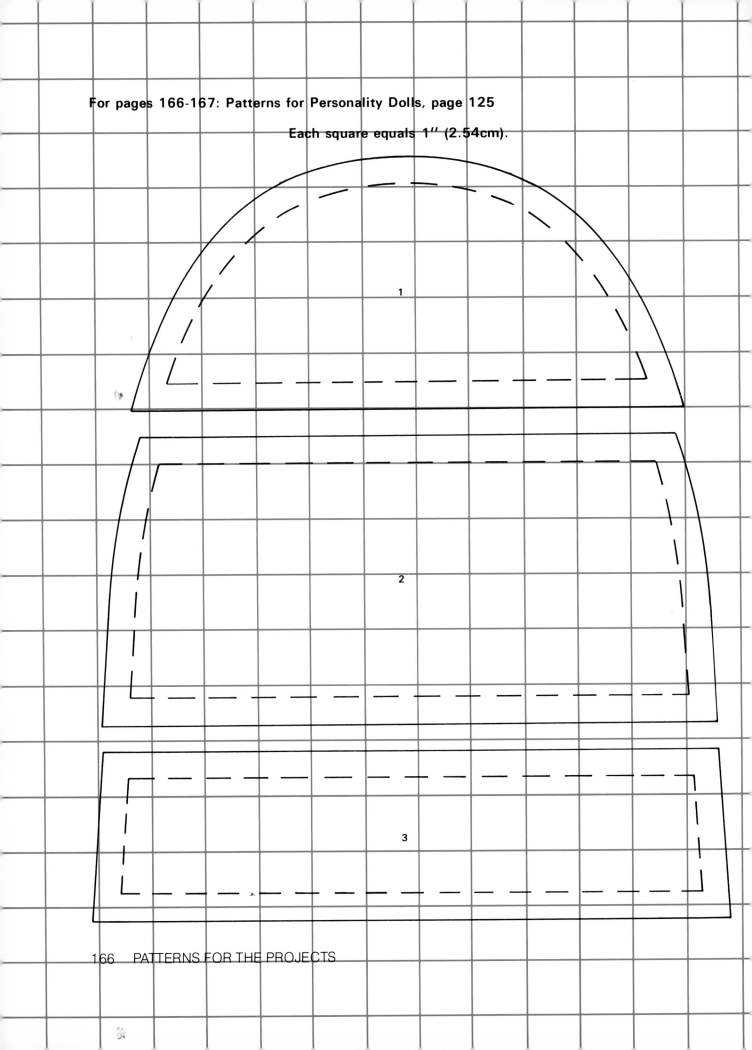

For pages 166-167: Patterns for Personality Dolls, page 125

Each square equals 1" (2.54cm).

1

2

3

Each square equals 1" (2.54cm).

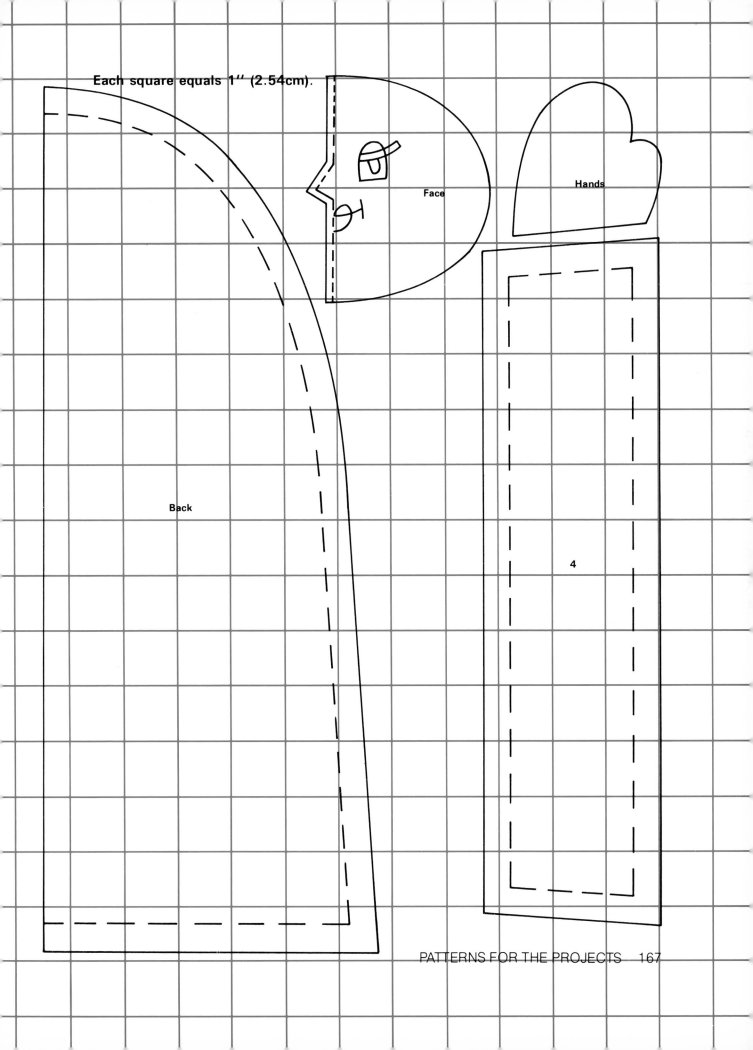

Face

Hands

Back

4

Machine Embroidered Pillow, page 129

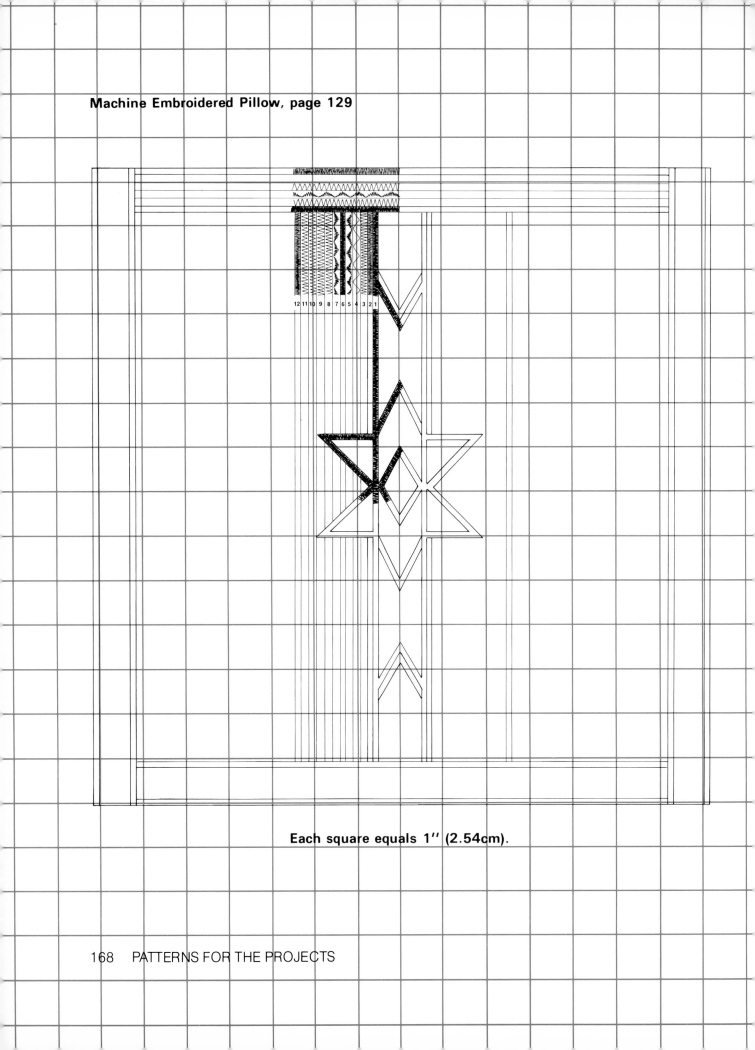

12 11 10 9 8 7 6 5 4 3 2 1

Each square equals 1'' (2.54cm).

Chart for Suburbia Needlepoint Design, page 130

Each square equals 1″ (2.54cm).

1″ (2.54cm) border

1″ (2.54cm) border

1″ (2.54cm) border

1″ (2.54cm) border

Pattern for Appliquéd Dove Pillow, page 131

169

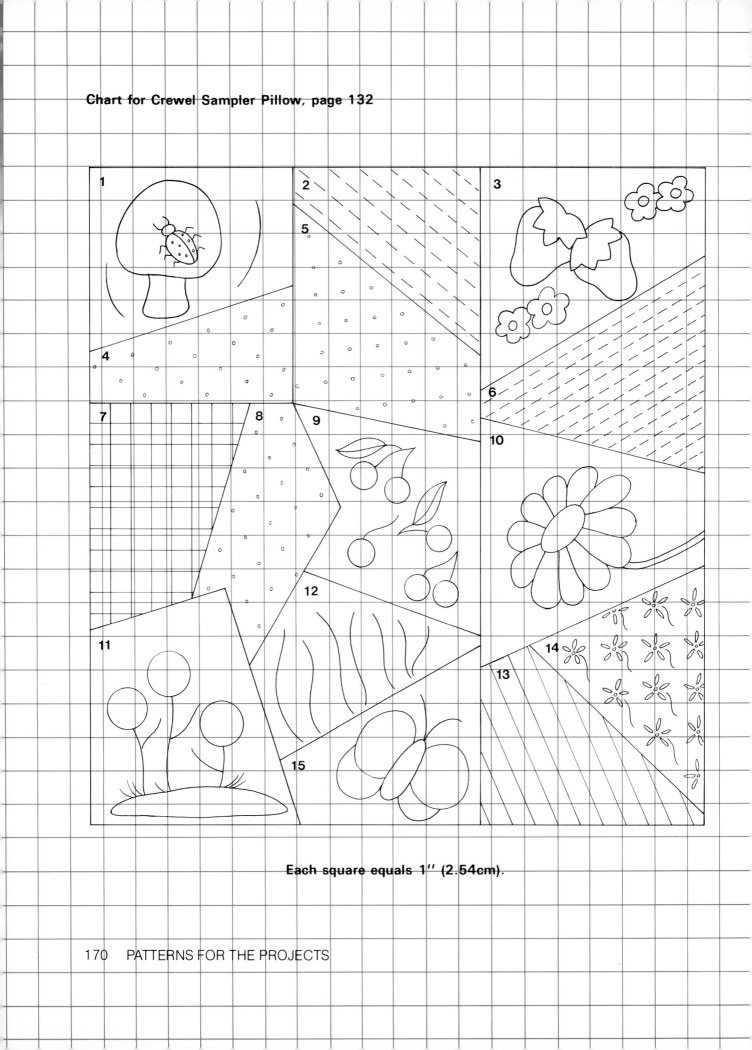

Each square equals 1'' (2.54cm).

Each square equals 1″ (2.54cm).

(Continued from page 141.)
grape. Come up at 1 and pull, down at 2 and pull, up at 3 and pull, down at 4 and pull, up at 5 and pull, down at 6 and pull. This completes one unit of the stitch. Go from number 6 to letter A. Come up and pull to start the next unit. If the stitch is done correctly, there will be an X across the back of each stitch.

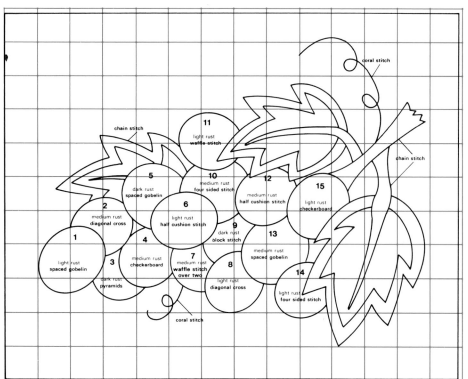

Each square equals 1" (2.54cm).

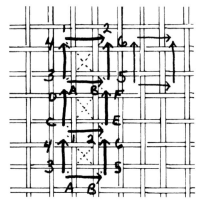

Four sided stitch

Pattern for "Oklahoma Trails and Fields,"

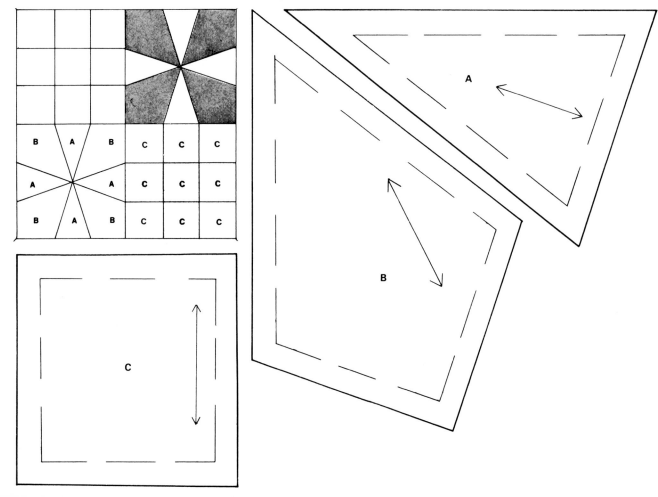

Pattern for "Wheels,"

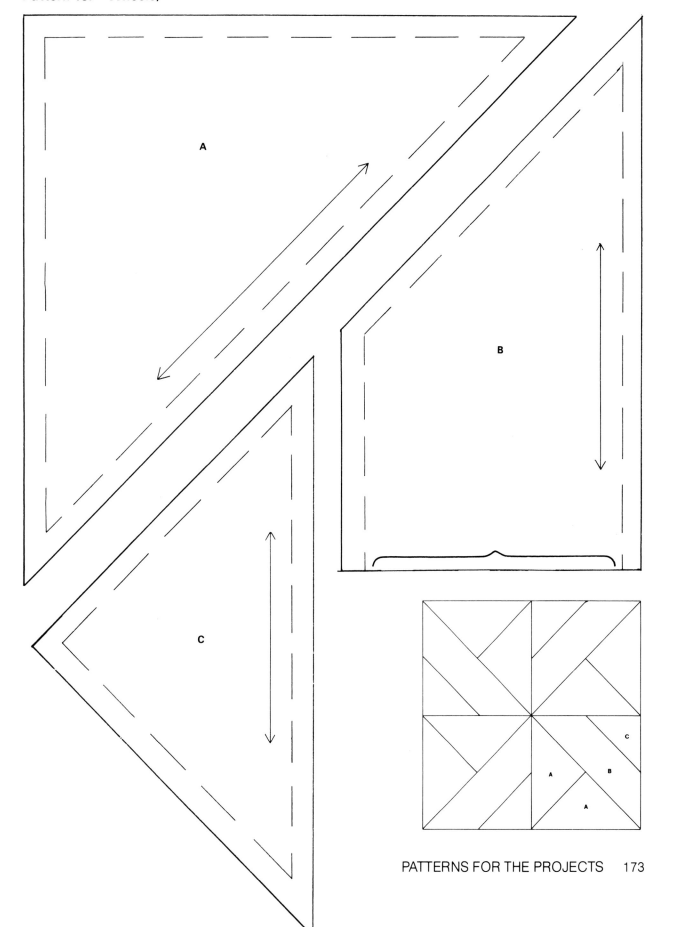

Graph for Painted Egyptian Cat Pillow, page 145

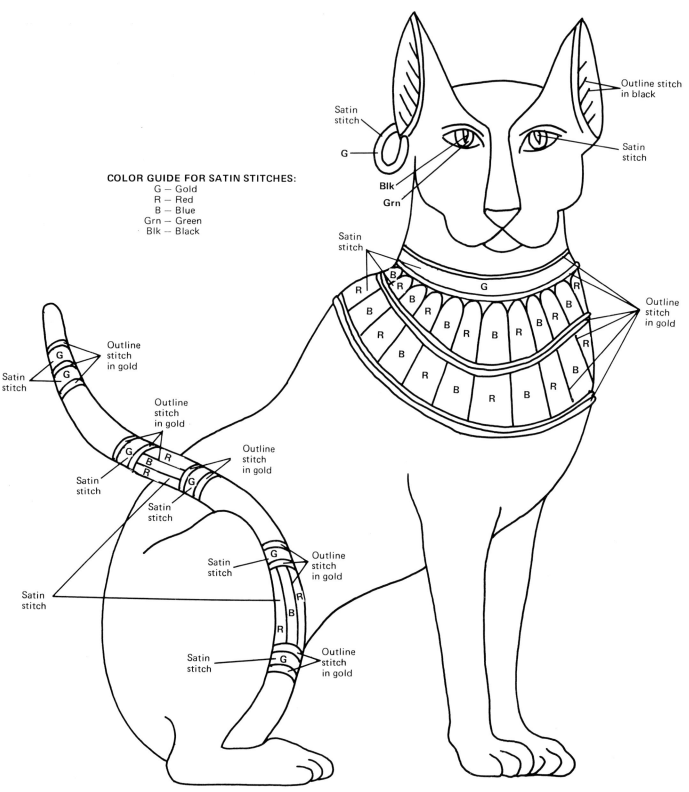

COLOR GUIDE FOR SATIN STITCHES:
G — Gold
R — Red
B — Blue
Grn — Green
Blk — Black

Outline stitch in black

Satin stitch

G

Satin stitch

Blk

Grn

Satin stitch

Outline stitch in gold

Outline stitch in gold

Outline stitch in gold

Satin stitch

Outline stitch in gold

Satin stitch

Satin stitch

Outline stitch in gold

Satin stitch

Satin stitch

Outline stitch in gold

Satin stitch

Outline stitch in gold

Satin stitch

Note: Complete outline of applique cat is done in black outline stitch. For cat on painted pillow, use gray outline.

Patterns for Bedtime Story, pages 134-135

Each square equals 1'' (2.54cm).

Each square equals 1'' (2.54cm).

sogni d'oro

Each square equals 1'' (2.54cm).

dormez bien

Patterns for Particular Pin Pillows, pages 142–144

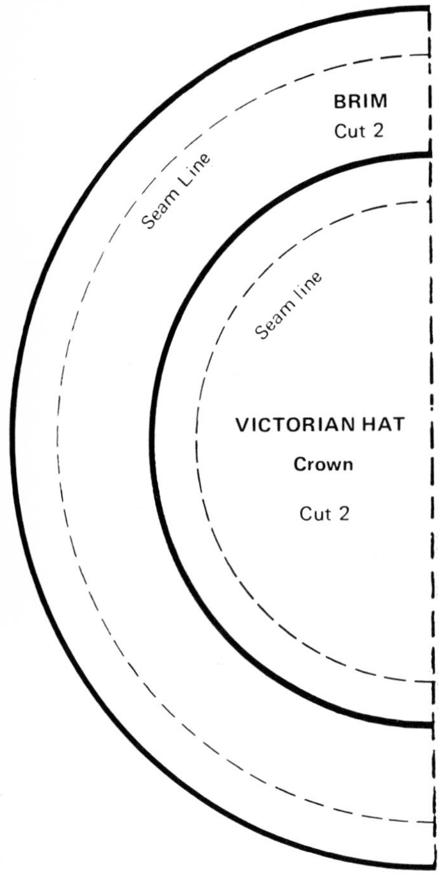
BRIM
Cut 2
Seam Line
Seam line
VICTORIAN HAT
Crown
Cut 2

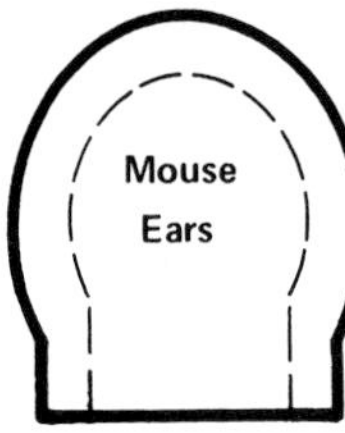
Mouse
Ears

Cut 2 Brown
Cut 2 Red

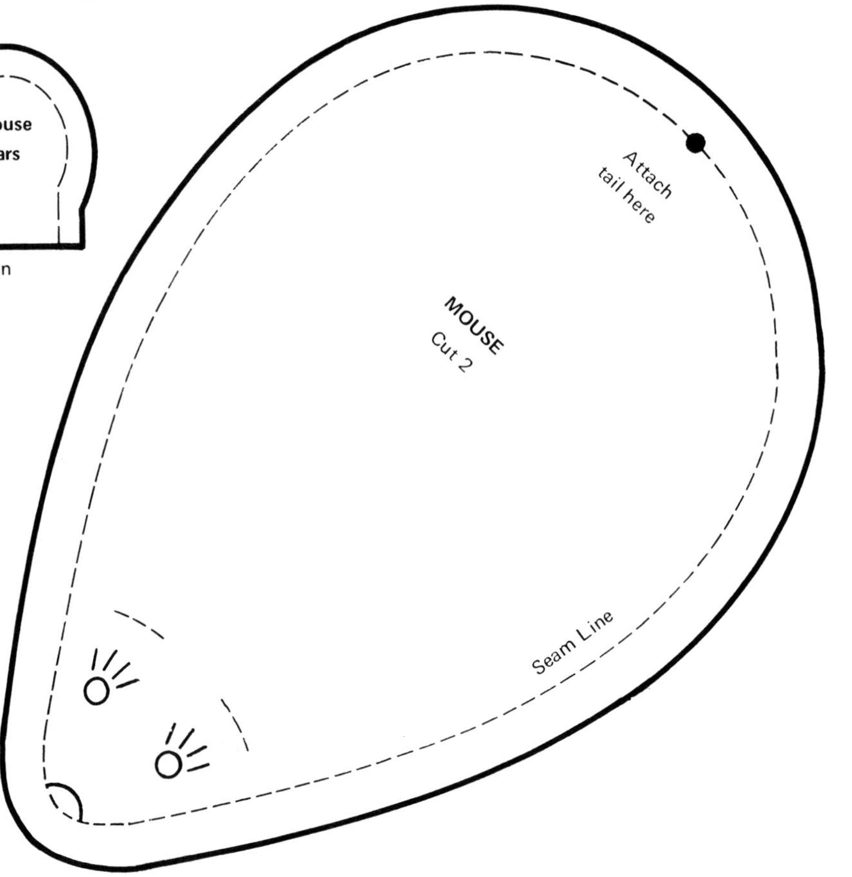
Attach
tail here
MOUSE
Cut 2
Seam Line

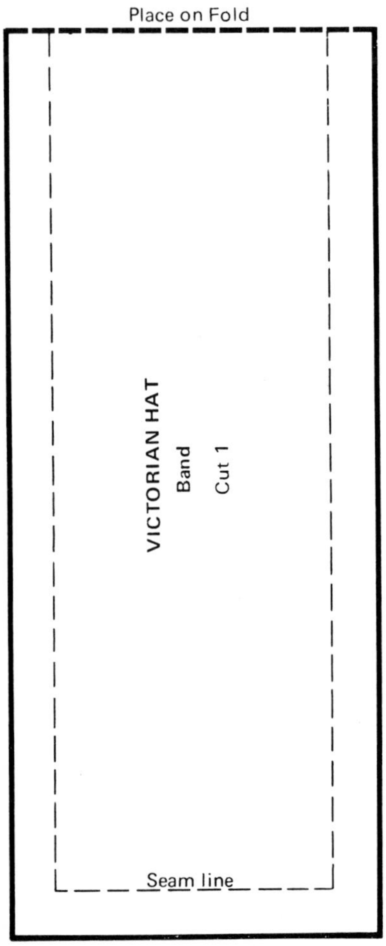
Place on Fold
VICTORIAN HAT
Band
Cut 1
Seam line

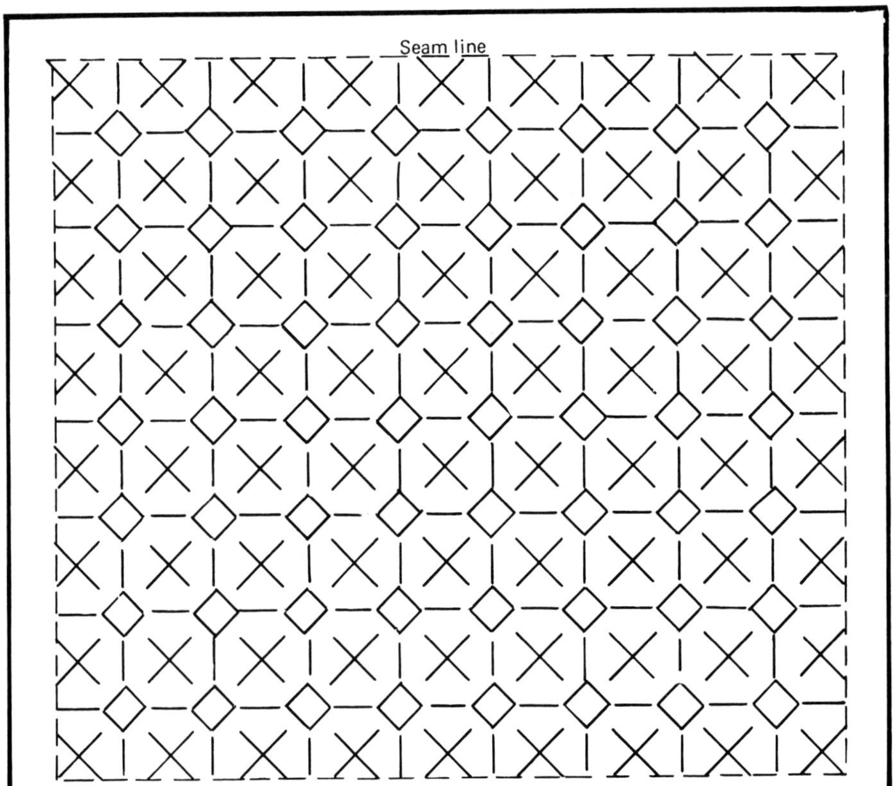
Seam line

TIC TAC TOE Cut 2
Transfer pattern onto 1/4" gingham, using square as stitch guide for embroidery.

MOUNTAIN DAISY
Pattern for stitch guide only (not actual size)

● Orange

○ Green

■ Red

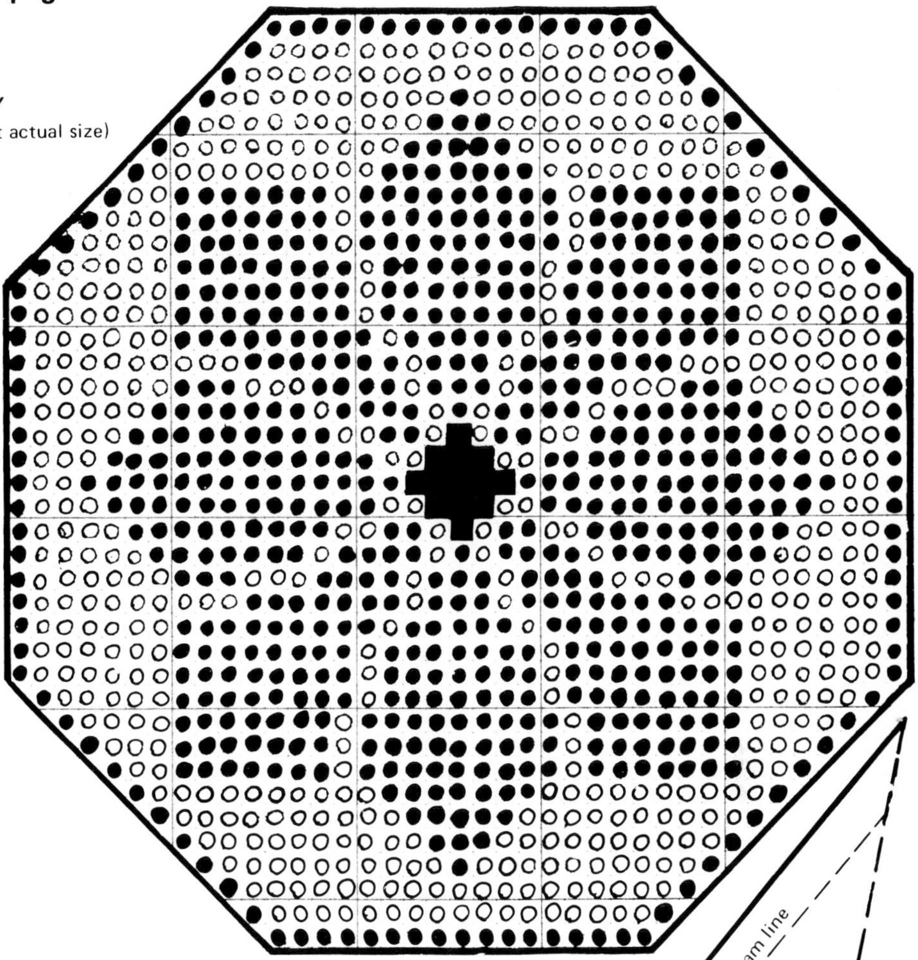

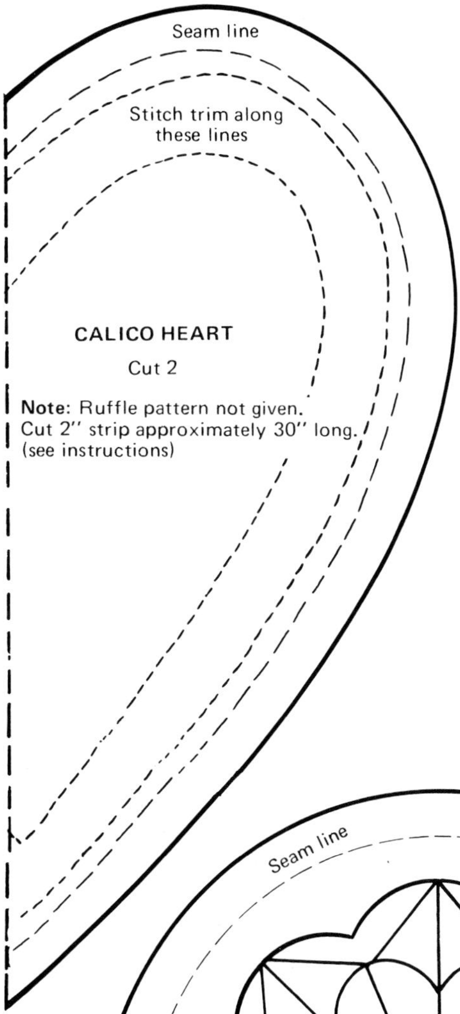

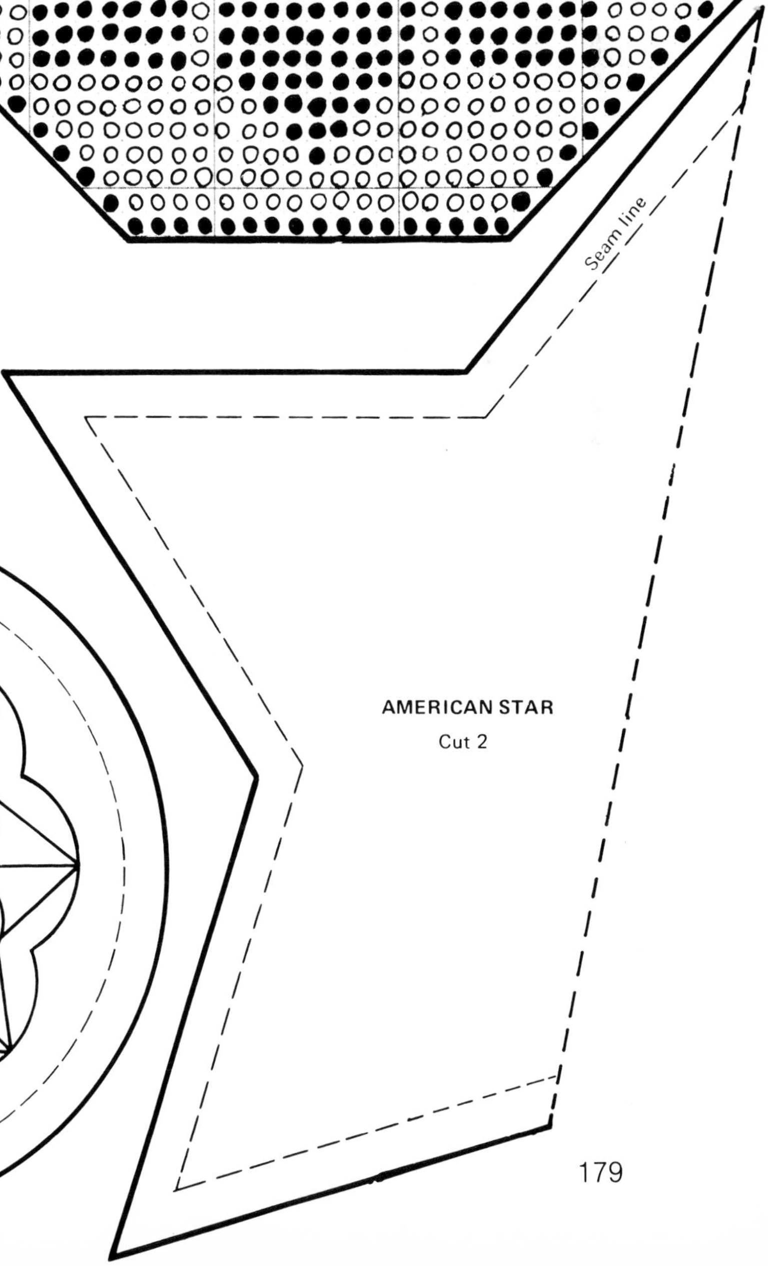

Seam line

Stitch trim along
these lines

CALICO HEART
Cut 2

Note: Ruffle pattern not given.
Cut 2″ strip approximately 30″ long.
(see instructions)

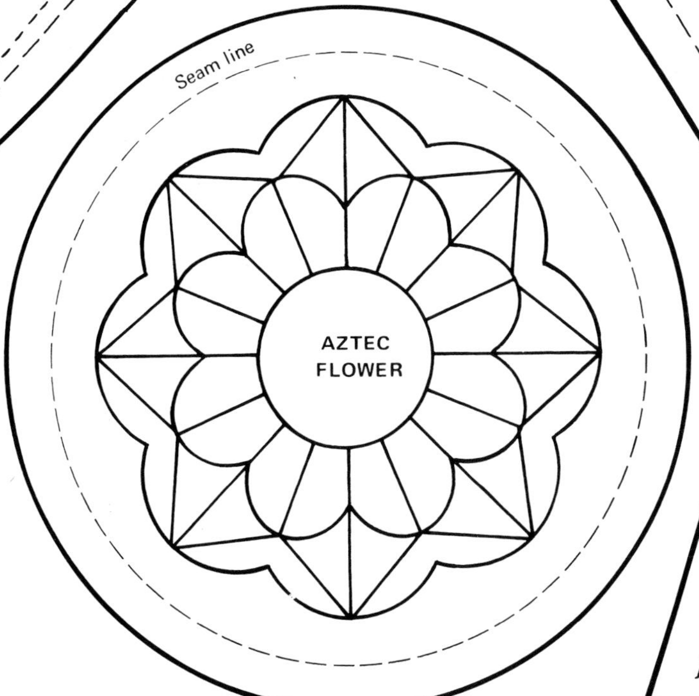

Seam line

Seam line

AZTEC
FLOWER

AMERICAN STAR
Cut 2

179

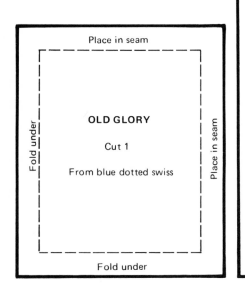

Place in seam

Fold under

Place in seam

OLD GLORY

Cut 1

From blue dotted swiss

Fold under

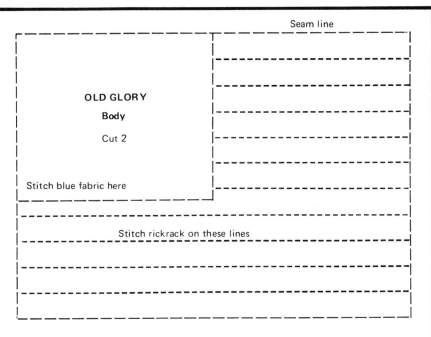

Seam line

OLD GLORY

Body

Cut 2

Stitch blue fabric here

Stitch rickrack on these lines

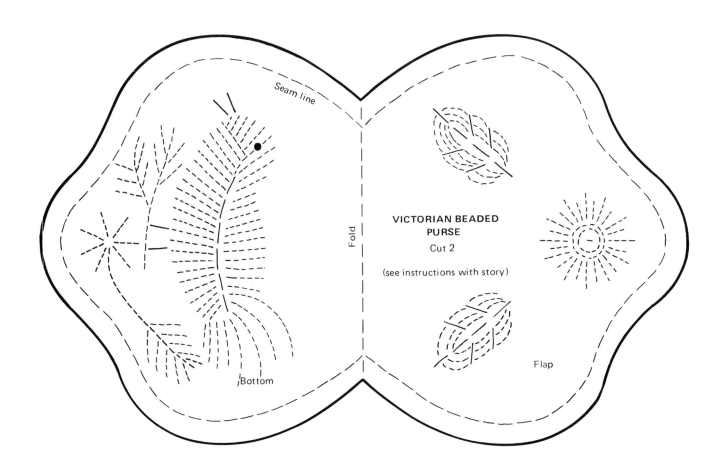

Seam line

Fold

VICTORIAN BEADED PURSE

Cut 2

(see instructions with story)

Bottom

Flap

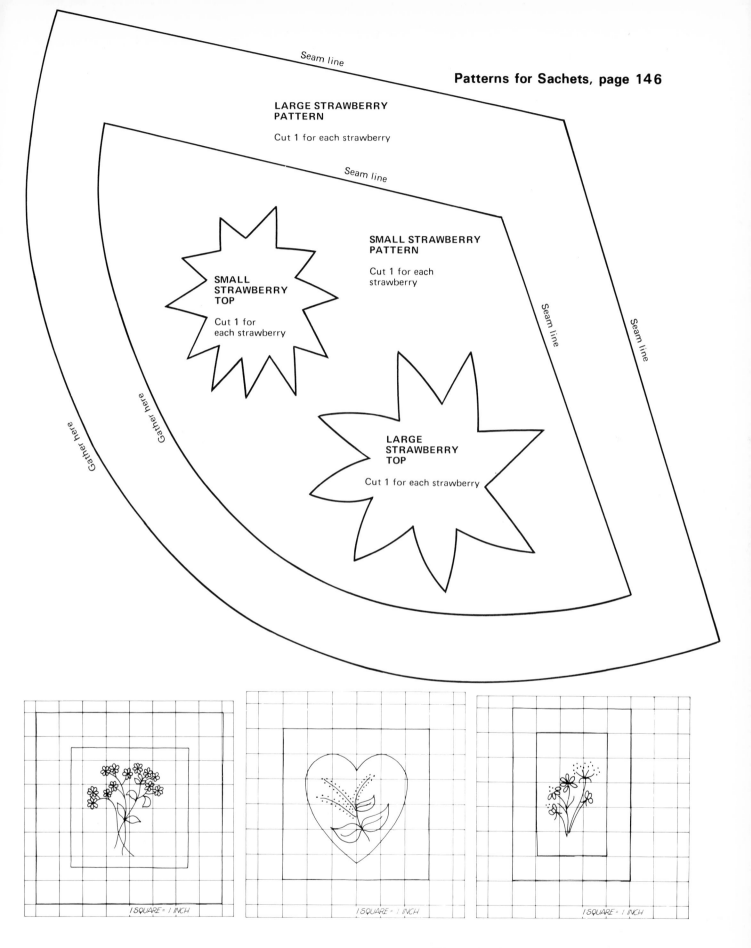

Seam line

LARGE STRAWBERRY PATTERN

Cut 1 for each strawberry

Seam line

SMALL STRAWBERRY PATTERN

Cut 1 for each strawberry

SMALL STRAWBERRY TOP

Cut 1 for each strawberry

LARGE STRAWBERRY TOP

Cut 1 for each strawberry

Seam line

Seam line

Gather here

Gather here

Gather here

1 SQUARE = 1 INCH

1 SQUARE = 1 INCH

1 SQUARE = 1 INCH

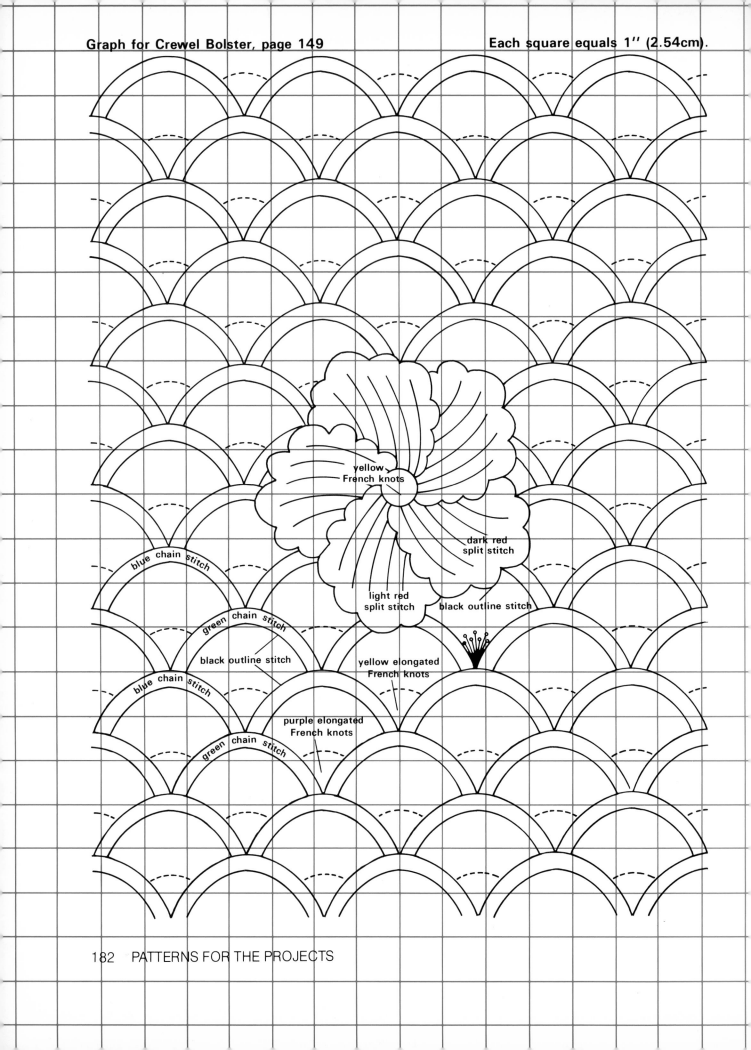

yellow
French knots

dark red
split stitch

blue chain stitch

green chain stitch

black outline stitch

blue chain stitch

green chain stitch

light red
split stitch

black outline stitch

yellow elongated
French knots

purple elongated
French knots

coral stitch

chain stitch

seeding

satin stitch

whipped
spider with
French knot center

woven spider

satin stitch

closed fly

buttonhole stitch

crewel
outline

French knots

stem stitch with detached buttonhole on top

APPENDIX

How to Work from a Charted Design

Please note that the words *graph* and *chart* are used interchangeably. They mean the same thing. The most important thing to remember in working with a charted design is that *each square on the graph represents one stitch.*

To determine the size of a finished piece that will be worked by following a graph, count the squares in the height and width of the design. Some of the charts in this book have twelve squares in an inch, with a darker line every sixth intersection, and some have ten squares to the inch, with every fifth intersection line darker. No matter how many squares there are in an inch on the graph, the design can be stitched on a canvas or fabric of any mesh you choose. (Mesh is the number of stitches allowed for in an inch of fabric or canvas.) A design charted on twelve squares to the inch graph paper may be stitched on ten mesh needlepoint canvas, 22 mesh petitpoint canvas, 14 mesh Aida cloth, 5 mesh quickpoint canvas, or any other mesh canvas or cloth that you want to use. The fact that the chart shows twelve squares in an inch does not affect the size of the finished work . . . the number of stitches you work in an inch determines the finished size.

Mathematics can be irritating when you are anxious to begin stitching, but it is necessary. If you do not figure carefully at the outset, you may find that you have bought much more material than you needed, or, much worse, that your stitches run off the edge of the material. In this case, the whole piece will have to be discarded and begun again. Here is a useful formula:

The number of squares in height of graphed design
divided by
the number of stitches in an inch of your needlework
equals
the number of inches high stitched design will be. The same formula works for determining the width.

When you know how long and how wide your stitched design will be, you must then allow extra material around the edges for background, plus 1 to 1½ inches all around for finishing.

Example: A charted design counts 120 squares high by 84 squares wide. To work in needlepoint on 12 mesh canvas, divide 120 by 12 and 84 by 12. The design will work out to be 10 inches high and 7 inches wide. If you want 1 additional inch of background stitches all around, the finished piece will measure 9 by 12 inches. Add 1½ inches for finishing; you will need a piece of canvas that measures 12 by 15 inches.

To work the same design in cross stitch on 22 mesh hardanger cloth, divide 120 by 22 and 84 by 22. Your answer will be 5.45 inches high and 3.8 inches wide. Round off the figures to 5½ by 4 inches. If you want an additional ½ inch all around for background material, the finished piece will measure approximately 6½ by 5 inches. Add 1½ inches all around for finishing and you know you will need a piece of hardanger cloth that measures 9½ by 8 inches.

To begin stitching from a charted design, remember that one square on the graph paper represents one stitch. If you have never worked from a chart, your first look at so many small squares of different colors or color symbols may discourage you. But, if you can see to do needlework, you can see well enough to follow a chart. The grids of the chart are not smaller than the mesh of the canvas or cloth you work on.

There are, however, ways to make counting the squares in the chart easier. A stitch finder can be used with the chart; it has metal strips that you line up underneath the row of squares you are counting. If you do not purchase a stitch finder, you can use a strip of poster paper in the same way. A standing clear plastic book holder is also an asset.

Charts can be either solid colored, color-coded, or both. There are advantages to each type of chart. A colored chart will give you a much better idea of how the finished piece will look, but it is sometimes difficult to see the lines of the chart. A color-coded chart has a symbol to represent each color in the design. If the color code indicates that the symbol x stands for gold, make a gold stitch for each x on the chart. Some color-coded charts are drawn in color—a green x stands for dark green, a green o stands for light green, a purple x stands for dark purple, a purple o stands for light purple, and so on. In this case, be sure to read the code key to get all the information available.

Some experienced needleworkers help themselves count on a color-coded chart by marking lightly with a pencil those squares they have worked. When the needlework is finished, the pencil markings can be erased so that the chart may be used again.

Work from the center out. Begin counting at the center of the chart and stitching at the center of the material. Usually it is easier to work up from the center and complete the upper part of the design, then finish the lower part. However, it may be easier to outline a central figure, beginning with, or close to, the center stitch, then fill in upper portions of the design, followed by the lower portions.

Find the middle of the chart by counting the number of squares up the height and the number of squares across the width. The place where the exact center of these lines cross each other is the center of the chart. Mark center point on chart.

Find the center of your canvas or cloth by folding it in half lengthwise, then again crosswise (Figure 1). Mark the center of the canvas or cloth. The safest method is with a sewing thread that can be snipped out after the work is begun. If you use a pencil, use it lightly. Never use a felt-tipped marker because it will bleed through the needlework.

The center of the chart may fall on one square of the design, or it may be somewhere in the background stitches. The center of the chart is not the same as the center of the *design*. You will, however, begin stitching from the center of the design. See the following examples (Figures 2, 3, 4) for how to start working a design from the center.

Work stitches, after the first stitch, to the right, left, or up, counting squares on the chart that are the same color and working the same number of squares in the same places on the canvas or cloth.

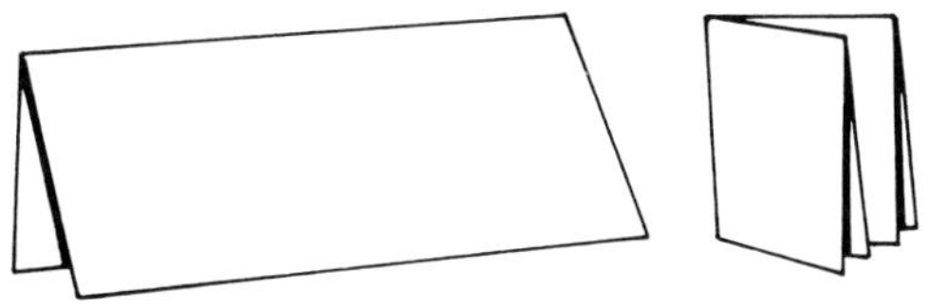

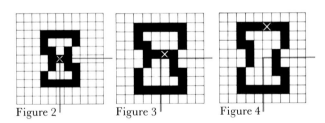

Figure 1. Find center of material by folding it in half lengthwise, then crosswise.

Figure 2   Figure 3   Figure 4

Figure 2. If the center of the chart is one square, begin by making that stitch.
Figure 3. If the center is a point where four stitches meet, choose either of the upper two squares and begin stitching.
Figure 4. If the center of the chart falls on the background, count up to the nearest design square and begin stitching there.

Guides for Working Cross Stitch and Needlepoint

In cross stitch, each under stitch of the cross should slant from lower left to upper right, and the crossing upper stitch should slant from lower right to upper left. You may work all of the under stitches first, then go back and cross each (Figures 5a and 5b), or you may complete each cross stitch before beginning the next (Figure 6).

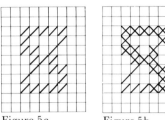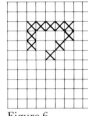

Figure 5a 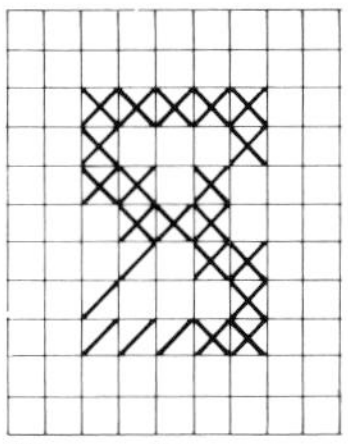   Figure 5b   Figure 6

For needlepoint projects, use a tent stitch to work the design and a stitch of your choice to fill in the background. A tent stitch is any stitch which covers one thread intersection on top of the canvas and two thread intersections underneath; there are several versions of the tent stitch. Sometimes it is necessary to change direction with your stitching; for example, you may need to change from working from left to right to working down. A half cross stitch will allow this to be accomplished. A half cross stitch in needlepoint covers one thread intersection on top of the canvas and only one thread intersection underneath. See the blue stitches in Figure 7 for examples.

When possible, in an area of many stitches of the same color, use the diagonal tent stitch, also known as the basketweave (Figure 8). This stitch is one of the strongest of the tent stitches and distorts the canvas less than most other stitches as it is worked.

A suggestion for a background stitch is the diagonal mosaic stitch. It fits in particularly well with the slant of the tent stitch and speeds up boring background work (Figure 9).

Topstitching, or backstitching, is indicated on a graph by lines. Finish the cross stitches or needlepoint stitches before working the topstitching. Use less yarn for topstitching on needlepoint by separating yarn strands, or use a full strand of embroidery floss. Top stitches may run along the sides, above, below, or diagonally across needlepoint and cross stitch stitches. They should be made by a "punch and stab" motion, not by "needle-through" (Figure 10).

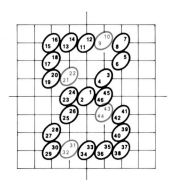

Figure 7. To follow any stitch diagram, bring the needle up from underneath the canvas on odd numbers (1, 3, 5), and put the needle through from above on even numbers (2, 4, 6). (Blue stitches indicate half cross stitches.)

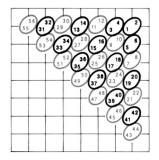

Figure 8. The diagonal tent stitch, also called the basketweave, should be used for backgrounds and any design areas that have many stitches of the same color. After the first three stitches, the rows drawn in black are worked diagonally down, with the needle put through the canvas vertically. Rows of stitches drawn in blue are to be worked diagonally up, putting the needle through the canvas horizontally. Remember that the needle comes up from underneath the canvas on the odd numbers and goes in from the front on the even numbers.

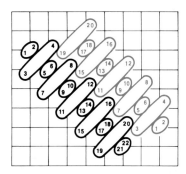

Figure 9. Follow the numbers for stitching the diagonal mosaic stitch.

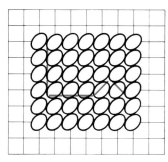

Figure 10. Embroidery stitches are worked after needlepoint is completed.

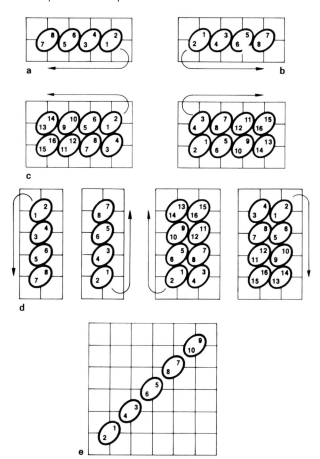

Figure 11. (a) This tent stitch is called the continental stitch. (b) If you must work from left to right, use a "stick and stab" rather than "needle through" method. Make sure each row of stitches slants in the same direction. (c) Two rows can be worked at once. (d) Illustrated also is how to work the tent stitch vertically, in single and double rows. (e) To work a single row of tent stitches slanting from lower left to upper right, use a "stick and stab" motion, not "needle through."

Choosing Colors and Materials

When selecting the materials that you use for needlework, rely on your past experience and the advice of other needleworkers. Penelope canvas with a woven vertical thread and double horizontal threads is the most durable. Antique (beige) colored canvas is less likely to show canvas through the finished work than white canvas. If you use a mono canvas, which is easier to see than penelope, make sure that it is interlocking. This will insure even stitches. The mono canvas used for bargello stitches is not suitable for needlepoint.

You may use tapestry yarn, spun for needlepoint, or Persian yarn.

There are many materials used for count-thread cross stitch. The only absolute requirement is that the cloth be evenly woven . . . that is, that there be as many threads in an inch horizontally as there are threads in an inch vertically. The number of threads from a strand of the embroidery floss that you use depends upon the weight of the cloth used.

Enlarging Patterns

It is seldom that you find a pattern that is exactly the size you need. Do not let this inhibit your creativity; enlarging or reducing a pattern is quite simple.

The very easiest way to size up a pattern is to have it photostatically enlarged. Simply instruct the photostat company as to what size you want the pattern pieces to be. The cost will vary and this service is usually found only in larger towns and cities.

You can easily enlarge or reduce a pattern yourself by using ¼'' (6mm) graph paper. You should be able to tell in advance whether or not the piece you want to enlarge will fit on one sheet of paper, or whether you must tape several pieces together to get the area you need.

First trace the design you wish to enlarge onto graph paper. If the design is to be twice as large, use two blocks for every one block on the original. Copy carefully, transferring what is in each square to the larger scale. It is helpful sometimes to outline the design with a series of dots, then connect the dots using your straight edge and French curve to make the lines smooth. Study the following examples carefully.

In Figure 1, we want to enlarge a "church

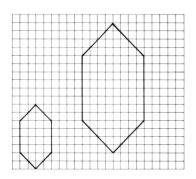

window'' from a quilt pattern. The original scale is that each block equals ¼'' (6mm). To make it twice as large, each space which is presently contained in one block must be stretched to two. The length of the church window from end to end is eight squares; the width is four squares. When enlarged, the length should be sixteen squares and the width eight. Count off sixteen in length and eight in width on graph paper as shown. Draw the lengthwise and crosswise lines every two blocks to give yourself a larger scale. Draw the church window onto the new scale, transferring exactly to the larger squares what is in each of the smaller squares.

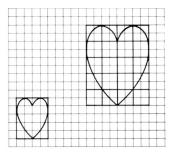

Irregular shapes are just as easily enlarged. Draw your new scale onto your graph paper, then copy exactly what is in each of the smaller squares. In Figure 2, you see how easy it is.

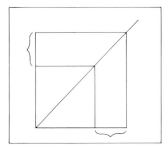

A regular shape such as a diamond or a square can be enlarged by merely extending the sides with a straight edge to the desired length , as shown in Figure 3.

Embroidery Stitches

Long and short stitch

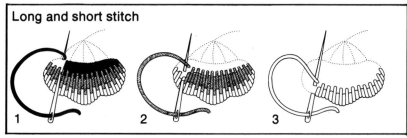

1   2   3

Running stitch

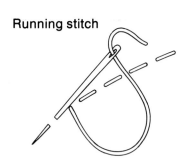

Seed stitch

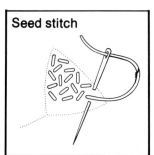

Seeding

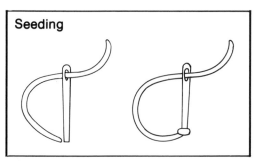

Back stitch

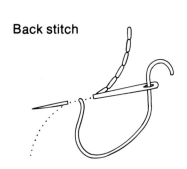

Arrow stitch

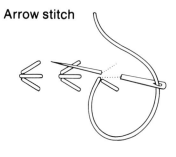

Lazy daisy or detached chain

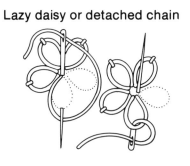

Straight stitch

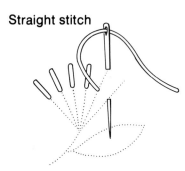

Cross stitch

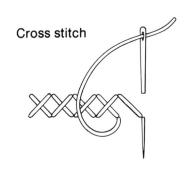

Herringbone stitch

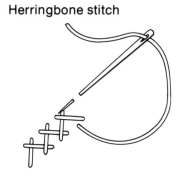

Satin stitch

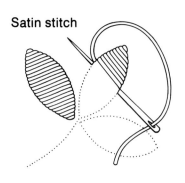

Chain stitch

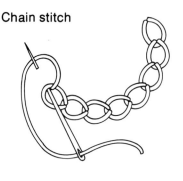

Chevron stitch

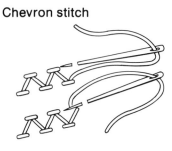

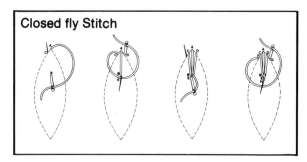
French knot　　　**French knot step 2**　　　**Elongated French knot**

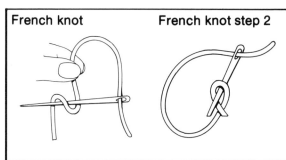
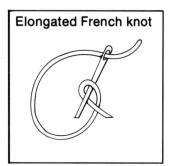

Coral stitch

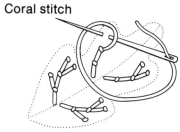

Split stitch

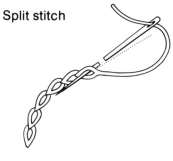

Feather stitch

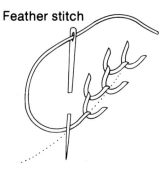

Couching

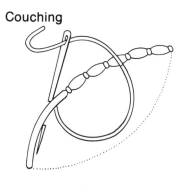

Stem stitch

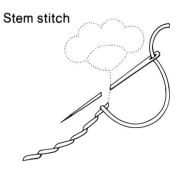

Bullion knot

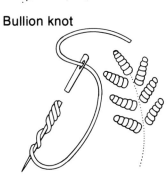

Buttonhole stitch

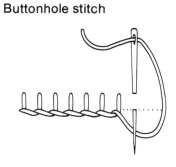

Detached buttonhole

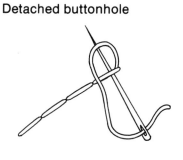

Padded buttonhole

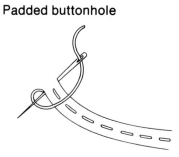

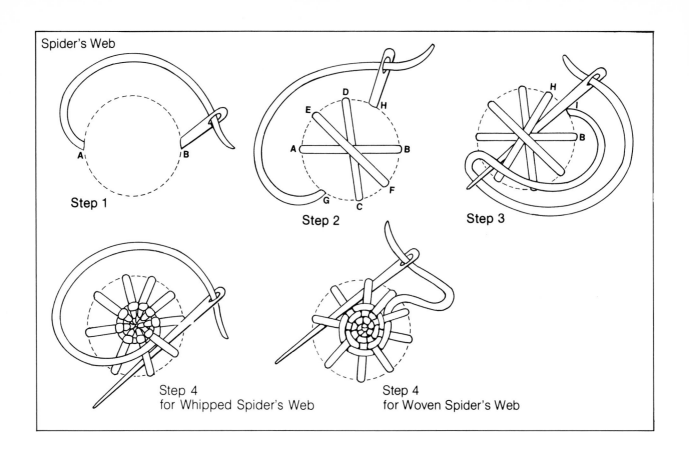

Spider's Web

Step 1

Step 2

Step 3

Step 4
for Whipped Spider's Web

Step 4
for Woven Spider's Web

INDEX